"Carey Walsh takes us into the thicket of Scripture, thorns and all, in order to 'chase' the divine mystery. Though trained as a scholar, she is less interested in textual analysis than in exploring those moments of disclosure when the Bible breaks open and breaks in. Reading a quirky Old Testament narrative can be aggravating as well as difficult. But for those who persist, she argues, joy awaits, a journey begins—a bumpy movement from disturbance to awe to contentment. Sharing her own experience, Walsh helps us see where the holy may be lurking unnoticed, waiting to be discovered."

—Peter S. Hawkins
Yale Divinity School
Author of *Undiscovered Country: Imagining the World to Come*

Chasing Mystery

A Catholic Biblical Theology

Carey Walsh

A Michael Glazier Book

LITURGICAL PRESS
Collegeville, Minnesota

www.litpress.org

A Michael Glazier Book published by Liturgical Press

Cover design by Jodi Hendrickson. Cover image: Thinkstock.

1   2   3   4   5   6   7   8

Library of Congress Cataloging-in-Publication Data

Walsh, Carey, 1960–
    Chasing mystery : a Catholic Biblical theology / Carey Walsh.
       p.   cm.
    "A Michael Glazier book."
    Includes bibliographical references and index.
    ISBN 978-0-8146-8069-8 — ISBN 978-0-8146-8094-0 (e-book)
    1. God—Biblical teaching.   2. Bible—Theology.   3. Bible—Hermeneutics.
  4. Catholic Church—Doctrines.   I. Title.

    BS544.W35—2012
    230'.041—dc23   2012029288

Contents

Where Did God Go?

I have no faith. . . . [S]o many unanswered questions live within me—I am afraid to uncover them—because of the blasphemy—If there be God—please forgive me. . . . I am told God loves me—and yet the reality of darkness & coldness & emptiness is so great that nothing touches my soul.[1] . . . just that terrible pain of loss—of God not wanting me—of God not being God—of God not really existing.[2]

The oppressive sense of the absence of God . . . has left its mark on us all today.[3]

These are the veritable road conditions for the person journeying in faith today. It is the condition in which I find myself as a biblical theologian whose very subject matter lies in the suspended animation of radical doubt. Vampires and wizards, it would seem, are more culturally viable than divine presence. A kind of doubt-fatigue hovers over all expressions of the living God in modern, secular culture, and this is true even for the heroes of the faith.

1. Mother Teresa, *Come Be My Light: The Private Writings of the "Saint of Calcutta,"* ed. Brian Kolodiejchuk (New York: Doubleday, 2007), 187.

2. Ibid., 192–93.

3. Pope Benedict XVI, *The God of Jesus Christ: Meditations on the Triune God,* trans. Brian McNeil (San Francisco: Ignatius Press, 2006), 15.

The first quotation above is from Blessed Mother Teresa; the second, Pope Benedict XVI. Mother Teresa gave her life to God by helping the poorest of the poor, the diseased people in Calcutta, India. Most of us simply assumed a robust spiritual connection lay behind her sacrificial lifestyle. She daily bore exhaustion, filth, and, as we learned some years after her death, a felt sense of God's absence for almost fifty years. Her experience of a dark night of the soul, then, was no solitary phase but rather lasted decades, virtually the entirety of her mission in Calcutta. Throughout that time, she did not experience even the relief of God's intermittent presence. Instead, darkness of the soul was for her a persistent, agitated state. Mother Teresa of all people did not enjoy a fluid, easy intimacy with God, which then fueled her service to the destitute. The pragmatist in me could not help wondering why she did not just book a flight out of there and serve in less severe conditions. And Pope Benedict, the head of the Roman Catholic Church, the man who may preside over Mother Teresa's canonization to sainthood, has also felt the dry sting of God's absence. He knows well the spiritual malaise that grips our age.

Why does God have to be so exasperatingly silent? Why can't we see him at least long enough to allay doubt? Our time is often referred to as the Age of Disbelief,[4] where religion, like everything else, is a matter of private choice. And the one place where people had found God in ages past was Scripture, but the rise of secularism has had a corrosive effect on biblical literacy. As a result, there are recent efforts to recover biblical knowledge for the broader culture beyond and within its houses of worship. Stephen Prothero's best-selling book *Religious Literacy* (2008) points to the desire for many to know more about faith, while the 2010 Pew Research Center poll on religious knowledge (where agnostics/atheists scored highest!) may well reflect a need. At the same time, there is a resurgence of atheism expressed in popular writers, such as Richard Dawkins and Christopher Hitchens, who relegate biblical faith to a best-forgotten past. Both responses to biblical illiteracy offer passionate, even moral claims. With the former perspective, "we *should* still know the Bible"; with the latter, "we *should* discard it in the name of progress." The Bible's iconic status is clearly used as a political football in a larger debate about religion in the public square. What is utterly glossed over in both these positions—surprisingly—is discussion, not of the Bible's historical impact, but of how Scripture remains holy, that is, "separate," divinely beyond the political discourse of any era,

---

4. Huston Smith, *Why Religion Matters: The Fate of the Human Spirit in an Age of Disbelief* (San Francisco: Harper Collins, 2001); Pope Benedict XVI, *Handing on the Faith in an Age of Disbelief* (San Francisco: Ignatius Press, 2006).

including our own. The Bible is frequently the subject of debate over its authority, canonical status, ideological premises, and use and abuse throughout history but, so far, not on what holiness actually means.

Surveys routinely show that the majority of Americans believe in God yet prefer to speak generally of spirituality rather than religion.[5] This trend is so prevalent that sociologists have coined a new acronym for it: SBNR, "spiritual but not religious." The market that has grown up around this SBNR demographic—with products like *Eat, Pray, Love*; *The Shack*; *The Secret*; Deepak Chopra books; etc.—does brisk business indeed.[6] Curiously, Americans prefer not to define who God is. Spirituality is the more general term about our inner life force and so can be defined in innumerable ways to suit individual tastes. It isn't surprising, then, that Americans, with our pronounced individualism, prefer the term "spirituality" to "religion," the latter a term tied quite literally to communal, historical definitions: it comes from the Latin *ligere*, "to bind, to tie."

Religion has commitment written right into its etymological DNA, and so Americans blanch at the term. In earlier times, believers "bound" themselves to a certain faith, willingly, not torturously. In today's choice-driven culture, free-ranging spirituality is much preferred to the constraints of religion. Yet the very fact that spirituality has such a booming market indicates a cultural restlessness for meaning. As Charles Taylor notes, the "ontic doubt about meaning itself is integral to the modern malaise."[7] At least some of the restlessness, the endless popular culture distractions, and the continued purchasing of spiritual books, surreptitiously or otherwise, express an inchoate religious hunger.

Increasingly, the enterprise of religious faith is a diminishing commitment in the West, to the point that scholars are quick to label our era as "post-Christian." They mean by this label not the extinction of Christians but rather an era in which Christians play no formidable role. While Christianity had profoundly shaped Western Civilization for two thousand years, its influence has now waned. Instead, varieties of secularism, pluralism, and multicultural tolerance hold sway in Western societies. Secularism, a world

---

5. Robert D. Putnam and David E. Campbell, *American Grace: How Religion Divides and Unites Us* (New York: Simon & Schuster, 2010); Robert C. Fuller, *Spiritual but Not Religious: Understanding Unchurched America* (New York: Oxford University Press, 2001); James T. Martin, "Spiritual but Not Religious—Not So Fast! Making the Case for Moving beyond Your Own Personal God," *Busted Halo: An Online Magazine For Spiritual Seekers*, http://bustedhalo.com (March 11, 2010).

6. Charles Taylor notes a "galloping pluralism on the spiritual plane" (*A Secular Age* [Cambridge, MA: Belknap Press of Harvard University Press, 2007], 300).

7. Charles Taylor, *A Secular Age*, 303.

without religion, as John Lennon imagined, marks contemporary culture in a way that Christianity used to.

Secularism itself is host to a variety of attitudes about religion. There are atheists, those who do not believe in God; agnostics, those who do not know if there is a God; and those SBNR types who reject organized religion but pursue spiritual wisdom in other fashions. In addition, there are the "cultured despisers" whom Friedrich Schleiermacher (d. 1834) spoke of, the educated elite who see religion essentially as backward and beneath their level of achieved culture. Unsurprisingly, these people proliferate in an Age of Disbelief, but they have always been with us. Today, these latter types thrive in positions in government, the academy, the entertainment industry, the news media, and they produce much of the popular culture we ingest: movies, books, television scripts, plays, etc. They distribute the goods that announce religion is passé and so are themselves active agents in the push for a post-Christian society.

Caught up in this sweep toward a supposed post-Christian culture, there is an absence of grief that I wish to note. Civilizations move slowly due to their enormity, so warehousing a two thousand–year Christian legacy in the last twenty-plus years says something quite deafening about the importance of God anymore. Where did God go that we could so blithely, so—I'll say it—guiltlessly relegate him to the past? Amid that, how does one still meaningfully relate to this biblical God? How does one grow deeper in love with God against the cultural currents of disdain and antagonism without the previous societal bulwarks—family, civic community, peer group—that used to nurture faith? Are theists caught in such a cultural shift all destined to adopt a page from the Amish playbook and set up communal outposts apart from corrosive, secular culture?

The stamp of "post-Christian" is premature and more likely the desideratum of eager forecasters with an atheistic bent. We have, at any rate, become too quick to call the time of death for cultural influences, as the proliferation of post-this, post-that attests. Why are we in such a hurry to get past each present moment? Doesn't our quick labeling of the near past as "post" suggest a disdain for history and a fortiori for the passing of our lives? Surely an epochal shift into cultural atheism merits, at the very least, considered reflection.

The Purpose of This Book

This book is an exploration into how the Bible negotiates the presence and absence of God in the hopes that its discoveries can forge a path in the modern situation where absences often seem more pressing than the presences. It is offered for those who truly and genuinely wonder if God could be real and, if he is, then why it should be so difficult to encounter the divine in our world. A theological question remains paramount to the study: *How* is God really present and not merely the product of our wish fulfillment, conceptual abstraction, and assertive fiats? It is instructive at the start to borrow from Walter Kasper's discussion on the nature of faith because it addresses the qualitative dimension of our faith, by delineating its affective, spiritual, and intellectual aspects. Kasper argues that faith in God has essentially three components: (a) to believe that God is, (b) to give credence to (to trust) him, and (c) to move toward him.[8] Kasper emphasizes that faith involves more than intellectual assent. He also provides a helpful diagnostic tool for assessing which parts of our own faith are solidly theistic and which might be more agnostic or even atheistic. I, for example, can teeter in the areas of b and c. My belief that God exists (a) is firm, but that belief can be distant. I believe God exists somewhat like I believe in the Milky Way; namely, they both exist but do not really concern me, even though both wholly sustain my existence! Such a belief in God is primarily cognitive; it is a box in my mind that I have checked yes to since I was little. In the Bible faith means trust rather than a set of beliefs, and so it spends the lion's share of its attention compelling readers toward b and c.

The adventure of faith feels a bit reckless and awkward, I think, because we would no more put our trust in a book character than fall backward for strangers to catch us. The idea seems absurdly daring. Why this Hebrew God and not Zeus, Athena, or the Tibetan Buddhism of the Dalai Lama? He seems remarkably content. Trust would take our control away, and this aspect troubles the modern psyche. But each desire to open the Bible and read for God's presence is itself a rather large act of trust. It is the fledgling surrender of some control, a little falling backward, a stumble forward, toward God. Prayer often reduces smart adults to wobbling, insecure toddlers because it too is a foray into trust. The mind's monologue, just to be clear, can look like this in prayer: "Are you there? Hi, I want to know you in my heart. What's for lunch? Am I just talking to fluorescent lights? Could you be real? Ooh, a squirrel! Do you ever speak? In the nameofthefatherandthesonandtheholyspiritamen." If this is a sampler of what the mind can do in prayer, imagine all the slicing and dicing it can do while reading Scripture!

8. Walter Kasper, *The God of Jesus Christ*, trans. Matthew J. O'Connell (New York: Crossroad, 1986), 122.

Biblical Theology

Amid the prevailing religious skepticism and restlessness, we must relearn the skill of trust in reading Scripture. Learn it with the same adventuresome spirit we would apply to any new meditation techniques or yoga positions; learn it as if it were a new, experimentally savvy thing to do. The aim is to experience God through holy writing. This approach to Scripture is vested from the start. It *wants* to discover God somehow, and so it is a form of biblical theology.

Biblical theology is a discipline within the broader field of biblical studies that emerged in the late-nineteenth and twentieth centuries, primarily in Germany and the United States.[9] It developed in response to a heavily historical emphasis in exegesis, which sought to uncover, in Paul Ricoeur's terms, "the world behind the text."[10] Biblical theology inquired into themes and ideas that were evident throughout the Old or New Testament as a whole.[11] Walther Eichrodt's seminal work, *Theology of the Old Testament*, argues that the concept of covenant is the central, distinguishing theme of Old Testament writings.[12] Gerhard von Rad, in his *Old Testament The-*

9. John W. Rogerson, *A Theology of the Old Testament: Cultural Memory, Communication, and Being Human* (Minneapolis: Fortress Press, 2010), 2.

10. Paul Ricoeur, "What Is a Text? Explanation and Understanding," in *Hermeneutics and the Human Sciences: Essays on Language, Action and Interpretation*, trans. John B. Thompson (Cambridge: Cambridge University Press, 1981), 159.

11. James Barr, *The Concept of Biblical Theology: An Old Testament Perspective* (London: SCM, 1999), 5, 14.

12. See Walther Eichrodt, *The Theology of the Old Testament* (Philadelphia: Westminster, 1967). This collection of writings is called various things. For Jews, it is most commonly the Bible or Tanak, from the acronym from the Hebrew for the Bible's three sections, TNK: *Torah* (Law), *Neviim* (Prophets), *Ketuviim* (Writings). For Christians, it is most commonly called the Old Testament to indicate a relation with the New Testament. I prefer this term over other scholarly created options such as Hebrew Bible, First Testament, or Early Writings because it indicates a relation with the second part of the Christian canon and does not stand alone. These recent terms were not used by communities of faith themselves nor in the history of tradition but meant to erase any pejorative connotations that the word "Old" has had. While I recognize the long, sad history of Christian supersessionism in biblical interpretation of the Old Testament, I understand "Old" simply to denote a historical difference with the New and intend no pejorative sense in my preference for "Old Testament." I hope this becomes clear by my treatment of the materials, rather than my use of a traditional term for them. In addition, since this is a work that engages the entire Christian canon, it is less cumbersome and more familiar to refer to the two sections of it as the Old and New Testaments, rather than, say, the first and second testaments, the Hebrew and Greek Literature, etc. I am sympathetic to efforts to excise prejudices in language uses, but given my canonical

ology, argues for a "theology of recital," wherein certain creedal formulae (namely, Deut 26:5-9; 6:20-24; Josh 24:1-13) help to fashion the biblical stories of a God who acts.[13]

More recently, Samuel Terrien traces the specific theme of divine presence through the various types of literature in the Old and the New Testaments and argues that God's presence is elusive.[14] Brevard Childs's work emphasizes the final, canonical shape of the Bible for the Christian Church as constitutive of exegesis.[15] And Walter Brueggemann's many works have had a tremendous influence on thinking theologically about the Old Testament. His own *Theology of the Old Testament: Testimony, Dispute, Advocacy* concentrates on the role of imagination and witness in the language of the Old Testament.[16] Biblical theology, then, concentrates primarily on what the biblical materials say about God and how they say it.

What distinguishes biblical theology from other lines of inquiry in biblical studies is, first, its emphasis on the normative and enduring testimony about God and, second, its inclusion of two levels of meaning: those for the ancient Israelites and that of the contemporary reader.[17] One advantage of this perspective is its focus on meaning in the "world in front of the text" rather than that behind the text, which historical criticism works to discover. As Christopher Seitz notes, "The problem with historical criticism was that it had failed to do constructive theological work involving the identity of God in the most basic sense."[18] In the discipline of biblical

approach and the fact that the Christian Bible is a dual corpus, the traditional terms are apt despite their misuse in the past by some, though not all, interpreters.

13. Gerhard von Rad, *Theology of the Old Testament* (San Francisco: HarperSanFrancisco, 1962). G. Ernest Wright was influenced by von Rad's earlier work, *The Problem of the Hexateuch and Other Essays* (New York: McGraw-Hill, [1938] 1966), in his *God Who Acts: Biblical Theology as Recital*, Studies in Biblical Theology 8 (London: SCM, 1952).

14. Samuel Terrien, *The Elusive Presence* (San Francisco: Harper & Row, 1978).

15. See especially Brevard S. Childs, *Old Testament Theology in a Canonical Context* (Philadelphia: Fortress Press, 1985); and *Biblical Theology of the Old and New Testaments* (Minneapolis: Fortress Press, 1992).

16. Brueggemann especially notes the theological promise of metaphor, which enables a "playful, open quality of Israel's most serious speech and its theological imagination" (*Theology of the Old Testament: Testimony, Dispute, Advocacy* [Minneapolis: Fortress Press, 1997], 70).

17. Ibid., 1–114; Leo G. Perdue, Robert Morgan, and Benjamin D. Sommer, *Biblical Theology: Introducing the Conversation* (Nashville, TN: Abingdon, 2009), 55–124, 209–34; Wright, *God Who Acts*.

18. Christopher R. Seitz, *Figured Out: Typology and Providence in Christian Scripture* (Louisville, KY: Westminster/John Knox, 2001), 4.

theology, matters of relevance, meaning, and enduring truths, irrespective
of history, are pressed. These scholars have offered comprehensive analyses
of all types of theological content of the Bible, and their influence is incal-
culable to the field and in shaping my own scholarly interests.[19]

My aim with this book is more circumspect. It is to offer a work in biblical theology that, while not comprehensive of the Old Testament writings,
yields insight into the very liveliness of the God of the Bible. My attention is
ambitious but deliberate. It slows down and zooms in to the site of reading
Holy Scripture, where divine presence is depicted on the page and transmit-
ted to the reader. It is my contention that the pages do not simply *describe*
divine presence. That would be a matter for semantic and literary analysis.
They *offer* and help to *evoke* it in the process of reading. Not all the time,
certainly not predictably, but enough to warrant a trust. The Bible necessarily involves us experientially and so is a matter of mystical discernment.

Mysticism is that aspect of religion concerned with a direct or immediate consciousness of the presence of God.[20] Mystical experience, as William
James notes, was both transient and passive, something that happened to
a person at key moments but is not constant.[21] Nevertheless, it gives shape
to the general meaning of a life that includes faith in God's presence, *even
when it isn't felt*. The absences are endured along with the memory of intermittent presence. Hence, though painful, Mother Teresa's experience was
a part of her mystical faith rather than a damning clue that she should have
heeded about God's nonexistence. Indeed, the absence of God has proven
a strong catalyst for rich classics of spirituality, from the book of Job to St.

19. Prominent examples from this century are Eichrodt, *The Theology of the Old
Testament*; von Rad, *Theology of the Old Testament*; Wright, *God Who Acts*; Rudolf
Bultmann, *Theology of the New Testament* (Waco, TX: Baylor University Press, 2007);
as well as the more recent works by Brevard Childs, Walter Brueggemann, and James
Barr. See notes 15–16 above.

20. Bernard McGinn, *The Foundations of Mysticism: Origins to the Fifth Century*,
vol. 1 of *The Presence of God: A History of Western Christian Mysticism* (New York:
Crossroad, 2004), xi. For a helpful review of mystical experience, see Robert S. Ellwood,
Mysticism and Religion (New York and London: Seven Bridges Press, 1999). For Christian mysticism, McGinn's *Foundations* remains the classic study. Among the many books
on Christian spirituality, the one-volume anthology, *Light from Light*, offers an especially
clear overview and analysis of the major traditions within the history of Christian spirituality: Louis Dupré and James A. Wiseman, eds., *Light from Light: An Anthology of
Christian Mysticism* (New York/Mahwah, NJ: Paulist Press, 2001).

21. William James, *The Varieties of Religious Experience: A Study in Human Nature*
(New York: Macmillan, 1961), 372. Consequently, spirituality will entail the psycho-
logical dimension of human maturation; see Michael Downey, *Understanding Christian
Spirituality* (New York: Paulist Press, 1997), 8.

John of the Cross[22] to Elly Hillesum,[23] to name but a few. Absence doesn't make the heart grow fonder so much as it breaks it, making it cry out in prayers no longer optional but unavoidable. Whatever else Mother Teresa's internal world held, she never stopped praying. While actual mystical experience of presence is intermittent, it nevertheless makes claims on the entirety of one's life by insisting that divine presence is genuine and possible.

I explore a selection of scriptural texts, primarily from the Old Testament but also the New, where mystical experiences of holiness occur in the hopes that such encounters can then spread like wildfire into the reading of other biblical texts and into our reading of the world around us. It is therefore a sustained reflection on the moment when profound meaning is made clear—*revealed*—in the text and existentially grasped by the reader.[24] My goal is to strengthen the heart's reading competency, the arena in which divine-human encounters occur. There is a barely perceptible yet real, potent shift from reading the Bible for information to finding oneself dropped into it, changed by it. The interactive dimension of reading for the holy is essential to this project. The texts indicate a fluid, pulsating presence; they do not merely predicate one. In some respects my focus is simply to ask anew the traditional question of what precisely divine inspiration in text is: what makes the Bible holy? For it is all text—Scripture and the world—made by this Hebrew God, but seeing it as such requires active participation. Biblical theology in this understanding is about the meaning that matters, then for ancient Israel and now for us.

A Note on Absence

It is a fundamental assertion of biblical faith, Pope Benedict notes, that God is invisible.[25] This would be unremarkable except that we live in an era that privileges sight, sense-data, and empirical ways of knowing, and so the Bible becomes problematic. Absence does not mean nonexistence to the

22. Saint John of the Cross, *Dark Night of the Soul*, in *The Collected Works of St. John of the Cross*, trans. Kieran Kavanaugh and Otilio Rodriguez (Washington, DC: Institute of Carmelite Studies, 1991).

23. Etty Hillesum, *An Interrupted Life: The Diaries, 1941–1943, and Letters from Westerbork* (New York: Henry Holt, 1996).

24. The philosophical underpinnings to this process of meaning are substantial. A most helpful description is given in Sandra M. Schneiders, *The Revelatory Text: Interpreting the New Testament as Sacred Scripture* (Collegeville, MN: Liturgical Press, 1999). Also, Paul Ricoeur, "What Is a Text?"

25. Pope Benedict XVI, *Introduction to Christianity*, trans. J. R. Foster (San Francisco: Ignatius Press, 2004), 50.

biblical mind. The Bible shows a God in the mess of life, never reified into concept. God is all over the place and not statically defined. You cannot catch this God. You catch instead traces in the witness testimonies of the Bible. "The proximity of God," Terrien argues, "created a memory and an anticipation of certitude, but it always defies human appropriation."[26] There is throughout a textual cadence: God was here; God went that way; No, that way; God-is-with-us, "Immanuel" (Isa 7:14). God is elusive, fleeting, and eluding conceptual capture always. He is alive, lively, and in movement. Hence, divine absences are experienced from the human perspective of the relationship. They encode the divine élan. It is the modern mind that tends to read divine absence as nonexistence.

The Old Testament makes it hard to get a handle on God. Precisely so; that is its sacred charge. The lingering memories of God ignite yearning in the soul. Divine presence in the Bible is intricately woven with absence in a way that catches the tension humans have relating to the invisible—as their primary relationship! The sacred "envelops and transports man beyond his powers and wishes, but a true liberty takes offence at this uncontrollable surplus."[27]

This *should* strike us as absurd or, indeed, something brand new. The Old Testament is a library of human theological experiences that prompt us toward our own. It conveys the divine presence mixed in with a flawed humanity. It is not a pristine doctrine of God; it gives expression to what it is like to relate to the invisible by people who tried and failed and got up and tried again. What is revealed, then, is certainly much about God, but equally important is something deeply true about humanity; namely, how difficult trusting transcendence—that is, relating to God—actually is.

The wager for God in contemporary society has become more desperate, heartsick even, than it was for Blaise Pascal in the seventeenth century. At the exhaustion point of postmodernity, we believers sit vigil, like loved ones in an intensive care unit. Today, we pray beleaguered, against a dull, gnawing threat that faith could be delusion. At root, it is an existential wager in the callous modern situation where divine absence is assayed as divine irrelevance. As Pope Benedict is aware, "the believer is always threatened with an uncertainty that in moments of temptation can suddenly and unexpectedly cast a piercing light on the fragility of the whole."[28] The modern condition of fairly chronic uncertainty wears us down, abrading

---

26. Terrien, *The Elusive Presence*, 43.

27. Emmanuel Levinas, *Difficult Freedom: Essays on Judaism*, trans. Seán Hand (Baltimore: Johns Hopkins University Press, 1997), 14.

28. Pope Benedict XVI, *Introduction to Christianity*, 42.

our openness to the divine. Atheism is attractive if for no other reason than its sheer "relief of revolt."[29] In contrast, Pascal's wager had been primarily epistemological: one cannot know for sure whether God and eternity exist. Therefore it is judicious to wager that they do, because if right, one gains an eternity with God; if wrong, simply decay after death. Eternity and God, Pascal reasoned, are possible gains against mortal decay. Betting against God means that one bravely stays with the cards dealt, decay and annihilation, but if wrong, loses eternity.

My wager is a more immediate one: I am asking if the invisible God of the Bible is present now and not only after a life bet wisely with Pascal. Faith in such a long, delayed gratification in an afterlife would undoubtedly influence the decades of actual living we are here to do, but it would not imbue them. And this largely anticipatory faith—for the *after* of life—seems an odd arrangement for a God who made both earth and life, that is, for their putative meaning to take hold only after the fact. Like Pascal though, the wager focuses all and lays bare the commitment of *wanting* God to be there. It risks outright the no-show, as happens so famously in the play *Waiting for Godot*. As with all risks, there would have to be a point of no return, where silent absence, rather than real, divine presence, could well envelop me. A "relief of revolt" would come, as I would finally know one way or the other, but the steep cost would be an embittered soul.

The wager is this book's origins: a challenge to glimpse God's real presence. It is not a defense of faith against the fashionable atheisms of our day but more a proclamation of wonder at the divine possibility in our midst. Karl Rahner has said that a Christian of the twenty-first century will have to be a mystic, that is, one who has really felt an experience of God and not just inherited words about him.[30] Consider this work a contribution to the felt experience of God. It is at once experiential and existential, as it needs to be to capture the short, skittish attention span of the soul—our inner lives.

Too many books argue against atheism or map out ways to include the divine in daily, bustling life. Ecclesiastes called that game long ago: "Of the making of many books there is no end" (Eccl 12:12). Some are persuasive, strategic, and helpful. And they have aimed too low. One does not encounter God after reviewing the benefits package to religious belief. We are in the end and always searching for God to *be in our lives*, not for descriptions

29. Taylor, *A Secular Age*, 306.

30. Karl Rahner, "The Spirituality of the Future," in *The Practice of Faith: A Handbook of Contemporary Spirituality*, ed. K. Lehmann and A. Raffelt (New York: Crossroad, 1986), 22.

about him as host to some later fabulous afterlife. This, then, is no defense of God's existence, for defense concedes far too much. Theology at this cultural stage must be more than defense, more than academic punditry.[31] We have to raise our expectations, not lower them to what is achievable— say, agnostic savoir faire. Pascal at least wagered. Befuddled by secularism, we lack even that energy. This search for God amid presence and absence is more existential contact sport than cerebral puzzle. It is Jacob wrestling with the angel (Gen 32), a biblical theology with rascal sincerity.

St. Paul defined God best, though not conclusively: in God, "we live and move and have our being" (Acts 17:28). I say "best" not because he cleared anything up about who God is but because it is the truest expression of what the believer actually experiences, namely, a surrounding, gentle, suffusing presence. And so for the believer, an atheist is a pure curiosity, something like a fish who doesn't believe in water. The believer is talking on this embracive, encompassing level; the atheist is talking about a cartoon character sitting atop a cloud. To not believe in this enveloping, subtle love is like cutting yourself out of the place of being, the air, the oxygen, the very life force within and surrounding us. Trying to describe this theology of presence in words over against the cartoon Supreme Being is a bit like throwing suction cups at the tide or at sound. That is how awkwardly limiting, excruciating, and self-conscious constructive biblical theology writing is. "Theology," Jean-Luc Marion notes, "always writes starting from an other than itself. It diverts the author from himself."[32] Paul's description of a place in which "we live and move and have our beings" pinpoints where this mystery lies for the theologian.

The term "mystery" derives from the Greek *mysterion*. Its occurrence in the Old Testament, the majority of which was written in Hebrew, is confined to those books that were originally written in Greek: Tobit 12:7, 11; Judith 2:2; Wisdom of Solomon 2:22; 6:22; 14:15, 23. The exception occurs in Daniel 2:18-19, 27-30, 47. There, *mysterion* is used in the Septuagint, the Greek translation of the Old Testament, for the term *razeh*, a Persian loanword meaning "secret," of either a religious or social nature. In the New Testament, however, *mysterion* is used exclusively in a religious sense, often related to the term "revelation" (Mark 4:11; Rom 11:25;

---

31. Andrew Louth makes the case that the post-Enlightenment era severed thought (Rationalism) from feeling (Romanticism) and theology from spirituality, so that there was a dissociation of sensibility. *Discerning the Mystery: An Essay on the Nature of Theology* (New York: Oxford University Press, 1990), 2.

32. Jean-Luc Marion, *God without Being*, trans. Thomas A. Carlson (Chicago: University of Chicago Press, 1991), 12.

16:25-26; 1 Cor 2:7; 4:1; Eph 1:9-10; Col 1:26-27; 1 Tim 3:9, 16; Rev 10:7).[33] *Mysterion* is primarily a Pauline concept, and when translated into the Latin after the third century CE, it is "sacrament."[34]

While the actual word "mystery" or "sacrament" is rare in the Old Testament, the notion that the created world is filled with multiple meanings of the seen and unseen is a given. So much so in fact, that I hope to show that it requires no technical term. Again and again, the extraordinary comes through the ordinary, or, in the biblical idiom, "with God all things are possible" (see Gen 18:14; Job 42:3; Matt 19:26). This is as true for the surprising blessings in a farmer's life as it is for the incarnation of Christ. Even the contrast between effusive biblical praise and the actual humble subsistence conditions of ancient Israel suggests that something remarkable is going on at least attitudinally. Gratitude for the concrete stuff of life fills the Bible: crops, spring water, cattle, wind, wine, pregnancy, reunions, etc.

Biblical details about daily life matter, as does the perspective for seeing more in them than meets the eye. Biblical faith is decidedly not Platonic, that is, about the hidden true ideas or meanings at the expense of the concrete. The mystery of life is not found above or beyond the material world and history but is instead written right into them. This, then, is an incarnational faith in a broad sense, that is, that God is enfleshed in the world somehow and always. This itself is an astonishing claim! Somehow the Transcendent Author of All made contact with little humans. The Bible, through the details, is teaching discernment and even nimbleness in relating to the divine in our midst. Divine presence is in human life. God did not drop the Bible out of the sky or dictate its contents once *in toto.* Instead, he reached out and collaborated—mysteriously, to be sure—with entire generations and the Bible emerged. Even the biblical people cannot get over this, as the psalmist cries:

> When I see your heavens, the work of your fingers,
>   the moon and stars that you set in place—
> What are humans that you are mindful of them,
>   mere mortals that you care for them? (Ps 8:4-5)

In other words, why do *you,* God, care about *us?* We—it turns out— are better than we imagined: we are made in God's image. God's very

---

33. C. F. D. Moule, "Mystery," in *The Interpreters' Dictionary of the Bible,* ed. George A. Buttrick (Nashville, TN: Abingdon, 1962), 3:479–81.

34. German Martinez, *Signs of Freedom: Theology of the Christian Sacraments* (Mahwah, NJ: Paulist Press, 2003), 28.

attention gives us dignity. We are each, as Pope John Paul II said, "unique and unrepeatable."[35] We read the Bible, then, in part to recover our sense of dignity and encounter the holy. I see no downside here.

"God," in Paul's sense, is a much larger reality than a cipher for philosophical disputes about transcendence. God is the very precondition of our rational reflections and doubts, already there like air, as I "live and move and have my being." The purpose of this book is to detect that element scripturally as presence rather than absence, as life-giving as air and more so. The Holy Bible trains us to become attuned to God's hidden presence so that we "may have strength to comprehend with all the holy ones what is the breadth and length and height and depth, and to know the love of Christ that surpasses knowledge, so that you may be filled with all the fullness of God" (Eph 3:18-19).

Methodological Perspectives

At the outset, it is worth noting the larger perspectives that influence this work of biblical theology. Though they overlap, the three perspectives are canonical, Catholic, and sacramental. In a canonical perspective, the meanings and insights within Scripture, inclusive of both the Old and the New Testaments, are put in constructive tension with each other and are not viewed as isolated bits within one genre or historical period. In a diachronic view, history and the development of ideas matter. But the Bible's corpus of theological meanings does not end with diachronic development. Instead, the existing corpus functions as a rich chorale of theological voices, and their synchronic unity brings additional meanings to the fore.

A canonical perspective remembers that what texts meant to their original, intended audience is not always the most relevant meaning for subsequent hearers of the Word, who are reading the ancient texts for some illumination into their own faith lives. This is a method most identified with Brevard Childs who, as my teacher, has exercised a long-term influence on my thinking. As a *historical* matter, it is certainly important to know when Israel first felt God's absence and perhaps which character was most afflicted by it (Job). But as a *theological* matter, if we are interested in negotiating our faith lives through our own periods of absence and presence, then we let the synchronic riches of Scripture instruct. For, in the end, we want *ourselves* to engage the God of the Bible and not simply

35. "Christmas Message, *Urbi et Orbi*, 1979," cited in George Weigel, *Witness to Hope: The Biography of Pope John Paul II* (New York: HarperPerennial, 2005), 273.

read what the ancients said about their own engagement with the divine. In the end, we desire not the hearsay but the encounter itself.

Childs nicely articulates the paradoxical twist of biblical interpretation: "The true expositor of the Christian Scriptures is the one who awaits in anticipation toward becoming the interpreted rather than the interpreter. The very divine reality which the interpreter strives to grasp, is the very One who grasps the interpreter. The doctrine of the role of the Holy Spirit is not a hermeneutical principle, but that divine reality itself who makes understanding of God possible."[36] This idea that the Bible is interpreting us, rather than we it, locates the interpreter in a position of deference before the text.[37] It has its modern origins in the neoorthodoxy of Karl Barth, who insisted that the interpreter stands transformed as "Scripture interprets itself."[38] As instruction on how to read the Bible, however, it is quite opaque, though I hope to show in the course of these chapters how it nevertheless occurs. At any rate, it is the divine reality we seek and not the historical moments in which it is attested for ancient Israel. And, if God is anything like who the writers say, then God is not only back there in biblical times.

My perspective is also distinctively Catholic in at least three ways that are characteristic of, but not exclusive to, Catholicism. Indeed, as "Catholic" comes from *kata holos*, "from the whole" or "universal," I hope readers of various backgrounds share some of these same affinities. First, there is an emphasis on the complementarity of faith and reason. The Catholic perspective sees these two facets as essential in theology and not at odds. Hence, this work about God's presence is as much from the heart as it is from the mind. It is not only intellectual. Instead, it is, as St. Anselm defined theology, "faith seeking understanding." I am prepared for a good deal of mystery to envelop me. It does at Mass, amid the incense, candles, and holy presence of the Eucharist. And it does when I kneel to pray there: "Lord, I am not worthy that you should enter under my roof, but only say

36. Brevard Childs, *Biblical Theology of the Old and New Testaments*, 86–87.

37. Characteristic of the Yale school of hermeneutics represented by Hans Frei, George Lindbeck, David Kelsey, Chrisopher Seitz, Ellen Davis, among others. See Mark I. Wallace, *The Second Naiveté: Barth, Ricoeur, and the New Yale Theology* (Macon, GA: Mercer University Press, 1990).

38. Karl Barth, *The Word of God and Theology*, trans. Amy Marga (London: T & T Clark International, 2011), 19. The precritical interpreters of Scriptures, such as Jerome, Origen, Augustine, Martin Luther, Jean Calvin, etc., of course, had a pronounced deference toward the text as well. But as a rule they were not vexed by the problem of the *subjective* position of the interpreter, except insofar as guilt, worldly distraction, and unworthiness might impair it. They did not need the neoorthodox reminder that "Scripture interprets itself," because that was a given, which was directed by the Holy Spirit.

the word and my soul shall be healed."[39] That seals the deal for me every time. It brings me up short and shakes my attention back from its wanderings. It is truly a performative utterance that arrests inattention. There, I sense God's presence unmistakably.

In this present work I want to probe Scripture for that same, sure, sacramental presence. Biblical studies itself is currently split on an either/or dichotomy between historical criticism or popular piety. So-called spiritual readings generally fall into the latter category, along with the precritical exegesis of the early Church fathers. Biblical studies still privileges reason over faith, as it views them in conflict. Yet, one hallmark of the Catholic intellectual tradition is that the relationship between faith and reason is a source of dynamic theological and interpretive insight.

Second, there is in the Catholic imagination a predisposition to enchantment. Andrew Greeley has described this best: "Catholics live in an enchanted world, a world of statues and holy water, stained glass and votive candles, saints and religious medals, rosary beads and holy pictures. But these Catholic paraphernalia are mere hints of a deeper and more pervasive religious sensibility which inclines Catholics to see the Holy lurking in creation."[40] And we never confuse the paraphernalia with divine presence. Catholics cannot help themselves. We love the art and the kitsch in equal measure and never for the things themselves, as idols, but for the deeper things they signify. We are just grateful to have something to hold onto, to see and smell and touch to help us worship the invisible God. We tend to believe that we inhabit an incandescent world: where visible signs of invisible grace are not too few or hopelessly naïve but are real, where miracles and grace stand a fighting chance even in a skeptical age, and where the ordinary still opens up with the extraordinary. Everyone cheered in 2010 when the trapped Chilean miners were brought up to safety and life one by one. But to one given over to enchantment, it was not simply a feel-good human interest story. In fact, they never are. It was more. It was God— through cranes and pulleys and dedicated engineers—re-presenting Lazarus thirty-three times in a row for the entire world to witness.

39. International Commission on English in the Liturgy (ICEL), *The Roman Missal*, Third Edition (Collegeville, MN: Liturgical Press, 2011), "Invitation to Communion."

40. Andrew Greeley, *The Catholic Imagination* (Berkeley: University of California Press, 2001), 1. David Tracy offers a nuanced, theological comparison of the Catholic propensity to think analogously, in terms of things having a "both/and" quality, with the corresponding Protestant propensity to think dialectically, in terms of "either/or." David Tracy, *The Analogical Imagination: Christian Theology and the Culture of Pluralism* (New York: Crossroad, 1998).

The Catholic worldview is crowded. It deals in the both/and of possibilities, in multiple analogies; it is rich with symbols and art and reaches at times toward a sensory, emotional, and tradition overload, just on the chance that the holy lurks nearby. It insists on an incarnational vision that a God who became flesh in Jesus is still doing so today, that the divine and the human have, in fact, united in one person and that simply does change everything. My aim, therefore, is to present a strategy of reading Scripture, a Catholic hermeneutics, for Real Presence. For, the Catholic imagination of an enchanted world where elements always mean more than one thing, where truths can be invisible, where the both/and possibilities of analogy and metaphor trump the reductive either/or, and where astonishing beliefs are claimed of bread and wine, is certainly suited to the reading of Scripture.

Finally, I hope this work encourages specifically Roman Catholic readers toward increased familiarity with and appreciation of the Bible, especially the Old Testament, as this remains a great unknown for many Catholics. Christians, as Pope Pius XI said, are "spiritual Semites" who can encounter God in the Old as well as the New Testament but have a long way to go in claiming that lineage with Judaism. Catholics are notorious for not knowing our Scriptures, but it was not until 1943, with the promulgation of the papal encyclical *Divino Afflante Spiritu* (Inspired by the Holy Spirit), that biblical study was even sanctioned. Twenty years later, with the issuance of *Dei Verbum* (Dogmatic Constitution on Divine Revelation) by the Second Vatican Council in 1965, the church offered substantial instruction on how to read Scripture critically and spiritually. As a result, there is today an enhanced role of Scripture, both the Old and the New Testaments, in the liturgy and in papal pronouncements. Yet, there remains a considerable confidence lag in Bible study among Catholics, which is quite understandable. For, in terms of historical time, these developments in Catholic biblical interpretation are relatively recent—the twentieth century. In the sixteenth century, Martin Luther proclaimed *sola scriptura*—"Scripture alone"—as the font of divine revelation. He then translated the Bible into the vernacular language of his time, German, to give access for the laity. Since then, the Bible's importance has loomed understandably large in the faith life of Protestants. As a result, Protestants have enjoyed a rich tradition of personal discovery of Scripture, evident today in the host of Bible versions targeted to specific audiences, for example, men, women, African Americans, teenagers, people in recovery, etc. Protestants tend to have a much greater familiarity with the Bible than Catholics. When I want to slyly gauge the ecclesiastical breakdown of a class, all I have to do is ask students to open their Bible to Isaiah. The prolonged rustling of pages is all Catholic.

As a further extension of the Catholic perspective, my focus is overtly sacramental. Augustine defined a sacrament as "a visible sign of an invisible grace."[41] Biblical texts contain (lots of) the visible details of what they are about—a flood, a pregnancy, a harvest, etc. At the same time, they have spiritual meanings that are not immediately plain but instead reveal themselves in reflection. When we read a story as an object about the past, that is, as an artifact, we are too removed for encounter. The important moments of the Bible are indeed descriptive of an ancient time, say, the Israelites on the edge of their Promised Land in Deuteronomy, but they also invite us to meet the living God. These tales, by their very nature as Scripture, are encounter material. Reading them takes on a performative aspect. It is my intent, then, to offer a hands-on biblical theology that is story-based rather than systematic in design. The Bible really is an interactive library, a place to wander around and react. Reading it is more like a steeping process where we abide in the scene, settling into it, fleshing it out, and browse with no sense of time. Slowly yet surely the graces emerge. The stories grant access to an enchanted world where, it turns out, this living God is real. Two textual interpretations will begin this trek for divine encounter. They are Deuteronomy 30 and Genesis 1. I chose Deuteronomy 30 because long ago it unexpectedly compelled me to interact with the Bible and Genesis 1 because it begins the Bible and offers initial clues for proceeding to read through its riches.

Deuteronomy's Choice

When I first crashed into the Old Testament, it was—by chance only—Deuteronomy, with its unabashed power and clarity. It was utterly thunderous and unapologetic about its God: "I have set before you life and death, the blessing and the curse. Choose life, then, that you and your descendants may live, by loving the LORD, your God, obeying his voice, and holding fast to him. For that will mean life for you, a long life" (Deut 30:19-20). Now that's writing! These words did not seem easy, just clear. "Choosing life" and "holding fast to God" seemed quite daunting, in fact, with their active, steep verbs. In one crystal-clear moment, all the sanctimonious preachers of memory shrank down to their true, puny size. There will always be these kinds of Christian spokespeople who use the Bible, lock and load, and take aim to judge others. They detract from this faith. Really, no sentence, religious or secular, should begin, "You should . . ." It stymies any chance of

---

41. Augustine, "Sermon 272," in *Augustine in His Own Words*, ed. William Harmless (Washington, D C: Catholic University of America Press, 2010).

encounter. Here, by contrast, in Deuteronomy, was a God offering life and love, even to the point of holding fast! This was no timid, furtive, aloof God. No one on those plains of Moab would have been in any doubt about who was addressing them. Even as it is Moses speaking for God, the unabashed clarity is Godlike.

The quest Deuteronomy offered, the adventure of a lifetime, where we choose every day between life and death, was enchantingly strange. The adventure seemed almost epic, and it is, as big and rollicking as *Moby Dick*. A kind of time warp of gratitude stretches from Moab to me to Mass: "It is truly right and just, our duty and salvation, always and everywhere to give you thanks, Father most holy."[42] The offer itself was life-giving as much then to the Israelite generation who had just walked across a desert as now for people caught in a rapidly secularizing culture. Today we endure distraction instead of desert, a dizzying array of options, packaging, and products on hand to choose from, but this raw, booming God of Deuteronomy is not one of them. He has either been put into storage or whittled down to bland, feel-good prosperity gospels.

"Choose life over death" is clamoring, clear policy, Zen-gong clear. It is profound wisdom predating by millennia the abortion debates in which it is currently invoked. Choose life over death every step of the way, from conception to natural death, as Catholics like to say, for every person. Every step of existence is a life or death issue, not only the heartrending dilemmas. Choose life and keep choosing it until the day we die. It was, incidentally, only that part of the Deuteronomy passage I could take hold of and awkwardly practice. I was worlds away from "holding fast to" God or even knowing who God is. But the baby steps of choosing life over death in everyday decisions got me in the door toward God. And, freakishly, it worked. It was helpful, like instruction (Hebrew: *Torah*) should be.

This ancient desert instruction slowly illuminated the death pockets all around me: in narcissistic friends, hostile traffic, off-color jokes, unremitting cynicism, angers, groupthink, gossip, multiplying addictions, careless behaviors, etc. Deuteronomy afforded a choice and with it a restoration of my dignity. In fact, it was *revelatory* of both, namely, that we genuinely have a choice and a God-given dignity. I lost my aptitude for death pockets, which did not let me "live and move and have my being" but had instead constrained me. It was an oddly tiny moment for a conversion. I felt awkwardly out of step with the culture, like those baby ducks you see crossing a highway of speeding cars with their mother. You just know this

42. ICEL, "Preface Eucharistic Prayer II," in *The Roman Missal*.

can't end well. And then it does. It did. Theologians call these tiny moments redemption.

St. Augustine, the moment before his dramatic conversion, merely opened the Bible like he had done so many times before, often with some literary disappointment.[43] But this time a phrase stuck to his conscience, altering his life irrevocably. The phrase that caught him up short was from the New Testament: "not in orgies and drunkenness, not in promiscuity and licentiousness, not in rivalry and jealousy. But put on the Lord Jesus Christ, and make no provision for the desires of the flesh" (Rom 13:13-14). Augustine remarks in his *Confessions*, "I had no wish to read further, and no need. For in that instant, with the very ending of the sentence, it was as though a light of utter confidence shone in all my heart, and all the darkness of uncertainty vanished away."[44] St. Augustine had heard God both through the voice commanding him to "take up and read," and in the Romans passage he then took up to read. These were not discrete experiences. Instead, they were the holy breaking through in his garden meditation, in voiced guidance and Scripture. God was *unmistakably* present for St. Augustine. It was real presence, through and through, nourishing his soul. For St. Augustine, the block to reading Scripture had been pride; the Bible, in his estimation, was inferior to Cicero's *Hortensius*. The modern disposition to reading Scripture is, like St. Augustine, also affected by pride. Reading Scripture too often can seem like an assignment, chore, bore, history lesson, or historical-critical puzzle. We are quick to judge materials for their entertainment value. *Our* interest must be kept. In addition to these considerable obstacles, for modernity the very idea of encountering living, divine presence in the act of reading is at best a distant, inchoate hope.

In the Beginning

> *Then God said: Let the earth bring forth every kind of living creature: tame animals, crawling things, and every kind of wild animal. And so it happened: God made every kind of wild animal, every kind of tame animal, and every kind of thing that crawls on the ground. God saw that it was good. (Gen 1:24-25)*

In the Bible's beginning, Genesis 1, we learn at least three things for discernment. First, the world we inhabit is more than a world, a planet, third

43. Augustine, *The Confessions*, trans. Maria Boulding (Hyde Park, NY: New City, 2001), 3.5.9.
44. Ibid., 8.12.29.

from the sun in a line of eight. Second, it is teeming with variety: species, flora, fauna, astronomical glitterings, crawling things, flying things, beasts of all sorts. It is plentiful, varied, teeming, dazzling. Third, the divine judgment on all of this display is affirming. After each day God pronounces it good. And on the sixth and final day of creation, God "looked at everything he had made, and found it very good" (Gen 1:31). The opening chapter has just reoriented our view of the world as the treasure trove that it is. Our vision is recalibrated into a kind of ecological tenderness, as the poet Galway Kinnell has envisioned:

> for everything flowers, from within, of self-blessing;
> though sometimes it is necessary
> to reteach a thing its loveliness,
> to put a hand on its brow
> of the flower
> and retell it in words and in touch
> it is lovely
> until it flowers again from within, of self-blessing.[45]

Except that in Genesis, it is God who gives the blessing and God who will reteach *everything* its loveliness. The Scripture here, Genesis 1, would retell the world "in words and in touch it is lovely." Its creation account of humans, from the Priestly source, unequivocally celebrates humans made *imago Dei*, in the image of God (Gen 1:27). You are good. You are very good. It is balanced by a second creation account, from the Yahwist source, that follows in Genesis 2. There, humans are made from dust and shall return to dust, but they have the breath of God for life: "the LORD God formed the man out of the dust of the ground and blew into his nostrils the breath of life, and the man became a living being" (Gen 2:7).

This second account is a tempered anthropology, that is, that without God, we are but dust from the ground. Humans are both/and. We fall when we deny our dependence upon God or misuse our majesty for domination. I don't think I fully understood this story until I went scuba diving. There I quickly learned how dependent I was on breath. I could either keep panicking or accept it and marvel at the delightful dolphins chirping and dancing around me. Gratitude had not even been a possibility for something I had hitherto taken entirely for granted. Dependency too, I discovered, can be liberating. It can beget beauties otherwise unseen.

---

45. Galway Kinnell, "St. Francis and the Sow," in *A New Selected Poems* (New York: Houghton Mifflin, 2001), 94.

This teeming, very good world described in Genesis 1 is the proper starting point for how to read Scripture. It is not merely descriptive but suggestive of how to read the world as creation, as pulsating with all sorts of life. (Choose it!) But it also serves as a hermeneutical goad for how to read what follows. The Bible's sly program of wonder is being uploaded as we struggle to understand the genealogies, sheep, battles, and speeches as teeming with life and its variety. Biblical details such as these are evocative. We are not responsible for knowing them. Instead, they are instructing us on how to read life, ourselves, and the world. We might recall that the word "text" is from the Latin *textus*, meaning "fabric." This ancient text, then, is no monolith. Instead, it is rich, variegated, tactile, textured, with tears, corrections, and gaps between the threads to examine.

Creationists misread Genesis as descriptive, and so somehow scientific, rather than evocative. Genesis 1, though, is not a story of *how* the universe happened but *why*. As children, when we first saw the night sky camping, it *did* look like a lit-up show. A rainbow *was* spectacularly worthy of a gasp (Gen 9:13). Genesis is not bad science. It is getting at the wonder evoked by the world. Genesis 1 invites us to marvel, to drop down into its enchanted world. What could possibly be lost by a reverie of how good we are and how alive everything around us is?

The biblical people struggled hard to get by in the semiarid land of Israel and Babylon. All sorts of adversity—enemies, poverty, famine, devastation, and deportation—had gripped Israel. Yet, the worldview they paint in Genesis 1 is hymn-like, front-loaded with gratitude. It bespeaks an astonishing chutzpah of these hardscrabble writers. And something more, something revelatory: namely, that underneath even hardscrabble existence, there is meaning and beauty. This is perhaps a bit of divine chutzpah too, since it will prove so easy for atheists to dismiss.

Divine presence is written into creation itself. It is the foundational gift of God's self-communication, that is, grace,[46] that makes possible all other instantiations of it: an incarnation, a burning bush, forgiveness, peace, giggling with dolphins. But since the scientific revolution, we have objectified the world and disengaged ourselves from this organic, spiritual given-ness— life *as* gift—so that we no longer see grace all around us. The creation is now a mere planet; we humans are Homo sapiens, not images of anything grander than our species. We no longer use words like "teeming" or "incandescent." Instead, we have to look them up when we encounter them.

---

46. This view is Karl Rahner's, who emphasized the initiative and gratuitousness of God's grace.

Mystery and Modernity

The Issue of Invisibility

Why does God have to be invisible? And since God is, how can we experience and relate to him, still less explain the nature of faith, of trusting in the divine invisible? Ours is a decidedly materialist world that privileges, even adores, the seen, the spectacle available empirically. If something can be seen and the data back it up, then we accord it reality status. Religion is forced onto an untenable ledge between the real as empirically defined and the superstitious.

This work examines the interplay between God's presence and absence in the Bible, both the Old Testament and the New. The point of such a focus is not academic curiosity. It is written in response to the modern conditions of secular culture that make the idea of relating to a personal God seem so distant. It presumes that many people remain interested in the Bible but often do not know how to begin. My second objective, then, is instructive for how to read Scripture for soulful gain. I argue throughout that Scripture still has much wisdom to offer for understanding the meaning of our lives and addressing the spiritual problems generated by modernity. Much of that wisdom occurs in the sly tension between God's presences and absences. These occasions of divine presence and absence are not mere literary devices to heighten contrast. Rather, they function as instructional scene-scapes on how to spiritually withstand this tension and accede beyond it to mystery.

What is it to live before mystery, to live as if it is real, even more real than the empirical reality around us? Augustine came to discover about

God, "You were closer to me than I was to myself."[1] This confounding, true mystery, interiorly present, is, I believe, whom the Bible introduces.

For theists, living in the Age of Disbelief can be uncomfortable and a countercultural challenge. Religious faith is largely considered a matter for private life and has diminished greatly as an influence in people's actual lives. Western civilization was built on the Judeo-Christian heritage, and this is now receding fast. For theists, this is more bad news; for Western civilization, maybe worse. If current demographic trends continue, European populations may become predominantly Muslim within a few generations, with all the attendant cultural shifts that entails.[2] Islamic theism might become a countervailing force to Europe's secular drift, but this remains to be seen. It would also differ markedly from the influence that Judeo-Christian faith has exercised on the West. My concern here is primarily theological rather than political. Currently, in Western culture, secularism, a general attitude toward life without regard for religion, is quickly taking the place of a historically Judeo-Christian heritage. Doing theology in such a clime means, as Karl Rahner noted, working in the "wintry season" of modernity.[3]

A secular world, one where religion is in abeyance, has eroded our ability to distinguish between the sacred and the profane. The very categories no longer matter, as the profane is all-pervasive. The sacred is some other too rare sphere, evident in religious houses of worship. Without an understanding of these categories, the idea of relating to God recedes even further into the background. It is hard to discern who God really is. Not who he was. Most Westerners have a passing familiarity with biblical ideas about God being just, merciful, fatherly, sometimes wrathful, and evident in his son Jesus. But these, I suspect, remain largely the descriptions of a character in a book, albeit an important book. The God of the Bible rescues an entire nation from slavery in Egypt and goes around healing the blind and lame with just words. Why, then, is such a dynamic, scene-stealing God not considered a viable option for our own lives?

In this "wintry season" of religious belief, the idea of providence, that is, God's active presence in history and in our lives, is especially problematic.

---

1. Augustine, *The Confessions*, trans. Maria Boulding (Hyde Park, NY: New City, 2001), 3.6.11.

2. The combination of immigration policies and a birthrate below the replacement rate needed to retain Europe's demographic makeup is the cause. Christopher Caldwell, *Reflections on the Revolution in Europe* (New York: Doubleday, 2009); Mark Steyn, *America Alone: The End of the World as We Know It* (Washington, DC: Regnery, 2008). Steyn's term for the future Europe is the provocative "Eurabia."

3. Elizabeth A. Johnson, *Quest for the Living God: Mapping Frontiers in the Theology of God* (New York: Continuum, 2007), 43.

We might concede that divine interventions could occur or that something like faith healings are possible. During a crisis we might even pray for divine intervention. God may or may not be real, but we urgently pull out all the stops if he can come through just this once. People who never pray awkwardly start. They invoke God, Jesus, Mary, and Joseph. Once the crisis is over, our lives resume, maybe changed, mostly not, exhibiting a routine secular humanism where we are nice and try to treat others as we want to be treated. But if that should fail for some reason, then, well, game on. Cultural phenomena like road rage would be much harder to indulge if providence were a given. God is the neglected, dusty deity of a busy modernity. We plead for him to be real when needed, but not before. In such a clime, how could God be vibrantly present in a hospital room, much less in the goings on of our world? I think if we could articulate this harbored, inchoate assumption, it is that God used to be present in biblical times, and those people really knew their God. But today that same God is so silent that it seems obvious that he must be gone. "Christianity became a little church in a much bigger world."[4] How did we get to this place? How did we come with such breathtaking ease to lower our expectations about the divine?

Modernity's Worldview

The question of how we came to this attitude about God concerns modernity, roughly the time period from the seventeenth and eighteenth centuries, including the Enlightenment, to the present time. Much has been written about modernity, but for our purposes, I simply want to address the salient characteristics that changed our worldview from an essentially God-centered one of ancient and medieval times to a human-centered one of modern times. "Modernity" denotes a host of cultural shifts: the advent of the scientific revolution, capitalism, industrialization, mass media, increased population in cities rather than rural communities, and a "turn to the subject" in philosophy. What this latter phrase means is that philosophical speculation turned from the *outside* world of metaphysics, natural law, cosmologies, etc., to the *inner* world of the thinker, the subject, now a sovereign self over the world he or she would study.

With the turn, philosophy concentrated on epistemology, that is, how we know things, how the thinker thinks,[5] a much smaller domain of inquiry and, in fact, a *literally* self-centered one. Descartes's (d. 1650) pronouncement *Cogito ergo sum*, "I think therefore I am," typically signals this shift

4. Ibid., 27.
5. *The Thinker* by Auguste Rodin is unsurprisingly from the modern period, 1880.

to the self in philosophy. He could, in his "method of doubt," be certain
of only one thing, his own thinking. As we have said, a premium is put,
in the modern period, both on reason and on the individual subject who
exercises it. The scientific revolution privileged empiricism, namely, that
we can know and verify truths through our senses. The upshot to religious
faith in a transcendent, invisible Other is that it goes neglected. There is a
concomitant disengagement of the self from the world, which now, as an
objectified domain, loses it normative force in our lives.[6] The central arena
for modernity is humanity, the self, rather than God.

In the medieval period, suspicion about God's presence could not even
arise. God was a given atop the given hierarchy of being. He was as real as
the king above us and the beggar beneath. This Great Chain of Being was
itself proof that there was a God who had designed it.[7] It located the king,
peasants, animals, and plants all securely in their station in life as it located
God securely in his, on top. His presence, therefore, was manifest in the
evidence, the Great Chain of Being, all around us and engulfing us. The very
awareness of my station in life and others in theirs itself bore witness to divine
providence. The chain pointed so conclusively to God that his presence was
uncontested; the notion of invisibility was not problematic. The medieval
confidence was not wholesale, of course. Undoubtedly, there would have
been agnostic sentiments in society from the daring avant-garde thinking
outside their time period's box and in the sporadic, metaphysical musings of
daily life. Still, the medieval confidence in divine presence was nevertheless
characteristic of the age. It might be somewhat analogous to the confidence
we generally accord to family genealogical trees. These are taken on faith; we
certainly do not see the ancestors, exhume graves for verification, or contest
the genealogical searches we attain. The notion of genealogy looms across
centuries, yet there is no concern about *its* invisibility. It is curious that we
still do take many things on faith while reserving our skeptical acumen for
religion. With God, his invisibility has led to doubts about his very existence.

The effect of modernity on religious faith has been devastating. While
modernity heralded new and exciting advances for humankind, scientific
discoveries, new disciplines of knowledge, a belief in human freedom and
individual rights, etc., the idea of a God actively engaged in the world suffered. Deism—namely, the belief that God exists but created the world and
then essentially stepped back—became popular. As William Paley (d. 1805)

6. Charles Taylor, *A Secular Age* (Cambridge, MA: Belknap Press of Harvard University Press, 2007), 283.

7. Etienne Gilson, *The Spirit of Mediaeval Philosophy* (South Bend, IN: University
of Notre Dame, 1991).

famously argued, God was the divine watchmaker whose agency consisted in the initial windup; he set the world in motion, but is no longer involved in its goings-on. From Deism, it was but a short jump to secularism, the disinterest in religious faith altogether.[8]

Modernity's potent cocktail of individualism, skepticism, secularism, and empiricism all combine to make religious doubts acute. With so many options and competing beliefs, there is a "nova effect," with the result that meaning is harder to lock down or even find. It can feel like a fractured culture,[9] where people of faith are viewed as throwbacks to a bygone era. Alternately, they are seen as the last holdouts in a dying enterprise or as having negotiated for themselves a pleasant denial for the sake of societal harmony. God becomes a mere shadow of who he used to be. As the theologian George Stroup argues, "At best God has become the postulate that accounts for the human experience of transcendence rather than that holy reality before whom faith and theology live."[10] The "turn to the subject" happened as well in theology. Even in theology—study (*logos*) about God (*theo*)—we have made it all about ourselves, that is, "the *human experience* of transcendence." Hence, it is a very modern question I pose here, self-referential and catering to individual experience: Does my faith signal a presence *other than me*, or is it simply *my need for an Other*—any will do—to effect my experience of transcendence? Is something or someone there when I pray or am I displaying Freud's repetition compulsion, just the pitiable need to pretend *as if* someone cares?

Secularism manifests in our times in a variety of ways. Charles Taylor details these ways in his authoritative work, *A Secular Age*: (a) the loss of God in the public sphere, (b) a decline in belief and practice, and (c) new shaping to the experience of belief.[11] The latter two elements occupy our attention more so than the first civic change, though that too is an important shift. Taylor asks throughout the work, why was it virtually impossible not to believe in God in 1500, while in 2000 it is easy to, even inescapable?[12] My central questions here are related, though concentrated on the Bible: First, why was God so present in Scripture and why is he so absent today? And, second, its rather more troubling corollary: "were the biblical writers mistaken about the existence of a transcendent being?"[13]

8. Charles Taylor argues that Deism, with its view of God as architect, rather than as interacting with his creatures, is the intermediate stage to an "exclusive humanism" (*A Secular Age*, 221, 270).

9. Ibid., 299.

10. George W. Stroup, *Before God* (Grand Rapids, MI: Eerdmans, 2004), 14.

11. Taylor, *A Secular Age*, 20.

12. Ibid., 25.

13. James Crenshaw, *Defending God* (New York: Oxford University Press, 2005), 26.

Secularism, then, is this Age of Disbelief in which both the believer and the nonbeliever swim. It displays an antagonism to God and mystery. Since some manner of empiricism and skepticism is the dominant lens through which moderns perceive the world and its meanings, the sense of mystery is precluded. It is even resented as a sort of system failure for the powers of reason. What you lose in the secular age is any pronounced awareness of transcendence, namely, that there is something wholly other than us and much vaster. Or it becomes the merely privatized aim in an individual's general pursuit of happiness, achieved variously through worship, rock climbing, ecotourism, meditation, and the like—all experiences we select. An important exception is twelve-step programs such as Alcoholics Anonymous and Al-Anon that overtly espouse belief in a higher power beyond the individual. Otherwise, transcendence often goes unnoticed, unwanted.

At the same time, an entire lucrative self-help industry is built on the transformation of the self. We strive to be the best self we can be. Both terms—*trans*cendence and *trans*formation—concern a "beyond" to the self's limitations. But the difference is how they affect the self. Transformation bolsters the self, the ego, while transcendence is unconcerned with it. There is opportunity for growth in either case, but with transcendence, I relinquish my ego as I come to recognize how tiny it really is. This is a taste of Jesus' teaching: "Whoever finds his life will lose it, and whoever loses his life for my sake will find it" (Matt 10:39). In front of the ocean, for instance, I am *transformed*; brought out of daily worries, attitudes, and thoughts, I gain a renewed energy. But something else happens as well. I sense how small my own self is and this awareness is peaceful rather than threatening. I can surrender my self to the transcendent moment. It is the difference, I suppose, between "getting a rush" and having an awareness. The rush benefits the self. I am pumped up by it and so it is utilitarian, as the ocean essentially becomes an instrument for my relaxation response. In contrast, the awareness has no measurable benefit.[14] Transformation ultimately is limited by how far the self in principle could go: "Be all you can be," but no more. Transcendence, however, is unlimited. It will be around the ocean long after I am dead. It is a limitless horizon. With transcendence, you can be redeemed, that is, restored back to who you were meant to be.

---

14. There is a well-known Zen koan that makes this difference with respect to the self clear. It is about a man who is hanging over a cliff with tigers above him and a steep drop beneath him. He sees a beautiful red strawberry but would have to let go to get it. What does he do? The answer: he eats the strawberry and it tastes delicious. In other words, his self is killed, but the strawberry brings him transcendent joy.

Nietzsche (d. 1900), the reigning bad boy of philosophy, championed a modern humanity that no longer bothered with the limitless horizon of transcendence. A believer in God during modernity is, in Nietzsche's estimation, a "madman":

> The madman jumped into their midst and pierced them with his glances. "Whither is God" he cried. "I shall tell you. We have killed him—you and I. All of us are his murderers. But how did we do this? How could we drink up the sea? Who gave us the sponge to wipe away the entire horizon? What were we doing when we unchained this earth from its sun? Whither is it moving now? Whither are we moving? Away from all suns? Are we not plunging continually? Backward, sideward, forward, in all directions? Is there still any up or down? Are we not straying as through an infinite nothing? Do we not feel the breath of empty space?"[15]

Nietzsche's story is a cautionary tale about the fate of transcendence under modernity. The madman is not Nietzsche; it is the pained, public spectacle of a man who actually misses God. If the definition of a political gaffe is a politician who accidentally tells a truth, it would seem here that Nietzsche has done just this, made a cultural gaffe and told on modernity's murder. And it shouldn't even have surprised us. We had done it before in the first century, killed a God. There is no God for Nietzsche. There is only us, untethered, plunging "backward, sideward, forward in all directions," seasick with isolation.

The modern zoom lens on subjectivity relegates transcendence to blurry background. Nietzsche traded transcendence for the transformation of man into his most powerful best, an *Übermensch*, a Superman. Humanity itself is where meaning occurs, all by itself, with its creative freedom and progress. Meaning, then, is manmade, either manufactured or arrived at via human experience and consciousness. It is not out there for us to discover. It is what we create and choose, as social constructivists posit, that gives meaning to our world.[16] As Charles Taylor notes, in a "world shorn of the

---

15. Friedrich Nietzsche, *The Gay Science*, in *The Portable Nietzsche*, ed. Walter Kaufmann (New York: Penguin Books, 1968), 95.

16. David Bentley Hart argues that nihilism underpins this ethos of choice in modernity, because there is no foundation, just lots of options to exercise choosing (*Atheist Delusions: The Christian Revolution and Its Fashionable Enemies* [New Haven, CT: Yale University Press, 2009], 21). In a similar vein, Pope Benedict points out that having so many choices, one no better essentially than another, is not freedom but a "dictatorship of relativism." He first coined this phrase in a homily before the conclave that elected him, Joseph Ratzinger, pope in April 2005. John L. Allen Jr., "Benedict Battles the

sacred" we feel a new freedom.[17] But the cost of unfettered freedom for humanity, no longer tied to old beliefs about God, has been steep. We are alone, on our own, at the whim of brute nature, its laws, and the society in which we live, and we suffer the maturing grief that no one does look out for us. We might have the vague feeling that something transcendent was once there, a yearning, say, but it is the itchy persistence of a phantom limb. It isn't real. The only real left to us is all the human flourishing we can achieve on earth.

The Numinous Mystery of the Divine

Since I am chasing mystery, I want at the outset to define the term's contours while remaining alert to the surprises that blast them open. The mystery that involves God has to be more than a conundrum baffling the intellect. It involves a relationship with the living divine and so it matters existentially. Christian mystery involves an Other's presence as radiating love. The perspective is not whether I understand this mystery or, still less, whether I can persuade another of its presence. Rather, the focus is on a relationship and part of the reason we may not believe in God is due to our self-centered focus. Karl Barth offers a powerful corrective against the individualistic bias in modern theology: "In Christian faith we are concerned quite decisively with a meeting. What interests me is not myself with my faith, but he in whom I believe."[18] Barth insists that what truly matters is not our experience of God but rather God's experience of us. And the fact that this emphasis puzzles us speaks worlds to the myopic condition modernity can be. We have it exactly backward.

Ironically, the term "God" often obscures the sense of mystery. It becomes a too familiar noun, curiously without substance and bandied about with casual frequency. That "God is mystery" is true but vacuous, a mere tautology rather than a source of joy. Traditional Jews resist using the term "God" and substitute instead "G-d" as a way to revere the one to whom the term signifies. This reverence for the name has its origins in the ancient scribal practice of rendering God's name, YHWH, unpronounceable by scrambling the vowels. *Ha-shem* (the name) and *Adonai* (Lord) became

---

'Dictatorship of Relativism,'" *National Catholic Reporter* (September 16, 2010), http://ncronline.org/blogs/ncr-today/benedict-battles-dictatorship-relativism, accessed June 29, 2012; Jeffrey M. Perl, A *"Dictatorship of Relativism"? Symposium in Response to Cardinal Ratzinger's Last Homily* (Durham, NC: Duke University Press, 2007), 216.

17. Taylor, *A Secular Age*, 80.

18. Karl Barth, *Dogmatics in Outline* (New York: Harper Perennial, 1959), 15–16.

common acceptable substitutes. Such grammatical cues fostered a heightened awareness of mystery around the divine presence in the scriptural text. The impulse, it seems to me, is correct if God-in-mystery is not to be deflated by the commonplace noun, God.[19]

"God" is the idea that there is something mysterious and other, someone enchanting the world, but not provable. Rudolph Otto termed this quality the "numinous." The numinous is that reality that elicits wonder and awe in us. The numinous is the sublime, calming stillness that nevertheless feels full, because it fills the soul. Most of us have experienced this numinous quality at some point in life. The sensation passes, but for a moment it takes us out of the ordinary and rejuvenates us. It is fleeting, quick, and certainly not analyzed, but it is nevertheless real. You cannot tweet this stuff.

A costly weakness to modernity is that we no longer know how to discern the numinous. There is a saying that when you lose a sense, the other senses become stronger. Perhaps in modernity, the reverse has happened. We became so enthralled with the power of our senses to observe, test, and verify in the heady certainty of empiricism that our religious sense, that of discerning the divine, atrophied. We became primarily scientific minds mining the objectively verifiable. The numinous? No idea how to assess or even notice that. As T. S. Eliot once remarked, "we had the experience, but missed the meaning."[20] Pope Benedict laments the Catch-22 moderns find themselves in, where our empiricism precludes the God we search for: "There is no experience of God unless one goes out from the business of everyday living and accepts the confrontation with the power of solitude."[21] At this moment, I am in the library next to a student reading on his laptop, sipping a latte, texting on his phone, with iPod earbuds delivering music. All he needs to complete the sensory ensemble is a scent diffuser! We are techno-pods of activity, virtually hermetically sealed off from one another and from anything smacking of solitude. I am sure that even the pope is plugged in. How can solitude even begin to compete with all this?

Divine mystery is not a thing, some noun, but a living, wholly other being for whom language categories—noun, verb, adjective—are too small. Is there a presence surrounding me in prayer and in life who is somehow

---

19. The Roman Catholic phenomenologist Jean-Luc Marion seems to endorse this Jewish reverence for the divine by sometimes crossing out the noun's vowel, e.g., "G⊠d" (*God without Being*, trans. Thomas A. Carlson [Chicago: University of Chicago Press, 1991], *passim*).

20. T. S. Eliot, "Dry Salvages," in *Four Quartets* (Orlando, FL: Harcourt, 1971), 39.

21. Pope Benedict, *The God of Jesus Christ: Meditations on the Triune God*, trans. Brian McNeil (San Francisco: Ignatius Press, 2006), 21.

obliquely communicating and self-offering at any and every moment? That would be a Yes, and this mystery of divine outreach is what Christians mean by "grace." Elizabeth Johnson, for example, describes the suffusing love that grace is: "Anchored in history by Jesus Christ, the holy mystery of God takes the initiative to surround the lives of all human beings from beginning to end with redemptive love."[22]

This is a mouthful, certainly, and surely way too good to really be true. Way. Too. Good. It is flat out incomprehensible that an ineffable, eternal plenitude of love drew near to humanity in Christ. It is even harder to fathom that this subtle, nudging, unthreatening, yet transforming and loving presence is still coming close to us all the time and just as often in a blighted, secular world. Many decline the offer without even being conscious it could really be on the table. If I am hurt, worried about the world, lonely, scraped raw by exhaustion and banality, struggling with bouts of anger, resentment, impatience, and self-importance, I am already surrounded with love. This grace of enveloping love, frequently undetected, is divine mystery.[23] A chase, then, strictly speaking, is unnecessary. The same mystery that rendered Augustine "restless until we rest in Thee, Oh God" turned out to be present all along, when he proclaimed of God, "you were closer to me than I was to myself."[24] The chase, then, is to discover a mystery undetected, something as real as air, alive and loving me into creation. It requires the exertion of trust toward believing that silent, suffusing love *could* be present. Consider it a chase, then, from the head to the heart, where a mere ten inches or so can be the longest distance of all.

St. Paul is convinced of God's nearness to us, but he had not always been: "For I am convinced that neither death, nor life, nor angels, nor principalities, nor present things, nor future things, nor powers, nor height, nor depth, nor any other creature will be able to separate us from the love of God in Christ Jesus our Lord" (Rom 8:38-39). And, he is just as convinced that the enveloping love of God's presence has nothing to do with merit. We are not surrounded by God's love because we have worked diligently at being lovable. We are surrounded by a gift, like all of that breathing we have been able to do. This is what Paul means by the phrase "justified by faith" (e.g., Acts 13:39; Rom 3:24, 28; 4:2; 5:1; Gal 2:16; 3:24; Titus 3:7). God's love is all *God's* initiative.

---

22. Johnson, *Quest for the Living God*, 41.

23. Ibid., 42.

24. Augustine, *The Confessions*, 1.1 and 3.6.11, respectively. For Augustine, the search for God takes place in interiority. See also Denys Turner, *The Darkness of God: Negativity in Christian Mysticism* (Cambridge: Cambridge University Press, 1995), 55.

Paul and Augustine came to their convictions, then, not through effort, which had been a colossal failure for Paul, but through revelation. They came to see that "the divine mystery is manifest in the midst of our world."[25] Faith, then, is not a categorical assent but a choice of openness.[26] Theology differs from philosophy in this respect: it reflects on a Word given outside oneself, a revelation, whereas for philosophy, the thinking process is primary.[27] "In theology alone," declares Marion, "the Word finds in the words nothing less than a body. The body of the text does not belong to the text, but to the One who is embodied in it."[28] God is hidden and present, animating the Scriptures that embody him.

The theological notion of mystery has had a strange historical career from biblical times to modernity. Traditionally, mystery was viewed as a fundamental aspect of God, and a positive one at that. But with the Enlightenment, mystery became problematic, an impediment to reason, the primary arbiter of knowing. Knowledge itself came to be viewed as a rationalistic enterprise, where one gained control of—mastered—subject matter.[29] Where knowledge is understood to be essentially acquisitive in nature, mystery proves uncooperative. And, in debates about the existence of God, mystery is often considered suspect as just more temporizing by believers.

Mystery in the modern period is viewed mainly as an intellectual problem to be solved. It consists of those areas that science does not yet understand but will someday. In such a perspective, mystery is largely negative, provisional, and subject to reason's ever-advancing encroachment. This viewpoint led to the so-called God of the gaps about which contemporary atheists speak.[30] This is the God who once ruled the world before the scientific revolution but whose sovereignty now has dwindled to the remaining unknowns, that is, the "gaps" in our knowledge. The God of the gaps exists only on borrowed time, as reason conquers these unknowns and mystery too since it is inversely indexed to scientific discovery.

Theology, by contrast, never viewed mystery as a mere cipher for human ignorance, still less as a euphemism for more "primitive ways of thinking." The religious view of mystery is that it entails some element beyond reason's

---

25. Walter Kasper, *The God of Jesus Christ*, trans. Matthew J. O'Connell (New York: Crossroad, 1986), 116.

26. Ibid., 117.

27. Pope Benedict, *Introduction to Christianity*, trans. J. R. Foster (San Francisco: Ignatius Press, 2004), 91.

28. Marion, *God without Being*, 1.

29. Kasper, *The God of Jesus Christ*, 127; Gregory C. Higgins, *Christianity 101: A Textbook of Catholic Theology* (New York/Mahwah, NJ: Paulist, 2007), 127–28.

30. For a discussion of this God and the New Atheists, see chapter 7.

scope. It is a holistic term, involving "more than" our rational knowledge. Mystery exists beyond the human intellect and is wholly unconstrained by the concepts it is ever generating. The holy, notes theologian Elizabeth Johnson, is mystery laced with the promise of plenitude.[31] Mystery, then, is not a gap but an overdetermined surplus. It denotes a kind of plenitude and surplus of meaning within experience. In contrast to modernity's perspective, then, mystery is positive, not negative; eternal, not provisional; and not constrained under reason's subjugation.

What makes me gasp before the ocean is not how inscrutable large bodies of saltwater can be. It is the mystery suffusing the experience and eliciting my wonder. It is a potent, palpable peace. There exists some sort of communication with my being. In Abraham Heschel's terms, the experience is sublime: "it is the silent allusion of things to a meaning greater than themselves."[32] The ocean is one such silent allusion. Mystery is the enveloping munificence where wonder is elicited. And surely wonder is a human aptitude every bit as valuable as reason. In Heschel's view, wonder is a religious aptitude, "a way in which things react to the presence of God."[33] This experience of something beyond ourselves is not at all a rational failure or gap in human understanding. It is, instead, a threshold into a domain much vaster than we had envisioned where truly the holy lurks.

Mystery thus understood is a vast expanse, a detectable fullness. Pope Paul VI defined mystery well as "a reality imbued with the hidden presence of God."[34] It has weight, is laden, is imbued with presence. Biblical language conveys mystery's heft by the images surrounding God. For instance: "Bless the LORD, my soul! / LORD, my God, you are great indeed! / You are clothed with majesty and splendor" (Ps 104:1). Here, the nouns "majesty" and "splendor" connote real presence but remain themselves fairly enigmatic. In another instance, presence is indicated by a part standing for God's greater whole: "When my glory passes I will set you in the cleft of the rock and will cover you with my hand until I have passed by. Then I will remove my hand, so that you may see my back; but my face may not be seen" (Exod 33:22-23).[35]

Divine mystery is real presence in biblical testimony. Its substantial reality is conveyed through such descriptions of physicality and might. As

31. Johnson, *Quest for the Living God*, 9.

32. Abraham Joshua Heschel, *God in Search of Man: A Philosophy of Judaism* (New York: Farrar, Straus and Giroux, 1955), 39.

33. Ibid., 40.

34. Richard P. McBrien, *Catholicism* (San Francisco: HarperSanFrancisco, 1994), 262.

35. See chapter 4 for further discussion of this passage.

Karl Barth thundered, "It is the unmistakable fact that the presence of the God of grace and mercy is very different from that of a harmless supreme being."[36] Just as the biblical witness views creation as teeming with lively diversity, reality also teems with the hidden presence of God. Mystery is a summons to see reality as "more than," as imbued, pregnant with meaning.

Incomprehensibility and Hiddenness of God

Christian tradition over the centuries has insisted on the predicate of incomprehensibility for God. Theology is the odd intellectual discipline that concedes a failure of mastery at the start. As Thomas Aquinas long ago noted, "Man's utmost knowledge of God is to know that we do not know him."[37] Divine incomprehensibility conveys the idea that God can be known to some extent by human reason but never captured by it.[38] God exists beyond the purview of reason as well as within it. The psalmist celebrates his rational limits before mystery: "Such knowledge is too wonderful for me, / far too lofty for me to reach" (Ps 139:6). Humility before vastness is no defeat. And so, Aquinas could say at the end of his life, after having written the expansive *Summa Theologiae*, that it was all straw compared to the beauty revealed of God.

The Bible champions divine incomprehensibility, it does not bemoan it: "See, God is great beyond our knowledge, / the number of his years past searching out" (Job 36:26). St. Paul expressed a similar idea. His proclamation that Christ was risen from the dead, since wholly unprecedented, duly scrambled the brains of both Jew and Gentile: "Where is the debater of this age? Has not God made the wisdom of the world foolish?" (1 Cor 1:20). While preaching in Athens, Paul notices the altar "To an Unknown God" and tells the people gathered that they worship in ignorance what he is there to proclaim (Acts 17:23). Paul unmasks this unknown God, now known in Christ, who is the basis of all debates and so surpasses them all. Pope Benedict adds that in Christian tradition, the Holy Spirit has "largely remained the unknown God" since Scripture never really describes the third person of the Trinity.[39] The divine remains incomprehensible even as Paul

---

36. Karl Barth, *Church Dogmatics*, vol. 3, bk. 3, trans. Harold Knight, G. W. Bromiley, J. K. S. Reid, and R. H. Fuller (Edinburgh: T & T Clark, 1960), 489.

37. *De Potentia* 7.5 ad 14.

38. Henri de Lubac, *The Mystery of the Supernatural*, trans. Rosemary Sheed (New York: Herder and Herder, 1998), 171.

39. Pope Benedict, *The God of Jesus Christ*, 105.

mentions knowing someone who "was caught up into Paradise and heard ineffable things, which no one may utter" (2 Cor 12:4).

Paul does not advocate a fideistic retreat before divine incomprehensibility. Incomprehensible truth can paradoxically be known by reason. Gregory of Nyssa makes an astute observation about this: "Who has known his own mind? Those who think themselves capable of grasping the nature of God would do well to consider whether they have looked into themselves. . . . Our mind bears the imprint of the incomprehensible nature through the mystery that it is to itself."[40] This theological view of mystery is quite circumspect on the value of reason, the cherished aptitude of moderns. Faith and reason are held in tandem in Catholic theology in a creative tension that neither jettisons reason—which would be fideism—nor privileges reason above faith—as rationalism. The stress in Christian theology, particularly in the apophatic theology of the mystical tradition, has been on God's incomprehensibility—to humbly and forthrightly admit that the creature's mind could not grasp in any definitive sense the reality of the creator and that the latter vastly exceeds the intellectual capacity of the former. The notion of incomprehensibility was vital in the writings of Pseudo-Dionysus, Basil, Gregory of Naziansus, Gregory of Nyssa, and John Chrysostom who developed a doctrine of it.[41] Augustine too addressed it. And the fifteenth-century theologian Nicholas of Cusa perhaps best represents the apophatic view, where it is necessary "to enter the darkness, to admit the coexistence of contraries which exceed my power of understanding, to look for truth where there seems only to be impossibility. . . . The place, O God, where we can see you unveiled is surrounded by the coming together of all things contradictory; it is the wall of the Paradise where you dwell, and we can only enter it by conquering reason, which stands guard at the gate."[42] Even the human intellect is a limited aspect of creaturehood. It was Nicholas, after all, who quite comfortably called the theologian *Docta Ignorantia*, a doctor of ignorance—the studied, skilled ignorance that is oftentimes silent, even dumbstruck, before God.

In the suffusing orbit of mystery, God can be known but never grasped.[43] What is interesting is how Christian tradition and the Bible differ on this

---

40. Gregory of Nyssa, *De hominis opificio*, cited in de Lubac, *The Mystery of the Supernatural*, 210.

41. Kasper, *The God of Jesus Christ*, 126.

42. Nicholas of Cusa, *De vision Dei*, cited in de Lubac, *The Mystery of the Supernatural*, 173.

43. de Lubac, *The Mystery of the Supernatural*, 171; Karl Rahner, "Mystery," in *Theological Investigations*, trans. Cornelius Ernst, vol. 4 (Baltimore: Helicon Press, 1961), 133.

aspect of God. While tradition stresses God's incomprehensibility, the Bible speaks instead of God's hiddenness. Both tradition and Scripture are insistent that transcendent presence always dwarfs human intelligence. Yet, Scripture claims something more than incomprehensibility, which is defined in terms of human intellectual limitations. It instead professes hiddenness as a *constitutive* facet of God, irrespective of human understanding, as the following verses illustrate: "He made darkness his cloak around him; / his canopy, water-darkened storm clouds" (Ps 18:12); "Truly with you God is hidden, / the God of Israel, the savior!" (Isa 45:15). These biblical testimonies about hiddenness are themselves vital theological insights. They are not in any sense proto-atheistic displays of frustration. Isaiah, in the verse above, is celebrating his hidden God, not complaining.

The biblical idiom that "God hides his face" signifies divine presence especially during moments of pain and despair, as in the psalms of lament.[44] It conveys the assurance of God's presence during dark moments of human experience. In assertions about divine incomprehensibility, the claim is that God is inscrutable, that is, primarily a challenge for the human intellect.[45] With the notion of hiddenness, though, a sense of mystery beckons. God's very hiddenness is known only through revelation. That is, the hiddenness of God is part of revelation itself and not merely the divine remainder held back from revelation. As David Tracy explains, "God also comes as an ever-deeper Hiddenness—the awesome power, the terror, the hope beyond hope."[46] God's elusive nature is revealed in the Bible. Even with revelation, God remains in mystery as one "who dwells in unapproachable light, and whom no human being has seen or can see" (1 Tim 6:16).

That mystery, Barth argues, is about divine love, the love evident in why God decided to reveal himself at all.[47] Barth insists that, rather than incomprehensibility, "When we believe, we must believe in spite of God's hiddenness. This hiddenness of God necessarily reminds us of our human

---

44. Elsewhere, as we noted above, God is depicted as invisible: Isa 45:15; Ps 139:6; Job 36:26; Rom 1:20; Col 1:15. There are also occasions when God reveals his face: Exod 34:20; Deut 10:8; 18:7; Ps 86:9. Samuel E. Balentine, *The Hidden God: The Hiding of the Face of God in the Old Testament* (Oxford: Oxford University Press, 1983), 49, 65.

45. The claim is epistemological and human-centered, and Johnson argues it reflects God's plenitude. Johnson, *Quest for the Living God*, 37.

46. David Tracy, "Approaching the Christian Understanding of God," in *Systematic Theology: Roman Catholic Perspectives*, ed. Francis Schüssler Fiorenza and John P. Galvin, 2nd ed. (Minneapolis: Fortress Press, 2011), 110–27, at 125.

47. Karl Barth, *Church Dogmatics*, vol. 2, bk. 1, ed. G. W. Bromiley and T. F. Torrance (Edinburgh: T & T Clark, 1957), 179ff.

limitation. We do not believe out of our personal reason and power."[48] Our cognitive limitations are not the point. Instead, the divine love that exceeds them is. All revelation remains mysterious, sacramental, a visible sign of an invisible reality, and this mystery is understood not at all as purposeless or random but as salvation.[49]

> *No one has ever seen God. The only Son, God, who is at the Father's side, has revealed him. (John 1:18)*

Vatican I had emphasized that the very existence of mystery is why revelation is necessary in the first place.[50] God *IS* who no one has seen. The revelation of this God who hides himself but nevertheless reveals himself out of love is central. As Kasper notes, the primary aim of divine revelation is not to solve a mystery but rather to guide us deeper into it.[51] Mystery is a gift of God's plentiful presence, the surplus enveloping us, eliciting faith "so that people might seek God, even perhaps grope for him and find him, though indeed he is not far from any one of us" (Acts 17:27). The game for us, with divine mystery, is always afoot, as God eludes our grasp. At the same time, though, there is a homing sense to our yearning, a sense that it is responsive to something rather than nothing. The psalmist describes this directive yearning with evident tenderness:

> My soul yearns and pines
>   for the courts of the LORD.
> My heart and flesh cry out
>   for the living God.
> As the sparrow finds a home
>   and the swallow a nest to settle her young,
> My home is by your altars,
> LORD of hosts, my king and my God!" (Ps 84:3-4)

Through our yearning and God's gentle guidance, we come to discern the life-altering difference between a plummet downward and a nest for home.

---

48. Barth, *Dogmatics in Outline*, 20.
49. McBrien *Catholicism*, 263.
50. Karl Rahner, "Mystery," in *Sacramentum Mundi: An Encyclopedia of Theology*, ed. Karl Rahner, vol. 4 (New York: Herder & Herder, 1968), 133–36.
51. Kasper, *The God of Jesus Christ*, 268.

Holy Text and Revelation

Access to the Bible

The Bible is clearly a major element in our own imaginative tradition, whatever we may think we believe about it. It insistently raises the question: Why does this huge, sprawling, tactless book sit there inscrutably in the middle of our cultural heritage?[1]

The Bible is a sacred canon, ingrained in Western civilization and overwhelming in its presumed authority. But on the microlevel, that is, for the individual, it is puzzling, a "huge, sprawling, tactless book" in Northrop Frye's honest words. Are the biblical texts still relevant today or are they primarily historical legacy, like, say, the *Epic of Gilgamesh* or the *Odyssey*? The Beatitudes, for instance, are a beautiful, stirring part of Jesus' Sermon on the Mount (Matt 5:1-12). The first is "Blessed are the poor." I can easily see how that would have cheered the poor who were listening to Jesus, but what can it have to do with me? In my efforts to live the gospel, I might venture a quick interpretation, laced with duty: be kind to the homeless and act grateful when I become impoverished in some fashion. But such quick interpretations obviously do nothing to nourish the

---

1. Northrop Frye, *The Great Code: The Bible and Literature* (New York: Harcourt Brace & Company, 1982), xviii.

soul and may likely instill both a faint resentment toward the homeless and a falser self, one cheered by poverty. Nietzsche argued that Christianity's Beatitudes make a virtue out of weakness and thus debase us all.[2] I trust that I am not alone in my assumption that the Bible is prescriptive for how Thou Shouldeth Improve and so can be one thudding, onerous tome.

"Within the Bible," Karl Barth announced in 1916, "there is a strange, new world, the world of God."[3] Since that time, the estrangement between us and the Bible, yoked though it is with curiosity, has continued. As we saw in chapter 1, there is modern interest in knowing the Bible, but the focus is generally quite scattered. The estrangement between the Bible's world and modern readers is not only the problem of the sheep, wheat, beggars, and all the other trappings of ancient agrarian life. That world can indeed start to look like an ancient version of the "it's a small world" Disney ride. It is also that we cannot relate to the Bible, let alone gain any real sustenance from it. The problem is fundamentally interpretive. It is the question of how to relate the meaning of what happened then to the meanings happening now. We might well resolve to read the Bible at every New Year or during times in the liturgical year, such as Lent, but resolutions rarely stick even with the zealous marketing assistance of products that slice Scripture into sections for forty or 365 days.

The idea of an adventure—in reading—is unthinkable, yet this is a book that has stirred souls for centuries. I want more than skimming through this of all books, this book of books. I want exactly that, a stirring, my soul seared by reading something holy. I want to be opened up, broken apart, and lovingly put back together again. The Scriptures are not pristine, pious dictates we swallow whole or neglect. They are the site for contest reading, engaged, all in, bracing disorientation. Access into the Bible is far easier when we expect nothing beneficially profound to happen. The information highway that we are all congested on is about speed, zipping through massive amounts of data, always multitasking, pausing almost never. Alas, Scripture demands a different approach. It is not a data source for yet more information, nor still for applicable lessons to life. That, after all, would be just another app. The goal in biblical reading is somehow more diffuse. It is to slip and fall in and let the lesson, the question, the searching itself reframe our notions about life. The goal cannot be, say, to read ten pages or get the gist. And it is certainly not to read only when one feels like it. It

2. Friedrich Nietzsche, *Will to Power*, trans. Walter Kaufmann (New York: Vintage Books, 1968), 129.

3. Karl Barth, *The Word of God and the Word of Man* (New York: Harper & Row, 1957), 33.

is, instead, to get lost in the words, the very strangeness of it all, regardless of mood. It is radically existential in a way that quickly subsumes all those agrarian trappings.

Reading Scripture is slow, in solitude or friendship, and is best done in small amounts. We mull, chew over phrases, and allow wonder to be stirred. In the early centuries of Christianity, reading Scripture was done aloud, as a way to taste the words. Comprehension intrinsically involved the mouth, pondering and ingesting ideas through speaking them. We could adopt some of this ancient patience and physicality in reading Scripture. Then, in our slow, chewy disorientation, we would experience the dour, stark words coming alive, opening into a feast. Estrangement imperceptibly yields to familiarity—familiarity not only with characters and situations but with something subtextual that concerns the soul, our truest self. Our central core, the locus of our thoughts, feelings, and dreams, is summoned. That core does not go home the same again. The essence of the journeys, promises, foibles, and circumstances of biblical characters start to be familiar amid all the strangeness. It is a terribly difficult thing to admit to someone else of course, and even harder to describe, but something is definitely stirring.

The eucharistic prayer links those biblical people to us: "Remember also, Lord, your servants N. and N., who have gone before us with the sign of faith and rest in the sleep of peace" (EP I). They are present in the communion of saints who surround the eucharistic table and hover somehow with us as people of faith. That can't be yet somehow is. The church invites us to think *what if* there were more than the timeline separating people according to discrete historical periods. That idea is the communion of saints, as Christ's presence overrides chronology. The journey the Bible offers starts to truly become ours by a trick of complexity and strangeness. We get almost hoodwinked into caring about our souls and jolted by the profundity in the eucharistic prayer. The Bible is indeed an internal adventure story, an inside job.

Reading the Bible is disorienting, exasperating, uncomfortable, and tedious. It commands a muscled reading, pondering oddities, frowning incomprehension, puzzlement—the whole interactive works. But what it can yield is even more dazzling: frisson, joy, *jouissance*, a bumpy movement from disturbance to awe to contentment.

We recall from chapter 1 that this approach to reading Scripture is sacramental. It seeks real encounter, real presence, in holy texts, rather than the vicarious view of how biblical characters experienced God. The concrete elements of a sacrament, such as the water and oil at baptism, and the bread and wine at Eucharist, are the visible signs of an invisible grace, God's gift of himself. An analogous idea occurs with Scripture. As St.

Jerome, the patron saint of biblical studies, affirmed, "every word contains a sacrament, there are as many mysteries as there are words."[4] The words themselves are not the full meaning as they also announce something other than themselves.[5] They are symbols; they participate in what they point to. The Holy Spirit in this kind of reading "is not found in spite of the letter but through it."[6] Somehow the Holy Spirit animates the text, flowing through the spaces of its densely knitted fabric as *textus*, just as it animates the human being. There are three key texts that will frame our entry into reading mystery, that is, sacramentally, for the holy. It is my hope that these examples demonstrate how specific words point to more than the scene they describe. They are from Genesis, Matthew, and Luke.

Jacob Wrestles with the Angel

As an instance of encountering the numinous, there is no better story than that of the patriarch Jacob wrestling all night with an angel of God. Neither contestant lets go as they come to know each other. "Jacob was left there alone. Then a man wrestled with him until the break of dawn. When the man saw that he could not prevail over him, he struck Jacob's hip at its socket, so that Jacob's socket was dislocated as he wrestled with him. . . . Jacob said, 'I will not let you go until you bless me.' . . . Jacob then asked him, 'Please tell me your name.' He answered, 'Why do you ask for my name?' With that, he blessed him. Jacob named the place Peniel, 'because I have seen God face to face,' he said, 'yet my life has been spared.' At sunrise, as he left Penuel, Jacob limped along because of his hip" (Gen 32:25-32). Jacob wrestles through the night and does not come away unscathed. The divine opponent is strong, elusive, and full of divine stamina. He leaves Jacob wounded, aching for a name, a connection. Both beings are conspicuously present to each other and the encounter is tangibly rigorous. As a result of their contest, Jacob shall limp the rest of his days. And it was worth every flinch, for Jacob, the deceptive trickster, matures on the spot. He undergoes a name change as well from Jacob to the eponymous "Israel," which means "he has striven with God." Israel the nation, then, understands its very origins in this numinous encounter.

---

4. Jerome, *Commentarioli in Psalmos*, in Louis-Marie Chauvet, *The Sacraments: The Word of God at the Mercy of the Body*, trans. Madeleine Beaumont (Collegeville, MN: Liturgical Press, 2001).

5. Chauvet, *The Sacraments*, 45–46.

6. Ibid., 46.

The "man" wrestling Jacob is mysteriously also God and an angel of God. His elusive identity is numinous presence, that which is strange, powerful, and frightening. It has commanded all of Jacob's attention, all of his energies, and Jacob wrests from him finally what he has needed all along, namely, a blessing. Jacob's own identity, now as Israel, is forever linked to God. Knowing nothing about wrestling, I nevertheless know, like Jacob, worlds about the limping exhaustion involved in searching for God, pleading for a name, some sign of divine presence. I am too often duped into mistaking the silence for absence. An all-night contest of the sort Jacob endured might just be what it takes sometimes to disabuse us of our religious suspicions.

Ask and Seek

Jesus' instruction for divine encounter also involves contact with someone Other, this time in the form of willingness. "Ask and it will be given to you; seek and you will find; knock and the door will be opened to you. For everyone who asks, receives; and the one who seeks, finds; and to the one who knocks, the door will be opened" (Matt 7:7-8 [cf. Prov 8:17]). This is a simple, daring instruction from Jesus—one that tends to be ignored, for it really must be too good to be true. It certainly looks much easier than wrestling, but it may well not be. It requires a level of sustained trust that does not calculate rates of return. This instruction has to be practiced in order to be believed; untapped, it remains simplistic. These gestures of pure willingness work with Scripture, though not magically. The Bible commands us by its very strangeness. Having to ask, to seek, and to knock, then, shakes us out of self-possession. The subject's autonomy is relinquished, undone by openness. It requires an admission of the self's vulnerability, and, depending on how thoroughly we have bought into individualism as a supreme value, this trust can be harder than a wrestling match.

Jesus' guidance is more than wild, optimistic promise, for it is a summons to an ego-less adventure. "The Bible," Barth warns, "gives to every man and to every era such answers to their questions as they deserve. We shall always find in it as much as we seek and no more."[7] Now the jarring possibility emerges that Jesus' advice had not been optimistic at all and that hope had a much longer reach than we had dared to imagine. "Ask, seek, knock" to the modern mind, and the ancient one as well, looks naïve and wholly unworkable as a plan. It disturbs human comprehension, that is, coming across as impractical, perhaps because it *is* divine. Anything

---

7. Barth, *The Word of God*, 32.

genuinely revelatory would have to strike us as strange rather than familiar. Reading with openness to another, silent presence causes discomfort primarily because it requires the jostling and then surrender of our ego, the very self-interest that is always clocking whether we are bored. That restless tic signals something important, namely, that we, as nascent spiritual beings, are wholly adrift in judging, the distraction of having all our attention scattered outward. When Jesus taught his followers not to judge, he used a vivid analogy: "Why do you notice the splinter in your brother's eye, but do not perceive the wooden beam in your own eye?" (Matt 7:3). It is a striking, satirical image and not merely hyperbolic or illustrative of down-home carpenter wisdom. Using it, Jesus exposes the Poe-like grotesquery in how judging others defaces *us*. He illustrates how ridiculously off-balance we look carrying around the clunky, blinding burden of judging. Our distortive judging persists into how we would read Scripture too. We judge it as off-putting or impractical rather than look into ourselves for why we are put off, why we have not yet asked.

Losing Jesus in the Temple

Mary's ordeal, as the mother of Jesus, must have been formidable, selfless, and faithful. She endured pain we understand, the unendurable pain of watching her son executed, and all the other pains involved in a lifetime of loving and letting go of her enigmatic son. Simeon had warned her, "you yourself a sword will pierce" (Luke 2:35). One of those painful moments came when her child went missing for three entire days, surely an eternity for any parent. Jesus was twelve years old. She eventually finds him in the temple back in Jerusalem, listening and learning from the teachers, and quite naturally asks him, " 'Son, why have you done this to us? Your father and I have been looking for you with great anxiety.' And he said to them, 'Why were you looking for me? Did you not know that I must be in my Father's house?' But they did not understand . . . and his mother kept all these things in her heart" (Luke 2:46-51).

I can think of plenty of responses a caring mother could make here, but not the one Mary does. This scene, occurring as it does with Jesus himself gaining instruction, directs us on reading Scripture, on reading Jesus. Mary, the first disciple, offers the quiet hermeneutic of simply listening and "[keeping] all these things in her heart." Notice that her parental anxiety and incomprehension are not at all resolved by her son's response. In fact, for Joseph these must have increased as Jesus mentions his other Father. Joseph's ordeal must also have been formidable and quietly borne. The mystery before Mary is bigger than she can fully grasp, but she has made peace with this. And sometimes that is all we do with a biblical passage. Only later will it come to work on us, to connect with other events from Scripture, our hearts, and our lives.

Wandering in the Desert

All the Israelites grumbled against Moses and Aaron, the whole community saying to them, "If only we had died in the land of Egypt," or "If only we would die here in the wilderness! Why is the LORD bringing us into this land only to have us fall by the sword? Our wives and little ones will be taken as spoil. Would it not be better for us to return to Egypt?" (Num 14:2-3)

The Torah or Pentateuch, the first five books of the Bible, contains the story of Israel's long trek across the Sinai Desert, from Egyptian slavery to freedom in the Promised Land. While in the desert, the people periodically voice their distress—grumble—to Moses (Exod 15:24; 16:2; 17:3; Num 14:2, 29; 17:6; Ps 78:17-18). Okay, they frequently do so. Even though the people have just been God's beneficiaries in a momentous exodus to new, free life, they grumble almost immediately about their desert discomfort. Panic and fear render them querulous to the point that oppressive Egypt starts to look good. And that detail alone reveals worlds about obdurate humankind. This grumbling tradition of the wandering in the desert is instructive on the nature of the divine-human relationship. It shows just how fast distrust intrudes and distorts memory. The people forget 430 years of slavery and consider returning to Egypt (Exod 12:40). Human resistance to change is so strong that slavery can look preferable to freedom; sameness seems better than whatever requires effort. Even with God providing daily deliveries of food, the people routinely panic. As Moses said, "When the LORD gives you meat to eat in the evening and in the morning your fill of bread, and hears the grumbling you utter against him, who then are we? Your grumbling is not against us, but against the LORD" (Exod 16:8 [cf. Num 14:36]). Theirs is a dance of ambivalence through and through, and I imagine that, for most modern readers of the Bible, ours is too. In our skittish desire to know God, we probably try many times to read Scripture but lack the follow-through. The Bible provokes our ambivalence. It is a strong emotion that, alas, must be crawled through.

Biblical studies has enabled us to discern in the desert tradition two levels of meaning operating for ancient Israel. The first is Israel's grumblings with Moses in the desert after their deliverance from Egypt. The second is the later exile of 586 BCE where the scribes, while combining materials for the Torah, undoubtedly saw new resonances in the texts to their recent situation. The desert grumblings in Sinai, then, also resonated for the restlessness of being in exile. The traditions are, in Brueggemann's terms, "recipherred as exile."[8] Biblical theology is informed by these dual foci but does not privilege one over the other. It adds yet a third new focus: that of the restlessness and grumbling condition of the current biblical reader in their cultural context. Imagination is at work in all three levels, with meanings trading back and forth for a multivalent text.

The drama of Israel leaving Egyptian slavery is easily more interesting than the desert tradition in which the law is given. Narrative allows the reader the posture of spectator; law, in contrast, demands reaction. We have to work for comprehension. The exodus story is gripping: the little baby pushed down the Nile, frogs jumping into homes, Egyptian wizards, a mighty pharaoh, firstborn sons dying, and lots of chariots. Then it happens; there is a screeching halt to all this dramatic action and a long pause to recite 613 laws, the fat middle of the Torah.

Entering this strange biblical world of law is an arduous adventure that both beckons and unnerves. It is akin to Israel's wandering in a strange desert in episodic rebellion and doubt. It can strike us that there does not seem really to be enough here, nothing really to sustain, let alone nourish. It is painful and often tedious, with moments of odd curiosity thrown in. For example, Leviticus can seem mind-numbingly baroque until something snags our attention, such as that tattoos are forbidden (Lev 19:28). This detail is remotely interesting, like seeing a scorpion in the desert. At least it isn't just another day of more sand and blinding light. The exasperation and impatience of wandering through these laws forces the reader into an analogous desert experience where it all looks the same, until something sticks out. In the case of tattoos, this was not simply a style prohibition. Tattooing, since it involves cutting, risks infection and mars the image of God that a human being is. God's people are too valuable to risk infection and too beautiful *as is* to cut into: "I praise you, because I am wonderfully made; / wonderful are your works!" (Ps 139:14). We may disregard the prohibition today—even Evangelicals sport tattoos—but surely we can appreciate that the law upholds human dignity.

The Bible does begin to question and rattle us, often in these little ways, provoking protests about its trivialities, violence, and sexism. Even reactions of disgust and annoyance are important, positive signs of engaged

---

8. Walter Brueggemann, *Theology of the Old Testament: Testimony, Dispute, Advocacy* (Minneapolis: Fortress Press, 1997), 75.

reading. We are *ambushed* by strangeness. In some ways, Barth did not go far enough. It is a strange, *assaulting* new world of the Bible. For example, the law stipulates which kind of winged insect among the four kinds that walk upon four legs is permissible to eat (Lev 11:22). How big of a problem *really* could that have been? Also stipulated are which fabrics cannot be worn together and which aunt if slept with counts as incest. Ditto.

The laws are a veritable onslaught of detail, with topics such as a neighbor's obligation when his ox trespasses, menstrual uncleanness, and various contagious skin diseases. The bizarre, for all its other properties, does hold our attention. We are dark-alley jumped by weirdness, like Jacob had been. One thing that becomes clear is that God is never domesticated, not even by biblical words, laws, and scenes. The laws remain turgid, impressively meticulous, maddeningly baroque, and all the while an intricate testimony of God's care.

The discomfort for the reader, once withstood, is performing a hermeneutic function: it excises complacency. That is a good sign, perhaps the first one that this Bible has begun to get under the skin. Scripture is dazzlingly subtle, sneaking past our tendencies to objectify material and use it for *our* purposes, which would domesticate the text into our busy schedule. Instead, it is the live wire, the spiritual current that jolts that schedule, jolts our soul. Hold on tight; the wrestling has begun. The Bible has just begun to open itself as an interactive encounter. Annoyance is the start of this, the sign that you are investing something. The winged insect clause, for instance, is part of kosher law, namely, what one can and cannot eat. It structures ancient taboos and helps to define social identity, just as American taboos against eating, say, dogs or cats, do for our culture. These laws are not binding today for a Christian, but they elicit at least a mild curiosity about food customs and their overall relation to identity.

And for Israel, it is yet another expression of gratitude to God. While Christians *say* grace before meals as a way of acknowledging God's bounty, the Jewish practice of keeping kosher *does* grace with the meal. It expresses gratitude by what is allowed on the table. In short, things that crawl, fly, and swim are generally considered kosher, with some expanded-upon distinctions and stipulations. The threefold structure of kosher law—crawl, fly, swim—replicates the structure given at creation. Humankind responds to the gift of creation, then, by eating gratefully from this selection. In such a posture of thanksgiving, there is no need to go wide of the boundaries or to experiment. God's bounty is already flourishing on the ground, in the sky, and underwater. Shellfish and grasshoppers are excluded from meals, not out of any slavish legalism bent on trying to please God, but because they are wholly unnecessary in a bountifully stocked creation.

The long legal section of the Torah in effect replicates the desert experience of ancient Israel. It throws us existentially into their situation. I do think this reader dislocation is intentional, even as various sources— Priestly, Decalogue, Covenant Code, Yahwist, Holiness—comprise the laws. We share in their experience of exasperating sameness and internal, infernal doubts. We experience as well the effort, stability, and the forced, focused stamina of being in the *in-between* place: *in between* slavery and the Promised Land, *in between* boredom with the Bible and grasping it as living Word. It forces us to move through exasperation to whatever is beyond, much as Israel had to do in the desert. Exasperation need not terminate an enterprise, though we would not know that strange, *inspired* idea yet, since it always has before. When anything bores us, we quite naturally stop it.

The unremitting sameness, the tedium, the effort, the ongoing disorientation, the cyclical fighting off of the urge to complain and giving in to the run of emotions is truly revealing of who *we* are. We identify with Israel. We are just like them, grumbling continuously amid divine presence, tempting and torturing ourselves with the seeming pointlessness of the process, dreaming of more pleasurable things to do, of places we would much rather be. Slavery at least had been dependable. Scripture is revealing of humanness as much as divinity. It is psychology well before the field was born. Richard Friedman has called the desert experience Israel's "incubation period," where the former slaves are forged in the desert as the people of God.[9] They are in no shape to be that yet. After slavery, the people are not even aware that they are covered in their slavery still. With no sense of irony, they dispute having to do without Egyptian garlic in this new freedom condition (Num 11:5).

The desert functions as spiritual boot camp, with all its attendant pains, to ready these people for the Promised Land, something unimaginably freeing. Reading the Bible is like that too. The laws are instruction on how to go from grumble to encounter. They teach Israel bit by slow bit what dignity for all looks like, namely, that you, your neighbor, your wandering ox, grasshoppers, and whoever is currently menstruating all have life in them. The Bible *is* trying to change us, and maybe that is why we protest too much, to preempt its power. Our complacency, our need to be entertained or pragmatic is being challenged, chiseled away in tiny, annoying chips. Efficiency, which seems to be the unnamed god we really serve, wreaks havoc on our spirit, and so totally that we remain unaware of it. For it always leaves us hungry, unsatisfied.

---

9. Richard Elliott Friedman, *The Disappearance of God: A Divine Mystery* (New York: Little, Brown and Company, 1995), 18.

The Bible is one artfully inefficient book. As Augustine knew, the Bible worked over its readers, "training them in truth by its hidden message . . . the hidden truths arouse longing; longing brings on certain renewal; renewal brings sweet inner knowledge."[10] It imitates its master, who is compassionately inefficient as well. Jesus spent what brief time he had in ancient Israel ministering to whomever he encountered, one by one, usually nameless on a road somewhere. God does the same for this one little broken band of former slaves. Forty years of the desert is, of course, nothing in God's eyes, but it still shows divine commitment to restoring this tribe from the slavery it had suffered (2 Pet 3:8).

A Hermeneutics of Trust[11]

There are two interpretive, or hermeneutic, questions to address in reading for the real presence of Scripture. Hermeneutics is the philosophical concern about *how* texts mean, *how* understanding occurs between reader and text. The first interpretive question is: What does it mean to say that the Bible is revelation by God? What exactly *is* revelation? And the second: Since God appears with some frequency to a variety of people in the Bible—no one is at risk for atheism—we might reasonably wonder, was God ostensibly more active in biblical times than he appears to be today? Did God manifest differently in the biblical period or at least in a more conclusive fashion?

Question One
The Bible is considered a primary source of revelation for Protestants, Jews, and Catholics. For Protestants, it is the sole source of revelation. For

10. Augustine, *Augustine in His Own Words*, ed. William Harmless (Washington, DC: Catholic University of America Press, 2010), 163.

11. This is a turn, borrowed from Avery Dulles, on the more familiar phrase the "hermeneutics of suspicion," from Paul Ricouer, which signifies an orientation of profound distrust and antagonism toward Christianity exercised by Ludwig Feuerbach, Karl Marx, Sigmund Freud, Friedrich Nietzsche, and their intellectual heirs. Avery Dulles, *The Craft of Theology: From Symbol to System* (New York: Crossroad, 1995), 7. Feminist biblical scholars have employed the phrase "hermeneutics of suspicion" to describe their own critical methodology in unmasking the androcentrism or patriarchal privilege in biblical texts. See Sandra M. Schneiders, *The Revelatory Text: Interpreting the New Testament as Sacred Scripture* (Collegeville, MN: Liturgical Press, 1999), 20; Elizabeth Schüssler Fiorenza, *Bread Not Stone: The Challenge of Feminist Biblical Interpretation* (Boston: Beacon, 1995), 15; Athalya Brenner and Carole Fontaine, eds., *A Feminist Companion to Reading the Bible: Approaches, Methods, and Strategies* (London: Routledge, 2001), 173.

Jews, the Bible, the Written Torah, and the Oral Torah codified in rabbinic literature, especially the Talmud, are the sources of divine truth. For Catholics, Scripture and tradition, the postbiblical heritage of doctrine, saints, theology, papal encyclicals, etc., are the prime sources of divine revelation. All three faith traditions deem the Bible holy, but how exactly did it come to exist? How does written holiness happen?

The Bible itself is a collection of writings spanning over a millennium, and so it is a library from a specific ancient people, first called the Israelites, then, after the exile, the Jews. In fact, the word "Bible" from the Greek, *ta biblia*, denotes the plural, "books."[12] The thirty-nine books of the Old Testament were composed between roughly 1200 and 164 BCE, while the New Testament's twenty-seven books date from the Common Era, from about 50 to 115 CE,[13] interestingly, well after Jesus' life, from about 0 to 33 CE.[14] Roman Catholic editions include seven extra books and additions of two others (Daniel and Esther), which Protestant editions do not. These books, which Catholics refer to as deuterocanonical, are Judith, Tobit, 1–2 Maccabees, Ecclesiasticus, Baruch, and Wisdom. Since these and a few other texts were written originally in Greek, rather than Hebrew, Martin Luther argued for their exclusion from the Old Testament. Today, Protestant editions collect these materials in the Apocrypha. The Bible itself was originally written in three different languages: Hebrew, Aramaic, and Greek. Hebrew and Aramaic are the languages of the Old Testament, while Greek is the language of the New, with scant phrases in Aramaic as well, the language of Jesus and the disciples.

Revelation, then, has a concrete, historical component. It occurs within a specific cultural context, that of the Israelites in Israel and Babylon and later, with Paul's journeys, in cities around the Mediterranean. The Bible is not the product of divine dictation at the hands of one appointed author as secretary, Moses traditionally, or God himself. Nor did it drop out of the sky on unsuspecting shepherds who then became the biblical peoples. It was not written literally by the "finger of God" as described in the origins of the Ten Commandments: "When the LORD had finished speaking to Moses on Mount Sinai, he gave him the two tablets of the covenant, the

---

12. The plural sense is easier to detect, for instance, in the term "bibliography" and in the Spanish word for "library," *biblioteca*.

13. BCE for "before the Common Era" (or the older BC, "before Christ") and CE for "Common Era" (or AD, anno Domini, "year of the Lord"). The newer classification acknowledges a less Christocentric focus while still reflecting Christianity's historical legacy in the formation of the calendar.

14. See chapter 8 for a discussion of this delay.

stone tablets inscribed by God's own finger" (Exod 31:18). Instead, revelation is best understood as a dynamic process involving centuries of oral storytelling, written sources, later editing, copying in scrolls, and, finally, the communal determination of what constitutes the canon—authoritative texts deemed holy—of sacred writings, Scripture. The fingers were human, the insights and truths both human *and* divine, and the result is a collection of disparate testimonies about a relationship between ancient peoples and a numinous presence.

The entire process, from God's self-communication in some manner to oral sharing to the transmission and collection of materials over centuries, comprises revelation. It presumes that all the unnamed people involved in producing the scrolls discerned holy presence in events and in transmitting written materials. The texts were holy in part because a community held them to be and because they contained some enduring truths about a presence greater than themselves—God. The emergence of the biblical books through this long, historical process is itself a demonstration of the Catholic understanding of tradition as the active conveyance of truths through the centuries.

Historical-critical scholarship has demonstrated the layered history behind the making of the Bible and so has enabled us to appreciate the complexities involved in revelation. For, if we presume that God essentially dictated the material atop a mountain to one man, then revelation is consigned to one point in time, far distant from our own. God's presence in such a view is conclusive, to be sure, but also singular. The model of revelation as a dynamic process involving people over centuries, by contrast, stresses the ongoing relationship between God and humanity, as characterized by the biblical notion of covenant. The word "testament" (from the Latin, *testamentum*) means "covenant," and so the Old and New Testaments reflect an ongoing covenant of divine and human relating. The dynamic view honors the historical recording of that relationship, while the dictation model does not.[15] Human intuition, discernment, and the transmission of materials all matter alongside God's initiative in the dynamic view of revelation. Avery Dulles describes the dual involvement, human and divine, well: "Revelation, as it takes root in human minds and lives, finds its way into literary sedimentation. To the extent that the revelation dominates the process of literary objectification, the books are inspired."[16]

---

15. An especially helpful discussion on the different views on revelation is Avery Dulles, *Models of Revelation* (1983; repr., Maryknoll, NY: Orbis, 1992), 193–210.

16. Dulles, *The Craft of Theology*, 7.

This dynamic process of transmission bestows a trust in human discernment as it reveals something characteristic but often ignored about
God. In a matter as important as revelation, God is humbling himself, as
it were, to trust that humans will get it right. In revelation, God exhibits
a patient trust in the human cognition of small, Semitic tribes. Egypt and
Mesopotamia had been the superpowers of the day, with Israel being viewed
as their land bridge. That revelation might be occurring in the dry, dusty
hills of that bridge did not concern the travelers passing through in the
least. Still, this isn't an argument against it having happened. Instead, it is
wholly characteristic of God to pick smallness for the scene of greatness:
Joseph, the best-dressed, second to youngest son of twelve, who survives
an attempted fratricide to land in Egypt's court and save the world from
starvation; Moses, an abandoned baby, a wanted murderer who stutters,
who leads his people from Egypt; David, the youngest son, so little he is not
even worth mentioning when Samuel comes to anoint a king; David, again
and paradigmatically, as the little warrior without armor or weaponry who
bests the armor-clad giant Goliath with nothing more than a slingshot; and
the birth of the Messiah in a manger in a backwater village of the Roman
Empire. This is kenotic in form, a self-emptying that is characteristic of
God: "he emptied himself, / taking the form of a slave, / coming in human
likeness; / and found human in appearance, / he humbled himself, / becoming obedient to death, / even death on a cross" (Phil 2:7-8).

This humbling God is not risk averse and is utterly open to vulnerability.
God allows vulnerability, as it were, in the very process of revelation by
having people heed truths and hand them down. It need not be shocking
or disappointing to learn that revelation was a process that involved humans over and against a divine literalism. It is somewhat charming to see
in God such kenotic trust and a lack of paternalistic dictation. There is no
control freak demanding, "Now read that back to me!" And it is immensely
affirming of us, of humans. Created in God's image, the biblical writers
were then entrusted to discern what was truest about life with God. This
is covenant where God too risks relationship. An unwed Palestinian mother
gets pregnant in a time when that was utterly scandalous. And God trusts
her to bring his child to term.

When God became human in the incarnation, humanity was ennobled,
even as it would often continue to act otherwise. In scriptural revelation,
humanity is entrusted with God's self-communication in some manner,
even as cultural biases, duplications, ideologies, and grammatical confu-
sions exist. The very product of Holy Scripture is a profound celebration
of incarnation—God and humanity united. In such a vital collaboration, a
kind of humility is expressed on both sides: God allows his communication

to filter through human understanding, language, and limitations; humans transmit materials carefully and in anonymity. The actual authorship of the entire Bible remains unknown, with the exception of the letters of Paul. The scribal tradition values holiness within the writings, because the message was vastly more important than authorial credit.

Biblical revelation is speech about God from a community, Israel,[17] who presumably got it from somewhere and felt compelled to fashion narratives, law, poetry, etc., in certain ways even beyond her own intentions. In legal terms, then, the Bible is hearsay and so would not qualify as admissible evidence in court. And this is where Scripture takes considerable criticism in modernity. For, if Scripture is essentially Israelite speech about God, how can it be reliable, let alone holy? We have, it would seem, less faith in humankind in this skeptical age than God had in all the nameless editors, scribes, and oral storytellers entrusted with the revelation process.

A relationship with a numinous, personal presence is of a different kind of truth than that satisfied by forensic evidence. Revelation is something bigger and different from evidence. It is testimony of a relating God. In an age of skepticism, one wonders what possible act of revelation would be able to qualify as such. If it were a miracle, it would have to be repeated for verification for each batch of skeptical eyewitnesses. But then the repetition would render the happening mundane rather than miraculous. If it were an ordinary sight, say, a flame, it would go unnoticed as just more background. It was never humankind's place to umpire which parts of the Bible are true and which are false. The collected testimony of Scripture results in a different sort of certitude than that of court judicial criteria.[18] It is reliable and true in that it gets at God's character, much as we truly know someone through the stories they and their loved ones tell on themselves and not at all by their fact-checked résumé.

Revelation in its simplest sense involves disclosing or unveiling to another. Somehow, God manifested himself to these ancient people and they intuited some awareness of divine presence; they were receptive to something, someone detectable. Further, this divine presence was a living one, willing to connect with humans. For biblical faith, the numinous is not merely a pleasant experience of some deeper plane of existence; it is interpersonal, a living presence. God initiates communication *and* someone is there to detect it. Someone is attuned to the numinous and can apprehend it as God. Otherwise it is lost. Even the revelation at the burning

17. Brueggemann, *Theology*, 118.
18. Ibid., 119.

bush, as we shall see in the next chapter, was not a dazzling, conclusive spectacle. Instead, something odd just caught the shepherd's eye, and the world changed.

Revelation consists, then, of Scripture's content as well as the mode of interaction—God with humans, humans with God—that is sketched out.[19] *Dei Verbum* (Dogmatic Constitution on Divine Revelation 2) clearly understands that mode of divine interaction as friendly, in that God makes known the divine will and "lovingly speaks to human beings as friends, inviting them 'into fellowship with himself.' "[20] By necessity, humans have to use language to describe this numinous quality. Hence, God "speaks," but not literally, that is, with vocal chords, tongue, and lips. Rather, this is an analogy to describe communication in a like manner to human beings. It makes sense that revelation entails lots of poetic imagery precisely because it is of a nature beyond our own. Always when we speak of God—in biblical times and today—we use, in David Tracy's terms, the "analogical imagination."[21]

"For what can be known about God is evident to them, because God made it evident to them. Ever since the creation of the world, his invisible attributes of eternal power and divinity have been able to be understood and perceived in what he has made" (Rom 1:19-20). One of those created realities is the writings in the Bible. Inspiration somehow works through their production by creatures who are gifted with discernment, memory, and writing. We cannot get any closer to the process of inspiration. But it is unlikely that God spoke with auditory sound to biblical peoples and not to postbiblical peoples. Always, "[God] dwells in unapproachable light" (1 Tim 6:16) and so revelation remains somewhat mysterious.[22]

This view of revelation as a process rather than a dictation in no way denigrates either Scripture or God. It praises God as mystery, incomprehensible, and so does not confine revelation to the words as stated in Scripture. To restrict God to the words themselves, as important as they may be, is to turn the Bible itself into a functioning idol. A literalist reverence to

---

19. *Dei Verbum* emphasizes the dynamic, interpersonal dimensions more than Vatican I had. Revelation need not be disruptive of human existence and can easily be nonecstatic in quality. By the Second Vatican Council, revelation was understood more as God's enduring witness of himself in created realities (*Dei Verbum* 3). See Avery Dulles, "Faith and Revelation," in *Systematic Theology*, ed. Francis Schüssler Fiorenza and John P. Galvin, 2nd ed. (Minneapolis: Fortress Press, 2011), 81.

20. Austin Flannery, ed., *Vatican Council II: The Basic Sixteen Documents* (Northport, NY: Costello Publishing Co., 1996), 2.

21. David Tracy, *The Analogical Imagination: Christian Theology and the Culture of Pluralism* (New York: Crossroad, 1998).

22. Dulles, "Faith and Revelation," 84.

Scripture is perhaps well-meaning but misdirected. It practices bibliolatry, preferring a thing—the Bible—to God.[23] Rather, the Bible bears witness to revelation. It is testimony, not transcript. God remains the subject of our worship and adoration, not the biblical page.[24]

Question Two

This discussion of language raises the second issue of whether God manifested himself differently in biblical times than he does now. Did God once speak in booming, unmistakable ways? Even if we grant that divine speech was not literal, did God nevertheless speak to the hearts of people in biblical times in much clearer ways than he does now? Was he more obviously present to the Israelites in the desert than he is to modern, urban populations today? Perhaps we assume this without ever having thought about it, namely, that people in biblical times, such as Mary, Joseph, Moses, Abraham, and David, enjoyed actual sit downs with the deity and we, well, do not. And so, of course, they are pillars of the faith. They had proof of divine presence; they had God accompanying them, and we are not at all sure we do today. Mary, for instance, had an angel talking her through an unwed, teenage pregnancy, so of course she believed in God! Yet, as we shall see in chapter 5, angels were not winged, cherubic creatures fluttering above humans in biblical times. That is an image drawn largely from Renaissance art. Angels (and demons) were not visibly distinct, supernatural characters in the Bible. They were simply "messengers." They were the source of a dream, an intuition, a decision, but when embodied, they looked like other humans. Real life—and biblical life is part of this—does not have sacred markers, halos and horns, to mark clearly the people we encounter.

If it is true that God spoke plainly to people in biblical times but now he does not, then we concede, I think, more than we mean to. First, we are claiming that God changed in history and is different from who he used to be. We would have to believe that God was loquacious during biblical times, namely, the Iron Age and Roman Era, but reticent in subsequent historical periods. And second, we would have to accept that it is just our cruel luck to be born in the wrong time period—the Age of Disbelief—to know God.

---

23. St. Benedict was after a similar caution about his Rule for monastic living. The Rule is, of course, important, but monks and Christians are still to "prefer nothing to Christ."

24. Even fundamentalist Christians will not need their Bibles in heaven, because they will be with God.

Torah and the Agility of Faith

Theophany

The Hebrew term *Torah*, as we have said, means "instruction" or "law," and so the first five books of the Bible provide instruction primarily on faith and what it means to trust a divine, invisible presence. Biblical theophanies—divine manifestations—obviously play an essential role in theological understandings of who God is for the biblical writers themselves, for their society, and for readers today. They portray God as manifest through nature, messengers, and cultic presence. In general, theology has traditionally emphasized God's immutable nature, namely, that he is impassable. This tendency has so marked our conceptions of God, in fact, that postmodern theologians busily challenge this traditional view of God by exposing its bias of stasis about God as the center or the Ground of Being. In a nutshell (which is always difficult to do with postmodern thought), the God of such "onto-theology," namely, Omnipotent, Omniscient, Omnipresent, and Omnibenevolent, is constrained by those concepts. For God as center or ground of a system of thought is not given to movement or dynamism. And because onto-theology valorizes stasis, it anchors and authorizes a status quo in cultural domains that privileges some while excluding others.[1] Fortunately, onto-theology does not occur in

---

1. Postmodern thought attends to the political and social consequences involved with reigning conceptual ideas that exert hegemonic pressure. For a considerably lucid

the Bible, and the four Omnis are nowhere to be seen. Instead, metaphors, indirection, and even shape-shifting abound.

The biblical ways in which God appears are varied and nuanced. The shape-shifting—from angels, fire, thunder, storms, glory, name, prophetic oracle—is characteristic of this divine entity throughout all three portions of the Old Testament, namely, the Torah, the Prophets, and the Writings. Even the angels are messengers who look just like human travelers, and it is only in hindsight that the protagonist knows something divine has occurred (e.g., Gen 18:13; 32:25; Judg 13:16). Biblical shape-shifting thwarts any onto-theological tendencies. It heralds not a changing God but a resistance to reifying the divine, to words themselves becoming idols. Israel had the difficult task of portraying a God who cannot be seen. Its tradition was aniconic—without icons, images—and this can be felt on the literary level as well. In fact, the sheer variety of depictions in the Bible instructs the reader in a supple dexterity of comprehending God beyond and through the text.

The Burning Bush

The paradigmatic tale of encountering the holiness of God in the Bible is the burning bush. There, divine presence was clear, and there, Moses had the theological certainty beyond all doubt that God was real, that he was alive and not only the God of his people's lore, "the God of Abraham." "When he looked, although the bush was on fire, it was not being consumed. So Moses decided, 'I must turn aside to look at this remarkable sight.' When the LORD saw that he had turned aside to look, God called out to him" (Exod 3:2-4).

Yet, for all its reputation as the exemplar of divine presence, this scene is not an obvious supernatural invasion into the natural world, indisputably evident to all. The bush is not shouting at Moses, or flagging him down, announcing itself as clear-cut miracle flush with God's presence. This famous little bush is neither irresistible nor overpowering as a bush on fire is not all that unusual in the desert. Brush fires flair up and die off regularly amid all the dry tinder scattered about. There is something unique about this bush, though it is not visually obvious.

Moses noticed something out of the ordinary, the subtlety of the branches not being consumed by the fire. This subtlety for him was worth

---

analysis of postmodernity and its influence on contemporary theology, see Paul Lakeland, *Postmodernity: Christian Identity in a Fragmented Age* (Minneapolis: Fortress Press, 1997).

a second look and would presumably take a few moments to notice. *Then* God called him. In other words, the scene depicts not overpowering divine presence but rather a relational give-and-take between God and Moses. God, as it were, waits for Moses to notice. Moses, for his part, did not read the bush as an object; he encountered it. Divine presence is inviting rather than coercive. Moses was someone who was paying attention. He has the makings of faith in him, the attentiveness. It is a test of sorts from God, a test for readiness, not merit, as if God were saying, "If Moses notices the difference, then I shall speak to him." While Abraham is known as the father of faith for the three monotheistic traditions (Judaism, Christianity, and Islam), I want here to propose Moses as a model for approaching holiness, specifically that of the Holy Scriptures. Whereas God initiates by manifesting his presence—revelation—Moses is receptive. There is something already primed in Moses to slow down and pay attention to the ordinary, from which the holy blooms. When we adopt this quality of attentive receptivity to reading Scripture as holy, our efforts are repaid. "When the LORD saw that he had turned aside to look, God called out to him from the bush: Moses! Moses! He answered, 'Here I am.' God said: Do not come near! Remove your sandals from your feet, for the place where you stand is holy ground. I am the God of your father, he continued, the God of Abraham, the God of Isaac, and the God of Jacob. Moses hid his face, for he was afraid to look at God" (Exod 3:4-6).

A moment ago, that "place where you stand" had been ordinary ground, indistinguishable from the rest of the desert floor. Now, it has all changed. Moses is taught how to approach holiness. Indeed, he *needs* to be taught it in the scene itself and he complies. There is much to admire here in Moses, but it too is subtle: readiness, maturity, alertness, curiosity, patience, and not least of all, openness to new experiences. Scripture operates like the desert terrain as well. We stumble onto a passage or verse quite ordinary, well-known or not, and then some shift occurs—nothing really, but still, something.

Lectio divina, reading for the divine, is the ancient practice of slow, deliberative, prayerful reading of Scripture. What is most instructive about this practice to my mind is the way it values the reader's pause. When reading Scripture slowly, there is a slight moment, maybe even not much more than that in Moses' deciding to take a second look, where we get snagged by an image or a phrase. *Lectio divina* encourages us at that point to stop reading, to mull it over and then let it be. We take just that image or phrase into the rest of the day. Reading in this fashion, then, is not labor but just the recognition of a pregnant pause. This is what happened when I read the Deuteronomy 30 passage discussed in the first chapter. Unwittingly, I had practiced *lectio divina*. Or, better, Scripture had practiced it on me. With this reading practice, we learn to read our own intuition better and to trust all the little snags in attention. They yield to holy encounter.

There is no question that Moses gains unprecedented access to God's presence and no longer has to listen for the snags. He enjoys an intimate relationship with God that begins here at the burning bush and lasts a lifetime. Indeed, "The LORD used to speak to Moses face to face, as a person speaks to a friend" (Exod 33:11). And Moses confirms it, saying to God, "You have said, 'You are my intimate friend; You have found favor with me'" (Exod 33:12). To know one another by name is a biblical idiom for intimacy. In John 10:3, the Good Shepherd knows every sheep by name, and they in turn listen to him because they recognize his voice. There is a relationship established. Later at the resurrection, it is not until Jesus uses Mary's name that she recognizes who he is (John 20:16).[2]

What Moses enjoys is the intimate presence of God over time. It establishes his authority for handing on the Torah. His encounter with holiness shapes his life and the lives of those whom he leads out of slavery. He is sure of God's presence. Moses' face even shows the effects of God's presence, in that it "was radiant" (Exod 34:35). Yet even with all of Moses' access, God still remains mysterious to him. After the conversation with God at the burning bush, Moses wants more. He wants a name, like Jacob had before him (Gen 32:30). He wants, in other words, to cement the friendship that must, however, remain elusive. Moses receives God's name, YHWH, but it retains its element of mystery. The name, from the verb *hayah*, "to be," denotes nothing specific, except that God is existence or life in some manner (Exod 3:14). *YHWH*—"I am who I am"—is a tautology that protects as it reveals. It connotes divine presence and mystery in active form but denotes nothing tangible. The Masoretic scribes later honor this theological impulse, by scrambling the vowels of the Tetragrammaton, that is, the four consonants of the name, as a deterrent to pronouncing it. For Jewish readers who want to retain the mystery of God's name, the Tetragrammaton has produced the resultant English conceits: The Holy One Blessed be He, Ha-shem ("the name"), G-d, and Adonai ("Lord"). The name YHWH—some sort of verbal causative—reflects God's animate quality, that he is in movement, that there is a *liveliness* to divine presence.

God's mystery remains intact after God tells Moses his name. Moses still yearns for it, more of the God he is so close to. When Moses later asks to see God directly, God replies, "But you cannot see my face, for no one can see me and live. Here, continued the LORD, is a place near me where you shall station yourself on the rock. When my glory passes I will set you

2. See chapter 8 for a discussion of this scene of encountering the holy.

in the cleft of the rock and will cover you with my hand until I have passed by. Then I will remove my hand, so that you may see my back; but my face may not be seen" (Exod 33:20-23).

The divine plan for Moses to catch a glimpse of God is tantalizing, eluding, and suggestive of an unintended anthropomorphism. Moses both sees and does not see God. Divine mystery is at once shared and protected. Gregory of Nyssa proposes that this scene is revelatory, not of something so trite as God's anthropomorphized backside, since the divine, being formless, would not have one. It is revelatory of the reverent posture of discipleship. Moses is correctly not face to face with God now but learning to follow him.[3] This too is a part of experiencing holiness; just as it merits taking off one's shoes, hiding one's face, it also involves following. Discipleship is no less miraculous than a burning bush, because the same divine presence has evoked response. There is, after all, someone whom Moses is following.

Approaching Scripture as holy requires a similar openness, attentiveness, and willingness to be led. We are not reading it; it is interpreting itself before us as we are invited in. Holiness is less decoded as it is encountered in a text such as the story of the burning bush. It redeems Moses, restoring him to who he was meant to be: not an identity-confused murderer, not a stutterer or adoptee, but a child of God. Holiness has restored him to his true self, and his response is then to follow God's moving, opaque presence wherever it takes him. Moses spends his life following God; the trek across the Sinai is his life. And once he is taught how to follow, he in turn teaches (with somewhat less success) those following him to freedom. The rest of the Pentateuch involves that following of God, through Moses, to the edge of the Promised Land. It is clear that divine presence, both manifest and mysterious, has had a profound, formative influence on the journey.

Yet, in terms of God's presence, a very strange thing happens in the Pentateuch. While God appeared in some sort of talking, visible form to the patriarchs in Genesis and to Moses in the first half of Exodus via the medium of angels and thundering climax in nature atop Mount Sinai, God disappears as the journey through the desert wears on. That is, after Sinai, divine potency downshifts and becomes manifest as "a column of cloud and of fire" in the journey through the desert to the Promised Land (Exod 13:21; 14:19, 24; 33:9; Num 12:5; 14:14; Deut 31:15; Neh 9:12, 19; Ps 99:7). Then, at the end of Exodus, divine presence is the cloud enveloping the tabernacle. God is still present with the people, still guiding them to the Promised Land, but in a much more diffuse form. In Deuteronomy, God's presence is clear, but only through the speeches of Moses that recount the

---

3. Gregory of Nyssa, *The Life of Moses* (New York: HarperCollins, 2006), 111.

history of divine action. It is only in the last chapter that God "returns" for one last face-to-face encounter with his servant Moses. We are left at the end of the Pentateuch, at the end of the journey to the Promised Land, to wonder what will happen next and what becomes of this elusive God.

The book of Exodus is ancient Israel's foundation story of who God is, namely, YHWH, the "God of your father, . . . the God of Abraham, the God of Isaac, and the God of Jacob" (Exod 3:6). Divine presence in Exodus is vigorous, decisive, and variable. In the delivery from Egyptian slavery (Exod 1–15), YHWH is portrayed with images of overwhelming power in a series of ten plagues devastating to the Egyptians.[4] And, right after Moses is called, YHWH "sought to put him to death" (Exod 4:24); the text is unmistakable. The short last words uttered by the bested Egyptians concede, with some understatement, YHWH's superior power: "All of us will die!" (Exod 12:33). At Passover, the people must remember to put blood on their doorposts lest the divine destroyer cause collateral damage to his own people, whom he is otherwise trying to save (Exod 12:7, 13). At Mount Sinai, the people send Moses in their stead, all too frightened to meet their God (Exod 20:19). Moreover, they themselves still have to take precautions, namely, of a three-day abstention from contact with women, before even standing at a distance from the divine presence at Mount Sinai (Exod 19:10-15). Divine presence is undoubted, even overwhelming, for Israelite and Egyptian alike.

Power descriptions are apt here, for this is indeed a contest, a battle for supremacy between two putative gods, YHWH and Pharaoh. Exodus is a rumble in the desert. These *theophanies* are all about power. YHWH's right hand shattered, his glory overthrew, and his wrath consumed Israel's enemies. When Exodus 15:11 asks "Who is like you among the gods, O Lord? / Who is like you, magnificent among the holy ones? / Awe-inspiring in deeds of renown, worker of wonders," it is rhetorical and high praise. For YHWH's commanding presence has vanquished all. When YHWH appears via miracle and warrior imagery, then, revelation *overwhelms* the natural world, irrupting into human history.[5] Providence occurs with considerable dramatic effect: mountains quake; rivers turn red; cattle die; eldest sons die; people tremble. Such heady interventionist attention, it should be noted,

---

4. T. B. Dozeman notes that elements of God's power dominate in chapters 1:1–15:21, while those of divine presence do so from 15:22–40:38. *Commentary on Exodus*, Eerdmans Critical Commentary (Grand Rapids, MI; Eerdmans, 2009), 44–45.

5. The poems widely held to be earliest in Israelite composition depict YHWH as an irresistibly powerful divine warrior in a contest for supremacy over nature, Israel's enemies, or other gods: e.g., Exod 15:3-8, 11-14; Deut 33:2, 26-27; Judg 5:4-5; Ps 68:4, 8-9, 33-35; 77:13-19; Hab 3:4-15.

stands in acute contrast to the slaves' own experience in Egypt, where God's absence extended 430 years before God "heard their moaning" (Exod 2:24).

Clearly these accounts take pains to render encounter with the divine as destabilizing and occasionally dangerous. This kind of divine manifestation is what Rudolph Otto meant by describing the holy as *mysterium tremendum et fascinans*, a tremendous and fascinating mystery.[6] Divine presence elicits a response of awe, what the Old Testament often calls the "fear of the Lord"—*yirat adonai*—a kind of gasping wonder.[7] The "fear of the Lord," it should be stressed, is not merely fear. The biblical God is not demanding a faith born in cowering. Awe is always just on the edge of fear, of palpable terror, because the holy *is* overwhelming. An encounter with God in these images, then, is dangerous not only because God may be angry or capricious but also because holiness by its nature is existentially overpowering to mortals and nature.[8] When God tells Moses that "no one can see me and live" (Exod 33:20), it is a function of the limits of humankind rather than divine punishment or restraint. Moses, in fact, becomes an intermediary as a way to mitigate the effects of this tremendous divine presence on the people who remain at a distance at the foot of Mount Sinai (19:17, 19; 20:18).[9] On the rare occasions when biblical characters do see God, they are surprised and filled with awe not so much at having seen God but at having survived the episode: for example, Hagar (Gen 16:13); Jacob (Gen 32:30); Moses, Aaron, and the tribal elders (Exod 24:9-11); Manoah and his wife (Judg 13:22-23); and Isaiah (Isa 6:5).

Mount Sinai

The theophany at Sinai (Exod 19–24) conclusively demonstrates the power of God apart from his engagement with an opponent, Pharaoh.

---

6. See the classic work of Rudolph Otto, *The Idea of the Holy* (1923; repr., New York: Oxford University Press, 1950). Otto highlights Exod 3:6 to suggest that Moses hides his face because he is afraid to look on God (75).

7. Terence Fretheim, *The Pentateuch* (Nashville, TN: Abingdon, 1996), 50–51; Brevard S. Childs, *The Book of Exodus: A Critical, Theological Commentary* (Philadelphia: Westminster, 1974); James L. Kugel, *The God of Old: Inside the Lost World of the Bible* (New York: Free Press, 2004), 6. For example, Exod 9:30; Deut 6:13; 31:12; Prov 1:7; Ps 22:24.

8. Walter Brueggemann, *Theology of the Old Testament: Testimony, Dispute, Advocacy* (Minneapolis: Fortress Press, 1997), 569.

9. Throughout the Torah, Moses as intermediary continues to experience divine presence directly, as YHWH himself makes clear to Aaron and Miriam when he says that with Moses "face to face I speak to him, plainly and not in riddles. The likeness of the LORD he beholds" (Num 12:8).

"Now Mount Sinai was completely enveloped in smoke, because the LORD had come down upon it in fire. The smoke rose from it as though from a kiln, and the whole mountain trembled violently" (Exod 19:18). Here, divine presence causes an attendant upheaval of nature with smoke, fire, quaking, thunder, and lightning (Exod 19:16), so dramatic, in fact, that it causes residual trembling in the witnesses (Exod 20:18). Various theories have been advanced to account for the origins of the theophany's specific images, such as volcanic activity,[10] borrowing from the Ugaritic traditions of the Canaanite storm god, Ba'al,[11] and cultic incense offerings.[12] These theories share the analytical intent to discern the *origins* of the Sinai imagery and tend to view the portable column of cloud and fire as largely derivative of Sinai's primary theophany.[13] In these views, the column of cloud and fire function primarily as literary contrivances. They are vehicles for the Israelites to take a bit of the original Sinai theophany with them as palladium, much as the tabernacle was a movable proleptic temple in miniature. The column then becomes a memento of divine power, fostering reminiscences of past divine potency. This perspective results in an odd

10. Martin Noth, *Exodus*, trans. J. S. Bowden (Philadelphia: Westminster, 1962), 159; Jörg Jeremias, *Theophanie: Die Geschichte einer alttestamentlichen Gattung* (Neukirchen-Vluyn: Neukirchener Verlag, 1965), 100–111; Claus Westermann, *Praise and Lament in the Psalms* (Louisville, KY: John Knox, 1981), 101; John van Seters, *The Life of Moses: The Yahwist as Historian in Exodus–Numbers* (Louisville, KY: Westminster/John Knox, 1994), 40; Hermann Gunkel, *Genesis* (Macon, GA: Mercer University Press, 1997), 181.

11. Cf., Pss 18:8-16; 29:7-8; 68:8-9; 77; Hab 3:5-6; Nah 1; Ezek 1:4; Zech 9:14; Exod 13:22; 19:16. Frank Moore Cross, *Canaanite Myth and Hebrew Epic: Essays in the History of the Religion of Israel* (Cambridge, MA: Harvard University Press, 1973), 157, 164–69. Thomas Mann, "The Pillar of Cloud in the Reed Sea Narrative," *Journal of Biblical Literature* 90 (1971): 17. For extensive analysis of Ugaritic parallels in biblical theophany scenes, see T. W. Mann, *Divine Presence and Guidance in Israelite Traditions: The Typology of Exaltation* (Baltimore: Johns Hopkins University Press, 1977). Terrien favors the idea of a seasonally late thunderstorm to display the experience of the holy and so argues that an ancient Near Eastern parallel is unnecessary; see *The Elusive Presence* (San Francisco: Harper & Row, 1978), 120, 128. Childs asserts that both volcanic and meteorological elements comprise the theophany; see *The Book of Exodus*, 344.

12. Walter Beyerlin, *Origins and History of the Oldest Sinaitic Traditions*, trans. S. Rudman (New York: Oxford University Press, 1965), 134, 156–57. Gerhard von Rad, *The Problem of the Hexateuch and Other Essays* (New York: McGraw-Hill, 1966). Von Rad cites other texts where theophany and covenant appear together: Exod 20, Deut 33:2-4; Judg 5:4-5; Hab 3.

13. Julius Wellhausen, *A Prolegomena to the History of Ancient Israel* (New York: Meridian Books, 1957), 20; Noth, *Exodus*, 109, 160.

theological development, though, for it implies that divine presence after Sinai has attenuated.

Given the preceding testimonies of providential force, there is a remarkable theophanic shift in Exodus. Divine potency downshifts, as it were, and becomes manifest as a column of cloud and of fire in the journey through the desert to the Promised Land (Exod 13:21; 14:19, 24; 33:9; Num 12:5; 14:14; Deut 31:15; Neh 9:12, 19; Ps 99:7). "The LORD preceded them, in the daytime by means of a column of cloud to show them the way, and at night by means of a column of fire to give them light" (Exod 13:21). This shift in presence elicits a series of theological conundrums about the nature of providence. Why do descriptions of God's manifest potency recede so quickly in Exodus? Why has divine presence shifted from forbidding, persuasive power to evanescence in the elements of cloud and fire? Was divine power ever really this overwhelming? Divine presence after Egypt has become elusive and portable.[14] Remarkably, this elusiveness holds true for the remainder of the Pentateuch, as the Priestly material dominates (the last halves of Exodus and Numbers and all of Leviticus) with its characteristic depiction of God's presence as "glory" in cloud.

From now on, divine power is primarily implied rather than witnessed. And it is typically punishing in nature (Num 11:33; 14:12, 22-39; 16:31-35; Lev 10:1-2). God's wrath at the golden calf incident is shared by Moses but is the cause for the deity *not* appearing to his people (Exod 32:11-14). Divine wrath is felt again with Aaron and Miriam, but Miriam's leprosy results only when God's "column of cloud" vacates the tent of meeting (Num 12:5-10). For the most part, these theophanies are restricted to members of Moses' family and are surgically precise microbursts of divine power. At any rate, they do not reassure the people of God's presence as their persistent grumbling indicates. Divine presence is implied as well when the skies rain down manna and quail for the people's provisions (Exod 16:4-8, 13-35). It is indirect enough, however, for the people to doubt their origins and to be anxious to horde them. Divine guidance for the rest of the desert journey, then, is assured via the firmness of the column yet nebulous in the evanescent qualities of cloud and fire.

This column of cloud and fire is not at all derivative of Sinai but constitutes a new form of theophany in the book of Exodus, one that offers at least three substantial theological insights unavailable in the upheaval and spectacular drama attendant with the Sinai theophany. As we shall see in a moment, these three insights have to do with human discernment of the divine. Upheaval and threatening, divine presence give way to a subtle,

14. Terrien, *The Elusive Presence*.

fleeting theophany of cloud and fire.[15] There is a general scholarly consensus that the cloud and fire imagery are from the J and E sources[16] while the images of a heavy cloud are from the P source.[17] Since clouds are common to all three, source analysis does not wholly explain the theophanic shift from images of potency to evanescence.

The Guidance of a Cloud

The shift signals an implicit theological instruction within the Torah, in that theophany becomes less about God per se and more about how and where to find God manifest. Theophanies manifest the divine, of course. But with the ephemeral imagery of cloud and fire, the role of human discernment is necessarily enhanced. A theophany of cloud and fire, then, signals where discernment should be focused, namely, in an aniconic tradition, in guidance, and in worship. The Priestly redactors offer theological instruction on discernment via the use of the column of cloud image. One key difference between the column of cloud and the other prominent Exodus theophanies of the burning bush and the revelation of law atop Mount Sinai is that it is addressed to the people *en masse* as audience and not only to a sole individual, Moses, who would then relay what he had heard to the people (Exod 13:22; 14:19-20; 19:9; 40:36-37; Num 9:17-18). The column of cloud, then, is a general revelation of God's presence, directly available to all people, no longer restricted to the divine intermediary. All of Israel receives instruction on how to discern the holy and follow God, as do we.

The first theological insight involves Israel's aniconic tradition. Since cloud and fire have opaque properties, they effectively mystify the divine

15. Terrien, *The Elusive Presence*, 128. Terrien's key issue is that the theophany of Sinai was "nature in tumult," and the column is not (*The Elusive Presence*, 120). Fretheim suggests that perhaps the origin of the column imagery is from brush fires, rather than a volcano; see *The Pentateuch*, 50–51. See also Brueggemann, *Theology*, 570. The importance of the imagery is to depict the awesome physical presence of YHWH. Brueggemann argues, contra Jeremias, that the theophany of Sinai in Exod 19:9-25 and 24:9-18 is not an upheaval of nature; see *Theology*, 569.

16. Exod 19:9, 18 is typically assigned to the Yahwist source (J); 19:16 and 20:18, 21 to the Elohist (E), with the pillar of cloud and of fire assigned to the Yahwist source (Exod 13:21-22; 14:19, 24; 33:9-10; Num 12:5; 14:14); Childs, *The Book of Exodus*, 220, 344–47.

17. E.g., Exod 40:34-38; Num 14:10; 16:10-11. Fretheim, *The Pentateuch*, 101–2. With the Priestly source (P), the element of cloud assumes prominence over that of fire; Childs, *The Book of Exodus*, 261.

presence they describe. Further, juxtaposing such ephemeral imagery with an architectural term, "column," preserves rather than exposes the nature of divine mystery. In this way, both the liveliness and the foundational firmness of God are suggested. Just as a (solid) column of (fleeting) cloud is hard to imagine, so too is this deity. The image manages to convey God as both elusive and immutable. This column of cloud marks divine presence precisely by what it *does not* describe.[18] It is, in essence, an oxymoron that preserves rather than captures the mystery of what it denotes. It is a metaphoric means to preserve God's ineffability. Theological discretion, in this perspective, accounts for the cloud and fire imagery,[19] which is, then, the original apophatic theology. A column of cloud and fire serves to mystify the mysterious and honor the aniconic tradition of the second commandment, namely, that Israel make no graven images.

The second theological insight has to do with the nature of divine guidance. Clouds and fire are dynamic elements intrinsically in movement in contrast to the stability of a column. They convey the dynamism of divine presence in imagery that approaches the ephemeral but not evaporation. God is going nowhere. Cloud and fire reflect a lively presence—silent, yet palpable—and are indicative of "God-with-us," *Immanuel* (Isa 7:14). The column of cloud imagery conveys, then, not divine attenuation after the exodus but rather a new aspect of divine revelation, namely, from miracle-working potency to the nudging guidance of a cloud. Guidance before this point had largely been by divine, verbal direction, for example, Noah (Gen 6), Abram (Gen 12; as Abraham in 18:22), and Moses (Exod 3–4). In a parallel with the New Testament, Israel could no more stay at the Sinai theophany than Peter could hope to remain in the certain light of transfiguration by building tents to reside in (Matt 17:4). Divine encounter, as central as it is throughout the Bible, nevertheless, yields to the guidance of discipleship, a journey in uncertain apprehension where "Faith is the realization of what is hoped for and evidence of things not seen" (Heb 11:1). The image of a cloud conveys, therefore, mystery, movement, and, perhaps most important theologically, the divine élan, the *liveliness* of God's presence.

God reassures Moses, "I myself will go along, to give you rest" (Exod 33:14). Even this detail reveals something about divine guidance that is supportive and sweetly attentive, but not to the obvious, such as the people's need for directions, their periodic panics, the upcoming hostilities with

18. Interestingly, later in the deuterocanonical Ecclesiasticus, the column of cloud actually *becomes* the throne for Lady Wisdom (24:4), which constitutes a twofold displacement of the divine—to throne and then to personified Wisdom.

19. See Psalm 29 for an early example.

other nations in their path, or pest protection. Rather, the divine is present to give the people rest. It recalls the newly learned third commandment for humans and animals to "Remember the sabbath day," that is, to "rest" (Exod 20:8; Hebrew: *Shabbath*). An entire commandment of the ten is given over to creaturely rest. And, in this experience, divine presence is discerned simply through imitating God's own rest in the Priestly creation narrative of Genesis 1. Its wisdom is so self-evident that this too should have been a no-brainer. It is altogether self-destructive that we pick even here to rebel, especially as we become increasingly exhausted running ourselves into the ground with activities. The theophanic shift from power to clouds and fire teaches a larger instruction for discerning a less evident God, one present where we might not have even thought to look—in rest.[20]

Finally, clouds and fire in the Torah and elsewhere are most often associated with the cult. Incense and fire offerings atop altars are described in the Priestly material in Exodus 25, 27, 30, and 37, where they are to be offered continually, "Morning after morning" (Exod 30:7). The law sections of the Torah are the least known area for Christians who tend to take a Pauline pass and say that they are under grace rather than the law (e.g., Rom 6:14). Yet Jesus does not see these divine realities as distinct. He differs from Paul here, in that he came to fulfill the law, not to abolish it (Matt 5:17). And, in his understanding, the laws became interior and more difficult to adhere to. For example, whereas the Ten Commandments prohibit murder and adultery, Jesus interprets those to include their milder emotional counterparts, anger and lust (Matt 5:21-30). Cultic legislation is also Holy Writ, and there is something instructive even to getting lost and bewildered in its thickets.

Worship in ancient Israel consisted of sacrifices from the provisions of daily life, for example, animals from the flock, grain from the harvest, olive oil and wine from the orchard. These foodstuffs likely symbolized social arrangements, such as a shared meal with the diety and the unity among various tribal groupings.[21] But, fundamentally, worship was the means to interact with God. Words float up, smoke floats up, and fire ascends. For instance, when Noah offers his burnt sacrifice, the smoke ascends, and God is pleased with the smell (Gen 8:21).[22] In addition, these incense and fire

---

20. Joseph Pieper, *Leisure: The Basis of Culture*, trans. Gerald Malsbary (South Bend, IN: St. Augustine's, 1998).

21. Jacob Milgrom, *Leviticus: A Continental Commentary* (Minneapolis: Fortress Press, 2004), 17–18. See also Mary Douglas, *Leviticus as Literature* (Oxford: Oxford University Press, 1999).

22. The scene has strong parallels to Utnapishtim's sacrifice in the Mesopotamian epic of *Gilgamesh*, where, upon smelling the "pleasant fragrance, the gods like flies gathered

offerings were likely more common in Israel than were animal sacrifices, given the premium put on meat for the Iron Age and postexilic subsistence farmers. The Priestly material legislates all types of sacrifice but says only of the incense and fire ones that these be offered continually (Exod 30:7).[23]

The smoke and fire offerings were likely considered a means of direct contact with God. Since biblical people envisioned God in the "heavens" or "sky" (Hebrew: *shamayim*) and saw clouds above, they might have understandably viewed their incense rituals as furnishing more of those clouds. Smoke offerings guided prayers, as a conduit to an invisible God. In this sense, Israel did not view clouds and smoke as God's absence, but just the opposite. These ephemeral images conveyed divine presence (Lev 16:12-13). This particular image of God's presence—cloud and fire—was in cultic practice now inscribed with the participatory presence of his worshiping people. Worship is the conduit of communication, and that is where the divine and human meet.

The column of cloud imagery, then, conveys both divine presence as guidance and Israel's *receptivity to God* via its worship, a willingness otherwise eclipsed by the desert grumbling traditions. Within the structure of the book of Exodus, narrative guidance of the divine yields to cultic guidance, where the depiction of God amid clouds—both in column and tabernacle—reinforces the Priestly agenda of the cultic activity of incense offering. In this understanding, the column of cloud and of fire functions not primarily as a reminiscence of Sinai. Rather, it affirms divine presence in cultic participation.

A central theme in the book of Exodus revolves around the notion of slavery and service, which in Hebrew is from the same verb, *abad*. The conditions of *abad* are "slavery" when the people are in Egypt under Pharaoh, but "service" when they gain instruction on how to worship YHWH. The trajectory of Exodus, therefore, has been to free the people from service to the wrong god and redirect it to the correct God. Understood in this way, the ten chapters on cultic legislation in Exodus, which come after the narrative of God's commanding deliverance from Egypt and the theophanies of the burning bush and Mount Sinai, do not *arrest* or *stall* the narrative of God's guidance. They *complete* it. And, they do so with some structural ingenuity. For the Priestly redactor uses chapters 25–31 (cultic instructions) and chapters 33–40 (execution of those instructions) as large brackets into

over the sacrifice" (Stephanie Dalley, *Myths from Mesopotamia: Creation, the Flood, Gilgamesh, and Others* [New York: Oxford University Press, 1998], 114).

23. For a detailed analysis of the incense offerings, see Kjeld Nielsen, *Incense in Ancient Israel*, Supplements to Vetus Testamentum (Leiden; E. J. Brill, 1986).

which he splices the golden calf story (chap. 32). This paradigmatic tale of idolatrous wrong worship is, then, framed (cushioned, perhaps) by the copious and repeated details of correct worship. The golden calf incident is a ritual disaster for numerous reasons, of course, but one reason is simply that its subject is inert. The dynamism involved in smoke and fire offerings would be utterly lost on a metal statue. To make this point, Moses grinds the statue up and forces the people to drink the metallic sediment, as if to say, "How would you like to get such offerings?" In contrast, smoke and fire offerings are not lost on God because worship is the conduit of interaction, and *God* is not inert.[24]

The book of Exodus concludes with a divine cloud and a divine fire determining when Israel moved in its journey and when it stayed put: "The cloud of the LORD was over the tabernacle by day, and fire in the cloud at night, in the sight of the whole house of Israel in all the stages of their journey" (Exod 40:36-38). The column of cloud and of fire had lent a stable guidance to the journey in the desert, even while protecting the ineffability of divine presence. So too does this Priestly image offer a corresponding stability through the continuity of divine presence in the cultic sphere. Throughout Exodus, clouds function as a "statement of faith in the continuity of divine presence. That presence is seen to transcend particular source strata and particular historical events or religious institutions."[25]

The issue at stake in the Priestly use of theophany revolves around the postbiblical distinction between *worship* and *theology*. With worship, one desires communication, encounter with God; with theology, one wants apt description of God. The column of cloud and fire symbolizes the people's ritual practice, their worship, and this for the Priestly editors is what truly guides Israel through the desert, because God is *really, palpably,* present

---

24. The incense would be burned on the tops of fairly wide cult stands, averaging anywhere between ten and twenty-five centimeters in diameter. Fire would burn in open-lipped lamps for multiple wicks that would cast a broad yet contained light. Hence, the visual effect from incense and fire offerings would be much more than a trickle or flicker and formidable in its own right. The smoke and fire of these offerings would, in effect, continue the shape of the cult stand itself. Amahai Mazar, "Cult Stands and Cult Bowls," in *Excavations at Tell Qasile*, Qedem 12 (Jerusalem: Hebrew University Press, 1980), 87–100; Nelson Glueck, "Incense Altars," in *Translating and Understanding the Old Testament; Essays in Honor of Hubert Gordon May*, ed. Harry Thomas Reed and William L. Reed (Nashville, TN: Abingdon, 1970), 325–41.

25. Leslie Brisman, "On the Divine Presence in Exodus," in *Exodus*, ed. Harold Bloom (New York: Chelsea House, 1987), 105–22, 106.

there—elusive (in a cloud), but solid (as a column).[26] Worship and miracles are both sites of divine revelation. But with miracles, such as the deliverance from Egypt, the people are *reactive* to God's tremendous power. Worship, by contrast, is *participatory*, even proactive, as the people ready themselves for divine encounter. In Exodus, miracle gives way to the mundane, with God revealed in both. Just as in the Mass where nothing ever changes but everything does, so the people of Exodus show up for the daily beauty, stability, and instruction worship offers, and it gets them across the wide Sinai desert to their Promised Land.

Hence, the incense and fire offerings prescribed in Exodus (chaps. 25, 27, 30, and 37) are not merely cultic appurtenances, whose functional efficacy rests in setting the mood for the holy. Instead, they reflect the dynamic connection between God and his people. Where there is smoke and fire, there *is* divine presence. God leads in cloud and fire, and by the end of Exodus, the people are no longer slaves, no longer even "the people." It is in the context of worship that the people finally receive their name, "house of Israel" (Exod 40:38). Slavery had infected and broken them; it had stuck to their souls. It had given them a mob's timidity so that they were not going anywhere without a leader who would speak for them.

The desert trek, the uncertainties, and the meticulous instructions on what it is to be Israel purified the Hebrew stragglers of the slavish gunk that had muddied them. Details after trauma are reassuring and anything but dull. They are a welcomed reminder that the trauma is over and that normalcy can either return or be reconstructed. Details such as these in the law, which are wholly given over to order, peace, security, stability, and the reliability of the world, are healing and restorative for the people in the post-trauma of slavery. *The people* are now highlighted as recipients of divine encounter through worship, with Moses relegated to background. Since we know that Moses will die just outside the Promised Land, in sight of it, at the end of the Pentateuch, the dynamic conduit of worship has replaced intermediary privilege in divine encounter. *All* the people experience God now. A single mediating hero is no longer needed as the people have been handed the means—worship—to interact with God in true "serving."

When we recall that the audience for this redaction is exilic and postexilic—that is, broken-down, dispirited people who lost their land and their God's temple and are refugees in a foreign land again—the reminder of God's real, elusive presence through the routine of worship must have replenished at least a few dry souls. The Priestly editor offers new hope

26. Joseph Blenkinsopp, *Treasures Old and New: Essays in the Theology of the Pentateuch* (Grand Rapids, MI: Eerdmans, 2004), 160–62.

shaken loose from an old story. The image of God's renewed guidance in a column of cloud would have heartened the people in exilic and postexilic communities in at least two respects: it recalled *both* God's guidance in the Sinai desert *and* the beloved temple where worship had once been access to the divine presence. With their hope rekindled, the people of these varying communities could remember that they had not been forsaken and that God just might lead them out of yet another foreign land (Babylon) or foreign occupation (Persian Empire) and once again take them home to *their* Israel.

With this important theophanic shift from miracle to guidance, the book of Exodus reveals a matured theology for the journey of faith. First, it reminds us that it is long, sometimes tedious, and that the details, routines, and periodic dullness of a life of worship are as much a part of the journey as is the story of conversion toward God, with its drama, leaders, setbacks, and surges. Second, it is no accident that the Priestly writer combines narrative and cultic material here and throughout the Pentateuch. God is revealed in both, as we are instructed. Priestly theology insists that worship be a central, steadying, regular facet of life, a way out of the despair of exiles and toward going home to God. Third, twenty chapters of detailed, intricate, repetitious cultic material—even as it pays homage to the temple—is still arduous reading. This teaches us the hard lesson about spiritual pacing. The slaves were not ready for the Promised Land. They grew, through God's guidance, into their identity, the house of Israel. Rhetorically, these chapters are the literary counterpart to the painstaking tedium of the desert trek. We are forced into the long haul along with the Israelites, and we are reminded that the journey is a lifetime.

The legal material of the Torah demands a less-is-more reading strategy, at least for Christians. When the Israelites in the desert start to complain about missing Egypt for its garlic, they have walked too far that day. When we become annoyed with the intricacies of ritual and our eyes glaze over in incomprehension and frustration, and I speak as one guilty, we have read too far. All of our questions about why we are doing this, what we will get out of it, etc., have to be drained from us before we can discern the holy. We have too much baggage, too many feedback loops, and too much personal narrative to hear beyond the tedium.

And just as worship, symbolized first in the column of cloud and then ensconced in the incense clouds of the tabernacle, guided and sustained Israel, so too is worship God's continued revelation, his presence through our lives of faith. This is a matured theology because it looks not to the miracle but to the proactive trust in meeting God through daily ritual.

Worship becomes the site where God is encountered. How could it be otherwise with an invisible deity? How can an armchair atheist possibly experience the venue for where God becomes real since it requires participation and not only observation? Believers put in the hours, the practice, the service, and it becomes habit. The routine energies involved in worship stabilize us to the mystery of presence. It habituates us to relating to the divine. This is never an easy venture and we can occasionally gauge that habituation as rote, but the routine readies us for deeper intimacies. Worship trains us to "Be still and know that I am God!" (Ps 46:11). The habitual sameness of service prepares us to discern mystery. It is perhaps the only place left that does that, though nature and music can too. We discern in the regularity, the details of worship, a light, silent sound of something greater, a love that embraces and infuses all the tedium, our tedium, and lifts it up. The tedium of life is holy too.

The entire time I might sit in a pew with a wandering mind, vaguely critiquing the homily and the sameness, God is present, accepting my own tedious skepticisms. To my "this just feels rote," God could well be saying the same to my doubts: "This just feels rote. You are always asking where I am, yet you're here. I'm here: 'Be still and know that I am God.'" The fidgeting child at Mass, I suspect, distracts me only because she is me. My adult restlessness is well socialized to go on the inside, where it then wreaks havoc with my attention span. The stability of worship teaches a fidgeting mind patience and acceptance, and the law is a welcomed scaffolding of dependability.

God is in the details of law just as he is in creation. Yet he is not contained by them. Any overly legalistic attachment on the part of his followers would seem to be stymied by the Torah itself. For when Moses breaks the first set of tablets containing the Ten Commandments, any temptation to idolize them is thereby averted. Perhaps this adventitious consequence helps to explain the curious lack of divine wrath over Moses' destructive tantrum.

The cultic legislation throughout the Torah also teaches perspective, for a lush appreciation of all the details in the world. It sharpens a spiritual discernment, now ready to gorge on the more of creation. The holy lurks in text and the world. Reading among the myriad legal details of the text in the end fosters a sacramental worldview where at any moment we might stumble into holy ground, as Moses had. The laws of holiness show us how to walk in the world as if it is holy ground, until we can see it for ourselves.

To read both the instructions for making a "variegated curtain of violet, purple, and scarlet yarn and of fine linen twined" (Exod 26:36) and their resulting display later (Exod 38:18) may lack much in the way of narrative suspense, but it focuses our attention to the beauty in worship and creation. The Israelites were lovingly exact with that curtain. The laws fashion the world as it looks in relationship, namely, spectacular and bedazzling.

Its sheer attentiveness to detail reflects no legal reductionism but is more like a lover who sets the table, *wanting* to get everything right. All the intricate decorations of the tabernacle—the sapphires, gold, vestments, water basins, purple curtains—reveal the eager anticipation of meeting. Desire shines through in the readiness. A sacristan today might appreciate these laws in a way few others can, simply for the company of saints who share her work, where, in fact, cleaning a chalice after Mass is not work at all but an extension of worship. All of these cultic laws devoted to describing the building of the tabernacle out in the desert also inspire the memory of the temple in Jerusalem. But the preeminent inspiration in this intricate material lies in envisioning the world itself as a tabernacle, with all its instruments, color, and design given over for the worship of God. This tabernacle is creation all lit up, in its Saturday or Sunday best, prepared and awaiting God's presence.

The Death of Moses

There is one last scene at the end of the Torah of God's intimate presence with Moses. It is a poignant scene, indeed, one of the saddest in the Bible. For here, poised at the very edge of the Promised Land, in sight of it even, Moses is told by his friend God that he shall not be entering. Instead, he will die outside of it, knowing that the people he dedicated his life to leading would enter without him. "The LORD then said to him, This is the land about which I promised on oath to Abraham, Isaac, and Jacob, 'I will give it to your descendants.' I have let you see it with your own eyes, but you shall not cross over. . . . [T]o this day no one knows the place of his burial" (Deut 34:4-6).

Moses enjoyed unprecedented access to God during his life right up until his last day. And when told that his death is near, he is silent. The man who had demurred with five different excuses when God first called him now silently accepts everything God tells him. He has learned to follow his God, even to the end of his life.

Angels, Holy Sites, and Prophets

The biblical ways in which God appears are varied and more nuanced than we might appreciate. The diversity of manifestation—from angels, fire, storms, glory, his name, prophetic oracle—is not wholly attributable to the existence of multiple literary sources, though these are there. It also preserves a theological insistence on God's essential mystery. God remains a numinous presence, even in the fairly clear occasions of intervention, such as with angels, prophets, and the climactic confrontation with Job. The presence of the holy, while evident, is still nebulous and expansive, always beyond the comprehension of the human character. In the Gospel of Mark, for instance, the disciples walk about with Jesus utterly clueless about who he is until the recognition scene halfway through the book in chapter 8.[1] Even angels, whom we might presume to be fairly obvious, are not. Nevertheless, we would be forgiven for assuming that biblical manifestations of the divine made it easier to be religious back then. Visiting angels would certainly stop at least the agnostic in his or her tracks. All of these manifestations are literary, theological reflections on a primary experience with transcendence. And this is the salient point: such experiences are not time-bound. They occur in modern times as well as in biblical ones. Nevertheless, there are certain occasions in the Bible when

---

1. Divine presence is, however, quickly evident to demonic forces in the Gospel of Mark. They recognize who Jesus really is long before the disciples get there.

the presence of transcendence is unmistakably clear. Holiness is conclusively present and active in certain types of beings and locations. Biblical testimony must portray this clear divine presence again without objectifying or domesticating it. Hence, this chapter examines how numinous presence is construed in scenes with angels, holy sites, and prophets.

Angels

The term "angel," from the Hebrew *malak*, means "messenger," and it is important to note that in Scripture this type of being is indistinguishable from humans. Biblical angels are nothing like the modern associations we have of them. They do not have wings or halos, and they do not sparkle, glow, or levitate when they announce themselves. Our associations of angels are influenced primarily by Renaissance art, which made them supernaturally obvious in scenes and often as cherubic (read: plump) babies.[2] Life does not have these beings flying at us. Instead, biblical angels look just like human beings and only hindsight makes it clear that the divine had been present (e.g., Gen 16:13; 18:13; 32:25; Judg 13:16; 1 Sam 3:4, in voice). In Genesis 18, for example, Abraham is eagerly hospitable to the three strangers who visit him, but he does not know they are divine (Gen 18:2-16). Jacob is faster than most, as he always has been, and understands mid-encounter just who his opponent actually is (Gen 32:27).

Mary is the exception. Remarkably, she takes a conversation with an angel—about her divine pregnancy, no less!—in stride (Luke 1:26-38). The initial greeting troubles her, but after that she engages simply on points of clarification, namely, how this could be since she has had no relations with a man (Luke 1:34). Her *fiat* truly is exemplary of a total trust in God, regardless of the details. And those details are considerable. She readily agrees to something that has, first of all, never been done before and, second, could cause her to be stoned to death on charges of adultery, to say nothing of the parental displeasure she would cause. Catholics venerate Mary because we recognize that she is much more than a passive vessel to God's will. She has given her consent, and the angel, for his part, has waited for it. Mary is exercising her own will in harmony with God's, the very aim of Christian living. Her example demonstrates how active acceptance and trust truly are.

---

2. Cherubs in the Bible are some type of strong creatures with wings akin to the winged creatures found in ancient Near Eastern iconography for palace guards. They represent the formidable power and range of God and so are anything but cuddly bundles of joy.

Just as important, Catholics venerate Mary in response to some deep, universal truth. If you love Mary, then you tend to notice moms more and the pained love it is to be one. Our veneration of Mary, the mother of God, boomerangs back to mothers and children all around us, which is everyone in one way or another. The veneration lights up the world of life-giving. We say rosaries, put her statue outside in a half tub, and bow to her on Sunday, all to adore the love of a mother that got us into this world as it got Jesus here. There is no minimalism in Catholicism. With so much to celebrate, why should there be? The veneration of Mary is more about the childlike glee that we were born than it is about defending Marian doctrines. The doctrines clothe her in mystery, rendering her brave, quiet holiness indisputable.

The nature of what is experienced in an angel encounter is not at first obviously religious but becomes so as human understanding catches up. When divinity becomes clear to the receivers of an angelic visit, they all do the same thing: they bow down and do obeisance, which is Bible-speak for "they drop to the floor." Catholics preserve this bodily impulse for reverence in genuflection while saving full-blown prostration for more solemn occasions, for example, ordination to holy orders or during the entrance procession of Good Friday. Biblical characters all know what to do before the holy. They are just caught wholly off guard when it visits them. James Kugel argues persuasively that this moment of perplexity giving way to comprehension before the divine is so frequent in the Bible that it must be saying something important theologically, namely, that the supernatural and natural world constantly intersect.[3] Discernment—the ability to know when something extraordinary has happened—then, is a skill that believers consciously practice in the world, while confusion would seem to be the lot of us all. For the Bible, the sacred and the profane are interwoven; the real is present constantly and in all sorts of domains, ever there for the noticing.

If this biblical testimony about the appearance of holiness is true, then the Ignatian practice of the *examen* is useful for reading the holy in modern, daily life. There, we review the events of the day with an eye to examining our behavior and the opportunities where God was present. The attentiveness to daily encounters conditions us to see, with the eyes of faith, that some of them were with angels who looked like people. I do not mean this in a sentimental way, in which angels are everywhere, in people and trinkets that look like them. Currently, angels are a boon industry, but they do not look like the trinkets; nor are they in many people we do encounter. They are found within the ordinary, but are not the ordinary. They are not banal.

---

3. James L. Kugel, *The God of Old: Inside the Lost World of the Bible* (New York: Free Press, 2004), 35.

Instead, we reflect in order to discern who in our day related to our soul and not just to us. Often, it can be an off-hand remark, not even an effusively kind one, but it aids an inner question or disquietude we have. A random cashier? The nurse's aide? Why not, if the holy makes it its business of love to intersect with the ordinary.

Holy Sites

As we recall from chapter 4, even the scene of the burning bush began in the ordinary—a desert brush fire. Moses does not see a blazing miracle on the side of the road. Moses is no more overpowered by divine presence than is Mary. Instead, something in the ordinary draws him in to take a second look. The second look, the curiosity, bequeaths the extraordinary, an encounter with God. That little desert spot becomes holy in an instant; Moses must remove his sandals because he is standing on holy ground. Then, just as quickly, the desert patch returns to normal and the sandals go back on. There is nothing special about the site. It is not even worth commemorating, marking the spot in some fashion. The holy vanishes just as quickly as it manifested. What Moses is taught is how to respond to the holy wherever it might occur. Before divine presence, he must recognize the spatial area as holy ground, different from the ground surrounding it, and then, just as quickly, let it return to profane ground. There is nothing supernaturally conditioned about any place or location. What is special is God's presence, made momentarily tangible but not taking up residence in a burning bush or, later, even in a temple in Jerusalem.

The Bible does mention a variety of cultic sites, such as Bethel, Hebron, Dan, Samaria, Jerusalem, etc., but is insistent that holiness is ever mobile. This helps to explain why storm imagery is used so frequently for divine presence in the Bible (Pss 18:8-16; 104:1-4; 68:8-9; Hab 3:5-6; Nah 1; Ezek 1:4; Zech 9:14; Exod 13:22; 19:16). The book of Deuteronomy legislates the centralization of worship but never once mentions *where* that is. Instead, centrality is the chief concern for the people's sake, so they are united in worship. Where they gather is less significant.

There are certainly pronounced strands within the Old Testament that posit centralization in the temple in Jerusalem.[4] The temple had been the biggest temptation for those wanting to secure God's presence to a place, but there remains as well a marked ambivalence as it comes under harsh prophetic critique. Jeremiah, for instance, offers a stinging invective against

---

4. Deuteronomy, 2 Samuel, 1–2 Kings, Ezra, Nehemiah, and Chronicles all especially tout the importance of a central temple for the people.

the complacency that arose by having a temple center (Jer 7). Ezekiel has to make the difficult point of God's absence in the Babylonian destruction of Jerusalem, including the temple, and so he envisions God's departure from Jerusalem in a chariot (Ezek 10). Overall, in the Old Testament as well as the New, there is nothing special about the places where humans encounter God. Jesus, for instance, is from the village of Nazareth but finds himself unwelcome there, run out of town, actually (Luke 4:29). His ministry, while predominantly in the northern region of Galilee, involves constant movement to various towns. He is, after all, an itinerant preacher: "the Son of Man has nowhere to rest his head" (Matt 8:20). The holy is fundamentally elusive.

There is a kind of religious genius or inspiration to this notion that the holy can never be contained in one place, for it engenders a universal and resilient faith. God is always elusive and free from the constraints of geography and religious machinations. A cultic site, a temple, a bush, a tomb, a relic does not contain the holy. Instead, holiness is experienced in the encounter itself; the relationship that it heralds remains vital long after the site of its occurrence does. Place is important for the establishment of relationship only. This is true even for the longed-for Promised Land. The Torah ends without the people entering it. The relationship between God and Israel was established outside the land, in the deserts of Sinai.

This biblical emphasis on God's dynamism enabled Judaism to survive the temple's destruction, not once (586 BCE), but twice (70 CE), and to thrive in Diaspora. And, without a necessary tie to the Holy Land, Christian faith could spread across the Gentile populations of the Mediterranean basin, largely through Paul's fervor. Faith, the response to holy presence, is on the fly; it is mobile. God too is not constrained to one place, be it a temple, the Vatican, or Mecca, though he is present and revered in these places. As Kugel notes, "The spiritual is not something tidy and distinct, another order of being. Instead, it is perfectly capable of intruding into everyday reality, as if part of this world."[5]

Divine presence in this lively, mobile, and elusive sense, then, is also not constrained by time or space. It did not just intrude in biblical times or over in the Middle East. People today who can travel to Israel are no more privileged with divine presence than those who cannot. It is not important where Jesus delivered the Sermon on the Mount, as the gospels themselves indicate: Matthew locates it "on the mount"; Luke, "on the plain."[6] It does

---

5. Kugel, *The God of Old*, 36.

6. The reasons for their difference are theological rather than historical. Matthew wants to portray Jesus as a second Moses, and so a mount serves that purpose. Luke

not matter where Jesus fell on his *via dolorosa*, or wept, or healed someone, or even where his tomb was. These are important devotional moments, as in the Stations of the Cross. A pilgrimage to the Holy Land can be spiritually meaningful because it provides an extended occasion for devotion,[7] but the Stations themselves remain meaningful everywhere they are walked.

The holy sites themselves offer inevitable disappointment, as they must. Jesus isn't on that *via dolorosa* anymore. He was back then, but only briefly. God was in the burning bush, but only briefly. God dwelt in the Jerusalem temple too, for a time, but not now. When Peter tried to extend the transfiguration, his desire—our desire—to make of holiness a fixture was on full display for all to see (Matt 17). Jesus gently instructs him again that the holy is free, uncontainable.

In a sweet irony brought on by the tourist industry, there are today two different tomb sites in Jerusalem for Jesus. The pilgrim, then, is confronted with a choice and the theological reminder that there is no "real" tomb. He or she is put in the position of Moses—is this a holy moment or a regular one? Consumer motives at each site serendipitously preserve the theology of holiness as a safety against turning the tomb into an idol, a fetish for the pious. The competition for tomb authenticity unwittingly upholds the resurrection theology of the Gospel, where at his tomb, Jesus tells Mary Magdalene, "Stop holding on to me" (John 20:17). Mary Magdalene wants holy encounter to last, as we somehow do too when we visit Jesus' pair of tombs. He is not there. To "stop holding onto him" is to stop fixating on place, to move on in faith and remember that a tomb is brief anyhow. The tourist goal is disappointed by the dual tombs, but the theological one is preserved intact.

Holy sites are not magically freighted with supernatural potential. They simply held something exceptional for a momentary time. Exceptional presence itself was never contained there. Much of the Bible takes place in movement and this is no coincidence. For it instructs a path of faith that is always a letting go of locations, fixed spots, and emotional needs for a certain kind of God and moving toward something greater and freer, to "have life and have it more abundantly" (John 10:10). Abraham is the father of faith who was first promised the land, yet even he spends the bulk of his life traveling around that land and never settling. His one poignant concession to place is his purchase of a burial plot for his wife Sarah at the cave

---

wants to show Jesus as the savior for everyone, so he puts him on a level plain, quite literally leveling the playing field for salvation.

7. And sometimes it is not, as the moneychangers have only multiplied since Jesus' day.

of Machpelah (Gen 23:9). Most of the Torah takes place in transit, from slavery toward a freedom with God. Moses would have to leave the bush, Peter the transfiguration, Mary the tomb, and even Jesus his life—all for something unimaginably and immeasurably greater. The angel stories always take place in fairly pedestrian, often unnamed locations. They teach us not to fixate—marking each and every spot as holy—but to discern, allow, and be open to its possibility at any point. It might even behoove us on occasion to eye each other suspiciously as potential angels in hiding and be as eager with our hospitality as Abraham was.

Prophets

Prophecy comprises the third section of the Old Testament, alongside the Torah and the Writings, and is an essential form of divine manifestation. There are the three large prophetic books, namely, Isaiah, Jeremiah, and Ezekiel, and the twelve books of the minor prophets, such as Amos, Hosea, Jonah, etc. Scripture throughout portrays a God resistant to imaging. The aniconic pressure impels a creative amalgam where elements from nature, anthropomorphisms, indirection, and aftereffects are all combined and reshuffled with ease.

The case of prophecy might seem to be the exception to the literary portrayals of divine mystery since prophets speak direct oracles or speeches from God. They serve as God's mouthpiece, giving divine voice to specific social and historical conditions in Israel. Prophetic oracles are the manifestation of divine presence through speech, shorn of a prophet's own agenda. At the same time, however, some ambiguity remains since the direct speech of God comes *indirectly* via the prophets' mouths. The ambiguity is conspicuous even in the prophets' own time as their audiences typically did not believe the oracles. Just because a prophet declared that he[8] spoke the word of God did not in any way guarantee a receptive audience. In fact, as often as not, it seemed to have the opposite effect as mobs often turned on the prophets. Hostility toward prophets was a proverbial commonplace by New Testament times as the murder of prophets is repeatedly mentioned: "Jerusalem, Jerusalem, you who kill the prophets and stone those sent to you, how many times I yearned to gather your children together, as a hen gathers her young under her wings, but you were unwilling!" (Matt 23:37; see also Matt 5:12; Luke 11:50). Further complicating matters, prophets often had rival candidates on

---

8. These literary prophets are all male. There were female prophets in ancient Israel too, but they do not have collected, written materials in their names. Deborah was one (Judg 4:4), as was Huldah (2 Kgs 22:14).

the scene, "false prophets," but, according to Deuteronomy 18:22, the only way to distinguish between a false and a true prophet was with the benefit of hindsight, that is, to ask if the oracles proved true.

The call narratives of the prophets depict divine presence through the literary technique of indirection. Since the prophet is held to be the mouth-piece of God, it is paramount that his authority be validated through a direct encounter with God. These narratives establish prophetic legitimacy while at the same time obscuring depiction of divine presence. In the case of Isaiah, his call narrative occurs in the inner sanctum of the temple, the holy of holies, where God dwells (Isa 6). The account is crowded with details, including smoke, the door frame, coals, coal tongs, wings of the surrounding beastly seraphim, a throne, and even the hem of God's garment. Everything, in other words, except God himself, is described. Isaiah is changed by the encoun-ter, much as Moses had been. As their mouths are readied for the task, the prophets move from insecurity and resistance to acceptance. Since Moses is "slow of speech," his words, which are God's words, are put in Aaron's mouth to deliver. The divine words, in his case, then, are twice removed from God (Exod 4:10, 15). In the case of Isaiah, his lips are purified for the job with a burning coal, that is, he is branded as God's mouthpiece (Isa 6:7).

For Ezekiel, indirection in depicting God occurs on the syntactic level. He loads his sentences about God with multiple similes—with the cue "like"—also to an obscuring effect: "And I saw something *like* polished metal, *like* the appearance of fire enclosed on all sides, from what looked *like* the waist up; and from what looked *like* the waist down, I saw some-thing *like* the appearance of fire and brilliant light surrounding him. Just *like* the appearance of the rainbow in the clouds on a rainy day so was the appearance of brilliance that surrounded him. Such was the appearance of the *likeness* of the glory of the LORD" (Ezek 1:27-28; emphasis added).

All of this indirect description creatively prevents any focused imaging of divine presence. Ezekiel also employs outright misdirection in his bizarre descriptions of what surrounds God, namely, a chariot whose wheel rims are full of eyes (Ezek 1:18), and, as if this were not sufficiently strange, flying creatures whose "faces were like this: each of the four had a human face, and on the right the face of a lion, and on the left, the face of an ox, and each had the face of an eagle" (Ezek 1:10-11). He then adds in masterful understatement, as if he hasn't just scared the bejesus out of his audience, "such were their faces" (v. 11). By this point we almost forget that this is a call narrative with God manifest somewhere in the scene, because Ezekiel has so effectively dragged our attention away from picturing God.

Still, it is Hosea, rather than Ezekiel, whose literary indirection about the divine is the most extreme. His call narrative involves no divine meeting or visual directly but occurs rather as an assignment where he gains vicarious experience of how God feels. Divine presence is manifest by proxy in Hosea's willingness, as it were, to step into God's shoes. God tells Hosea to marry a whore and experience God's circumstance with Israel: "Go, get for yourself a woman of prostitution and children of prostitution, for the land prostitutes itself, turning away from the LORD" (Hos 1:2). And Hosea proved obedient right down to naming the unfortunate three children of his union "God will sow,"[9] "Not-Pitied," and "Not-My-People" (Hos 1:4, 6, 9). God's presence to this prophet is indirect, established through forced empathy with the divine. While Hosea's call narrative entailed only the vicarious presence of God via imitation, Jeremiah's initial encounter with God is also construed with indirection in that it is lost to the prophet's conscious memory.

It is the prophet Jeremiah who receives the most intimate call of all from God, but since it happens prenatally, he has no conscious memory of it: "Before I formed you in the womb I knew you, / before you were born I dedicated you, / a prophet to the nations I appointed you" (Jer 1:5). This verse, for obvious reasons, is often used in the prolife literature. It supports the idea implicit in Genesis that we are all made in the image of God and mysteriously do not know when precisely that begins. In addition, the verse is suggestive that all people, not only prophets, have a vocation, a reason for having been born. A prenatal presence of God, before our conscious awareness kicks in, coheres well with Augustine's description of a God "nearer to me than I was to myself." Jeremiah and Augustine both experience divine absence, but only because they are not really present to themselves, to their own inner lives. Divine presence in these prophetic call narratives as well as in angel visitations is clearly evident, but, as we have seen, the literary means by which it is conveyed vary quite a bit at preserving God's ineffability.

Another means to portray divine presence is by the resulting aftereffect. In this case, the narratives take pains to describe the people significantly altered by a divine encounter that itself is not described. The presence and absence of the divine, its fluidity, is experienced or construed not by a statue or the plurality of a pantheon but by its impact. Examples occur throughout the Old Testament. Moses, as we saw in the last chapter, has spent enough time with God that his face shines radiant (cf. Num 6:24-26).[10] Reverence for divine mystery leads to the otherwise odd locution about

---

9. In the NABRE, the name is untranslated Jezreel. The translations from the Hebrew here are my own.

10. The Hebrew root, *qrn*, means both "to shine" and "horn," so early interpreters misunderstood the effect to be horns. See Michelangelo's sculpture of Moses with blunted horns on his forehead.

the temple as a place where God's *name*, rather than God, dwells (e.g., 1 Kgs 8:17-20; 9:7; 1 Chr 22:10). A life of wisdom is a clear effect of having known God (Prov 1:7; 1 Kgs 3:12). And, for Elijah, the light, silent sound in a breeze restores the exhausted prophet (1 Kgs 19:12). There is a deft artistry at work in such literary zigzagging, all to accord the numinous its rightful place of no place, to preserve its divine freedom.

All of these various means of describing the reality all around God's presence serve to cradle divine mystery. Since God cannot be portrayed, everything around him is, often in great detail. Noting the deity's hem as Isaiah does is the literary equivalent of averting the eyes. Even the descriptions of God's throne displace imaging the God who would sit there. Cloud, smoke, fire, simile, and so on mystify divine presence so that God can be understood as elusively substantial. It is a "both/and" presence. God, as we noted in chapter 4, was not in the bush or the fire but rather in the mystery of its not being consumed. When asked where the Torah was before it was given on Sinai, the rabbis asserted that it had existed always, written as "black fire on white fire."[11] This idea expresses the lively mystery of God and the fundamental indeterminacy of holy writing. The literary inventiveness of varying theophanies preserves God's freedom and keeps the human open to the numinous by decentering its subjectivity.[12]

The variety of divine manifestations in the Bible obviously plays an essential role in theological understandings of who God is for the biblical writers themselves, for their society, and for us today. Israel, Walter Brueggemann summarizes, "engages in a dense rhetoric that makes available the density of its God who refuses every exhaustible domestication."[13] The variety, we have been arguing, is a principal biblical witness to the fluid, lively, dynamism of God's presence. Insistence on any one concept, site location, or even a sequence of them would betray the liveliness of God and thereby threaten to petrify the holy. At the same time, traditional theology has tended to emphasize only God's unchanging nature, namely, that the divine is immutable.[14] Here, the Bible offers a continued corrective to theology, in order to preserve the wild freedom of God.

11. *Midrash Tanhuma Genesis*, ed. Samuel Berman (Hoboken, NJ: KTAV Publishing, 1996), 1JT, Shel. 6:1, 49d.

12. Samuel L. Terrien, *The Elusive Presence* (San Francisco: Harper & Row, 1978).

13. Walter Brueggemann, *Theology of the Old Testament: Testimony, Dispute, Advocacy* (Minneapolis, MN: Fortress Press, 1997), 67.

14. Thomas G. Weinandy, *Does God Suffer?* (Notre Dame, IN: University of Notre Dame Press, 2000).

The Problem with Omnipotence

In recent years, contemporary theology has critiqued omnipotence as a category for the divine because it both reifies divine presence as power and renders it static. It is a heavy given, unassailed, yet largely undetected, particularly in the modern and postmodern contexts. The conceptual abstraction of omnipotence, as well as the other Omnis of renown—omniscience, omnipresence, omnibenevolence—vouchsafes a divine all-ness that has to "be there." It illustrates Derrida's claim that Western philosophy has privileged the category of essence.[1] Abstractions about the essence of God reify the divine life force, its living freedom. The theological conundrum is and always has been that God cannot be captured by human articulation, no matter how precise. On occasion, readers might wish for the biblical God to be more stabilized, but that wish is not realized in the process of reading. The abstractions for God as omnipotent, omniscient, omnipresent, and omnibenevolent do not in any case really introduce the living God who is desired, prompting Pascal to cry out that he wanted the "God of Abraham, God of Isaac, God of Jacob, not of philosophers and scholars."[2] In other words, the qualities of relationship with

---

1. John D. Caputo, *The Prayers and Tears of Jacques Derrida: Religion without Religion* (Bloomington: Indiana University Press, 1997), 15.
2. Blaise Pascal, *Pensées and Other Writings*, ed. Anthony Levi, trans. Honor Levi (New York: Oxford University Press, 2008), 178.

this personal God and verbal actions are necessary aspects in theological description of the biblical God.

Wisdom literature, part of the third section of the Hebrew canon, the Writings, continues the biblical reticence for objectifying the divine. But its theophanies differ in considerable ways from those found in the Torah and the Prophets. They pointedly address the problem of relating to numinous presence and consider its impossibility in a way that earlier biblical literature had not.

The Contesting Theophanies of Wisdom

In general terms, Wisdom literature has received the least amount of attention in biblical theology,[3] to the point that Walter Brueggemann has lamented that it is the "embarrassing stepchild" of Old Testament theology.[4] Theophanies are far less frequent in the Wisdom literature for several reasons. First, its focus is given to the experiential, practical knowledge discerned in everyday human endeavors. Second, the devices used to convey divine appearance in the other portions of the Hebrew Bible—angels, law, oracles, glory—are nowhere to be seen. In Wisdom literature, theophanic witness has dwindled to infrequent discourse, that is, talk *about* God. Talk about God in the third person has replaced any overt descriptions of divine presence. In Proverbs 1:7, "Fear of the LORD is the beginning of knowledge," but after that, God stands merely as referent for what constitutes proper behavior in the teachings of wisdom; God is a footnote, albeit an oft-cited one, to the wisdoms conferred from parents to their children.

And third, since most of the Wisdom literature is relatively late in Israel's history, it innovates and questions God's presence in a way that earlier materials had not. After the catastrophe of the exile in 586 BCE, those believing in YHWH adapted to life under foreign rule and were themselves spread out in a variety of locations in the Diaspora, namely, in Babylon, Yehud, Samaria, and Egypt. The loss of political independence as a result of the Babylonian destruction of Jerusalem and Judah occasioned hard reflection on Israel's past and God's presence within it. Loss and recovery became important themes in Wisdom literature, as can be seen most clearly in Job, yet also in the book of Ecclesiastes, whose own journey consists of attainment, transitions, and dissatisfaction with the cycle.

---

3. Choon-Leon Seow, *Ecclesiastes* (New York: Doubleday, 1997), 54.

4. Walter Brueggemann, *Theology of the Old Testament: Testimony, Dispute, Advocacy* (Minneapolis, MN: Fortress Press, 1997), 334.

There are two appearances of God in the book of Job, but dialogues about God's absence fill the rest of its pages. It is an ambiguous testimony of a present God, as divine absence persists for the majority of the book. And Ecclesiastes is widely considered one of the least theological books in the Bible, the other major contender being the Song of Songs in which God is not mentioned.

Yet a comparison of the theophanies evident in Job and Ecclesiastes reveals an inner biblical critique—a proto-postmodern one, if you will—against omnipotence. Together the uses of divine power and its absence in these two Wisdom books further the aniconic literary tradition. The God of Job is caught in an idol of power while Ecclesiastes offers, through his use of the term "vanity" (*hebel*), a theological space for an iconic presence of the divine at the edges of human living. Further, the contrast between the two enables a discursive biblical caution against the dangers of *any* concepts becoming idols.

The manifestation of the holy or of its potential in Job and Ecclesiastes involves atmospheric phenomena: for Job, God manifests in a whirlwind; for Ecclesiastes, "vapor" plays a central role. Both books display innovation from conventional Wisdom literature, with Job's steadied theme of innocent suffering and Ecclesiastes, for his part, pushing at the very purpose of busy, toiling human affairs. Further, a pronounced absence of God marks both works, illustrating perhaps the insight of Emmanuel Levinas that "the path that leads to the one God must be walked in part without God."[5] The contrast between the two portrayals of God in these books is stark especially in conveying the possibilities of divine power. This difference suggests that Israel's own understanding about divine power was a source of contention, at least in the postexilic period if not before.

The Power Theophany of Job

The well-known theophany of Job occurs near the book's end.[6] God clearly appears to Job, is interventionist about it, and is utterly commanding in presence. From the whirlwind, God comes, booming a soliloquy on all he has created. It is a nature theophany, through and through.[7] Yet, even

---

5. Emmanuel Levinas, *Difficult Freedom: Essays on Judaism*, trans. Seán Hand (Baltimore: Johns Hopkins University Press, 1997), 143.

6. The Lord appears from the whirlwind, chaps. 38–41. Cf. Jer 23:19 and 30:29.

7. For a thorough analysis of the various types of theophanies in the Hebrew Bible, see George W. Savran, *Encountering the Divine: Theophany in Biblical Narratives*, JSOTSS (London: T & T Clark International, 2005).

in this potent, almost menacing, display of divine presence, the theophany itself is all words. God is the subject of talk, first between Job and his friends for thirty-six chapters, then by God himself for four more chapters. So much talk, so many words, that it is as if God is *not* there, narcissistically too full of his own presence to notice the Other, Job.[8] This narcissistic absenting is further confirmed when God's idea of restoration is to give Job a second batch of children to replace the ones destroyed in the celestial bet.[9] Divine omnipotence is clear, to be sure, yet it is wholly unimpressive.

More important, this whirlwind theophany delimits the holy to power alone. The whirlwind speech acts as a kind of conceptual idol. It is, in Jean-Luc Marion's sense,[10] an idol because it is fixed presumably by the gaze of what humans—the friends of Job and all subsequent Bible readers—want of their God, a mighty, all-powerful *deus-ex-machina* deity. Marion criticizes conceptual abstractions in theology because they limit God and are really only a mirror of our own wishes projected. The mirror function of the idol can only display as much as the human gaze can bear and return it, with the result that the divine is confined to the scope of the human gaze that sees it.[11] This God of Job, then, is frozen by the human need for divine, bring-it-on omnipotence. Feuerbach was correct to note that so much of theology *is* projection on a blank screen of what humans want God to be, need him to be.[12] Some of this projection for more power is occurring in the whirlwind speech.

The dialogues throughout the book have revolved around God's potency and the aptness of when it is deployed. The painful silence of God for thirty-six chapters follows with a four-chapter-long torrent of talk by him. This divine talking spree would certainly answer the silence that has pained especially Job. It meets the desired gaze or expectation for a deity in control of life, of fate, but is in the end an unsatisfying projection. Job's friends express a human desire for a God who can be reliably predicted to reward and punish. They want, essentially, a Greek god, a Zeus controlling the fates, to explain the fate of their pitiable friend. And so, in the whirl-

8. This inability to see the Other is a glaring weakness of the deity, in its refusal to have "renounced all claims to domination or sovereignty" (Levinas, *Difficult Freedom*, 8).

9. See chapter 7 for further discussion of Job's situation in suffering.

10. Jean-Luc Marion, *God without Being*, trans. Thomas A. Carlson (Chicago: University of Chicago Press, 1991), 7–18.

11. Christina M. Gschwandtner, *Reading Jean-Luc Marion: Exceeding Metaphysics*, Indiana Series in the Philosophy of Religion (Bloomington: Indiana University Press, 2007), 132.

12. Ludwig Feuerbach, *The Essence of Christianity*, trans. George Eliot (Lawrence, KS: Digireads, [1841] 2012), 20.

wind account, they get one. This mirror image of their own power-laden desire shows a God not only in control of the fate of humankind but one so thoroughly omnipotent that he even micromanages each sneeze of the Leviathan,[13] the flight of the raven, and the crude mothering instincts of the ostrich (Job 41:25; 38:41; 39:14).[14]

The whirlwind speech may be the climactic scene of the book of Job depicting the long longed-for presence of God, but as brute cipher for providential control over everything, it is functionally an idol, what Marion has termed the "low water mark of the divine."[15] An idol debases God; biblical discourse is fiercely insistent on this throughout. Here, though, in the book of Job, biblical discourse about idolatry gives way to an enacted occasion—a parable—of it.[16] Readers have long been unsatisfied and disturbed by the God of the whirlwind speech. Perhaps they are meant to be. The theophany is not theologically descriptive but rather provocative; not of what God *is* but of who he cannot *merely* be. The biblical image evokes protest.[17] It directly challenges the theological tendency to limit God to any one element, be it divine power, mercy, gender, etc. The exposé of God's power in Job serves, by its very overreach (e.g., ostrich nurturance), as a biblical critique of omnipotence for the divine.

In fact, Mrs. Job (she is nameless) may have been the only working theologian in that household when she said, "Curse God and die" (Job 2:9). The Death of God movement begins, then, not in the mid-twentieth century but back even further with Mrs. Job.[18] Curse *this kind* of God, she

13. The Leviathan is envisioned here to be some sort of large water beast, perhaps a crocodile, with allusions to the chaos monster in Ugaritic mythology. At the very least, it manifests the alien Other. Carol A. Newsom, *The Book of Job: A Contest of Moral Imaginations* (New York: Oxford University Press, 2003), 248–50; Mark S. Smith, *The Early History of God: Yahweh and the Other Deities in Ancient Israel*, 2nd ed. (Grand Rapids, MI: Eerdmans, 2002), 85–86.

14. Newsom suggests that the ostrich symbolizes not only an absence of wisdom but also an "anarchic joy," which may have drawn the attention of a dominating God (*The Book of Job*, 247).

15. Marion, *God without Being*, 14.

16. Sallie McFague, *Speaking in Parables: A Study in Metaphor and Theology* (Minneapolis, MN: Fortress Press, 2000), 66–91.

17. For a discussion of the multiplicity of voices and the dialogic character of texts over and above their descriptive elements, see Newsom, *The Book of Job*, 21–31; Barbara Green, *Makhail Bakhtin and Biblical Scholarship: An Introduction* (Atlanta, GA: Society of Biblical Literature, 2000).

18. Thomas J. J. Altizer, *Radical Theology and the Death of God* (Indianapolis, IN: Bobbs-Merrill, 1966); Richard L. Rubenstein, *After Auschwitz: History, Theology, and Contemporary Judaism*, 2nd ed. (Baltimore, MD: Johns Hopkins University Press, 1992).

would seem to be saying: the one who takes bets with the satan; the one who singles out the righteous for experimentation; the one who is bracingly omnipotent, *way* above their own pitiful sorrows, yet also curiously impotent. For, this all-powerful God had been vulnerable to the satan's questions in the first place, much as Eve had once been to the serpent's. Moreover, this divine speech about divine power thrums on for far too long. Job had conceded the issue at 40:4-5, but God continues for the rest of the chapter and the next for a total of sixty-one verses. This theophany dedicated to divine power, in effect, protests too much. If God is no better than an insecure mortal, subject to the dares of others far less powerful, or defensive to the point of overkill, or if God is merely divinized abstraction, namely, Omnipotence Unquestioned, then perhaps theology should heed Mrs. Job's counsel and "curse him and die."

A God, then, *reduced* to omnipotence is not a God worth knowing. He is an idol only of power, of what humans need him to be, namely, a security system against uncertainty. The whirlwind theophany in Job transgresses into the idolatrous because it restores the God of interventionist and retributive power, which the book otherwise takes such great pains to debunk. Marion highlights an important difference between Job and Ecclesiastes: Job complains for having lost his goods, while Ecclesiastes laments the nature, the vanity, of all goods.[19] Job's plight, in other words, is situational, while that of Ecclesiastes is existential. Job, in this sense, will settle for the gratifying fix of an idol. When Job's crisis is over, he can presumably return to the worldview he knew before. Ecclesiastes, on the other hand, is vexed and dissatisfied by the very sensibility of the world around him. He will hold out for an icon of ephemeral presence, even at the risk of a vaporous nothingness.

God's display of omnipotence in the whirlwind theophany may indeed soothe our anxiety about "who's in charge here, anyway?" but it leaves a distasteful ambivalence about encountering this hectoring Captain of Fate, who commands that we ready for battle by girding up our loins. Ironically, the friends of Job might have appreciated this encounter more than he himself could. The whirlwind God is an idol, almost a bully of one, where power is vouchsafed, but at the expense of other signal divine characteristics, for example, loving-kindness, love, covenantal awareness of the other, relational encounter, mercy, etc. Divine love exists in this whirlwind portrait but it is remote, evident in how God daily takes care of all the species he has made and how he has the sun and stars come to the skies. It is indeed full-time work for this creator to keep the diversity going: the whirlwind speech is essentially a curriculum vitae of the creator's efforts. Hence, while the

19. Marion, *God without Being*, 124.

divine encounter champions a creation theology, the price is steep, namely, a God isolated by divine power. It has the effect of reminding Job that his problems, as *one* member of *one* of these species, in the vast expanse of the universe God maintains, are quite small in comparison. The whirlwind theophany for Job is, at best, then, an exercise of divine "tough love."

Job perhaps catches up with his wife's perspicacity at the end when he says, "I disown what I have said, and repent in dust and ashes" (42:6). His response to the whirlwind speech is ambiguous, as ours might be. "Dust and ashes" signals the self-mortifying humility that accompanies grief,[20] while "disowning one's words" is biblically impossible (as surely the deity would know); it is the reason why there are strict biblical laws governing vows. Words, once spoken, are "out there"; they have reality and cannot be taken back (e.g., Jephthah's vow in Judg 11:30-31). Interpreters have long wondered if Job's contrition is genuine or a mocking dismissal of this brutish God, an idol of power, "By hearsay I had heard of you, but now my eye has seen you" (Job 42:5). If genuine, then, Job is cowed and appropriately reverent. But if mocking, then, his words overplay deference, with sarcasm really the covert dismissal of such totalizing power.[21]

The theophany in Job, in effect, deconstructs *itself*, forcing Job and his readers to seek some more real presence of the divine. Even the prose ending of the book, regardless of its source analysis, serves the idol of omnipotence. This God-in-charge gives Job new servants, new animals, and ten new children. Whereas the dialogues critiqued the notion of retributive justice, namely, that God reliably punishes the wicked and rewards the righteous, the God portrayed in the final chapter reverts right back to it, as if the new brood of children could possibly make up for Job's trauma. Tellingly, Mrs. Job remains silent. The wisdom of Job, then, is radically deconstructive. It offers in parable a critique of an omnipotent God. It exposes the limiting idol of God as all-controlling creator, hovering over creatures to manage each and every last detail, *except* the broken heart of his faithful servant, Job.

Ecclesiastes' Search for the "Vanity of Vanities"

By contrast, the book of Ecclesiastes is far more reticent on naming the divine, to the extent that its theological value has long been disputed,

---

20. As do the "sackcloth and ashes" elsewhere in the Bible.

21. In situations where the powerless are so completely outmatched by the powerful, they nevertheless find covert means of resistance through sycophantic playacting and mockery. James C. Scott, *Domination and the Arts of Resistance: Hidden Transcripts* (New Haven, CT: Yale University Press, 1992).

beginning with the rabbis who debated whether or not it should even be included in the canon of Holy Scripture. It shares the characteristic Wisdom focus on human experience and knowing, rather than God, and its well-known refrain, most commonly rendered, "vanity of vanities" would seem to forestall theological insight. The various other refrains too often help to qualify the work as a skeptical, philosophical treatise rather than theology: "there *is* no profit under the sun" (2:11); "all *is* vanity" (1:14, etc.); human beings and beasts "both were made from the dust, and to the dust they both return" (3:20). The existential weariness in the book led Gerhard von Rad to call Ecclesiastes a "practical atheist."[22] But while the futility of human effort certainly concerns the author, his skepticism does not necessarily extend to the divine. In fact, a subtle, sublime movement toward envisaging God is evident. Ecclesiastes in a sense picks up where Job had fallen silent. He restores the mystery of God, even at the cost of indeterminacy. Here, there is much less talk about God, but the silence is not absence.[23] The apparent downshift from booming powerhouse God to a barely detectable God is, instead, expressive of plenitude, a muted gain. Ecclesiastes has found something in the "vanity of vanities."

One striking feature of Ecclesiastes is that the personal name of God, YHWH, is never used.[24] Instead, he uses the generic term for "god," *elohim*, no fewer than thirty-nine times. Even stranger, thirty-one of those instances have the definite article attached: literally, "the God" (*ha elohim*).[25] Hence, discourse about God in Ecclesiastes is always the impersonal, grammatically distancing, "The God" or "a God." The very awkwardness calls attention to the divine noun, much as scare quotes do today.

The omission of the name YHWH itself is telling and could mean a number of things. It could signify spiritual distance, theological indifference, or merely an abstract knowledge of God. Alternatively, it could express a reverence, or at least a theological restraint, that Job certainly had not shared. We recall the scribal resistance to pronouncing the divine name, YHWH. In the postexilic period, the practice had developed of substituting "Lord" for YHWH, as the Septuagint, the Greek translation of the Old Testament, often renders YHWH as "Lord" (*Kyrie*).

---

22. Gerhard von Rad, *Wisdom in Israel* (Nashville, TN: Abingdon, 1972), 65.

23. Carey Walsh, "Theological Trace in Qoheleth," *Bulletin of Biblical Theology: Journal of Bible and Culture* 42 (2012): 12–17.

24. The other books of the Bible that do not mention God, namely, the book of Esther and the Song of Songs, are also from the postexilic period.

25. Thomas Krüger, *Qoheleth: A Commentary on the Book of Qoheleth* (Minneapolis: Fortress Press, 2004), 2.

Ecclesiastes may have omitted the divine name as a deterrent to profaning it amid his discussion of so much prosaic human activity. He is clear elsewhere that "God is in heaven and you are on earth" (5:1). His omission, then, acts as a gesture of reverence about God's name that the Masoretic scribes would later enshrine. The absence of the name YHWH amid the frequent and clunky use of "the God" indicates a belief in the divine more than it does dismissal. Ecclesiastes avoids any name theology in an effort to say something beyond the conventional religious ideas of his time. Theological traditions after catastrophic change cannot simply be recycled. They adapt in order to maintain their credibility or they die. Divine presence for Ecclesiastes is largely enigmatic or unknown, and it is understandable that his perspective would have struck a chord with the postexilic communities under changing foreign rules (neo-Babylonian, Persian, Hellenistic) who struggled to know how the God of the old Israelite kingdom, prophets, and patriarchs was still present to them. As such, it offers instruction for others who also feel disaffected in their piety. At the same time, while many things about human life are deemed a vanity in a book that uses the term *hebel* ("vanity") no fewer than thirty-eight times, "the God" *never* is.

From Vanity to Vapor

The term *hebel* occurs thirty-eight times in twelve chapters, and so it is clearly the dominating motif of Ecclesiastes. Unfortunately, the translation of *hebel* has had a distorting influence on how Ecclesiastes has been interpreted over the centuries. "Vanity of vanities" resulted first from the Septuagint translation of *hebel* into the Greek, *mataiotes*, "vanity," rather than *atmos*, "air,"[26] even as the root meaning of *hebel* is atmospheric: "vapor" or "breath."[27] The Septuagint translation then held sway in the Latin translation of the Bible, the Vulgate, with its use of the *vanitas*. The less pejorative connotation of *hebel*'s sense is that everything is vaporous, fleeting, and ephemeral.

Both senses of *hebel* are attested in other parts of the Old Testament (e.g., Pss 39:6; 62:10; Deut 32:21; 1 Kgs 16:13; Jer 8:19). If, however, we attend to *hebel*'s basic atmospheric meaning throughout Ecclesiastes, a theology emerges. Ecclesiastes' refrain of a "vapor of vapors," functions less as concluding assertion and more as a riff on a developing theme, namely, the limited and liminal nature of human doings. It is more jazz-like than we imagined and has more theological insight than expected.

26. Ibid., 42.
27. Ibid.

Twice, at the beginning and at the end of the book, Ecclesiastes uses the superlative construction, "vapor of vapors" (Eccl 1:2; 12:8), framing the book's content. The superlative construction is relatively rare, occurring only nine times in the Old Testament, most often in a sacred context. Hence, the "holy of holies," "heaven of heavens" (1 Kgs 8:27), "God of gods, the Lord of lords" (Deut 10:17), and "prince of princes" of the priests (Num 3:32). And of course, "king of kings" refers to Jesus in the New Testament (1 Tim 6:15; Rev 17:14; 19:16).[28] The Song of Songs may even have a divine hint in it. YHWH is nowhere mentioned in the Song either, but there may be an allusion. In 8:6, "Love is strong as Death. . . . flames of the divine"; the Hebrew phrase for "flames of the divine" is *esh Yah*. The theophoric *Yah* can be used simply as a grammatical intensifier, but it is also God's name, hidden right at the point where love is transcendent of death. Ecclesiastes' superlative "vapor of vapors," *could* signify a vacated God, that faith too is futile. But the holy of holies, we should recall, was also empty, and that was the central site for divine presence.

Both the "holy of holies" and "vapor of vapors" act as icons rather than idols of the divine precisely by including absences within them. That is, their emptinesses give rise to possibilities unnamed, mystery. In Marion's contrast, the idol is a mirror; the icon, a window. The icon is absolutely vital to theology because it can do the near impossible, that is, bring invisibility to visibility.[29] "Vapor of vapors" as icon allows the divine to saturate the visible without being fixed by it.[30] An idol can only block the divine. Where Job saw God as power player, Ecclesiastes sees only atmosphere, saturated obliquely by something more, something suggestively, possibly, holy.

A second phrase in Ecclesiastes is often coupled with "vapor," namely, a "chase after wind" (1:14, 17; 2:11, 17, 26; 4:4, 6, 16; 6:9). With the frequent use of "vapor," we learn that all human activity does not last, but with the second refrain, we discover initiative and desire nonetheless. People in despair simply do not give chase. But Ecclesiastes does. The full variety of human activities that Ecclesiastes addresses does not fully satisfy the human heart and that felt limitation fuels an ongoing chase. The reason for this is not that life is pointless or nihilistic or absurd but because God "has put the timeless into their hearts" (3:11). Yearning is in our spiritual DNA.

To "chase after wind," then, demonstrates effort toward transcendence, something beyond all human tasks (5:2), even as the pursuit is often fraught

---

28. Translations of these superlatives from the Hebrew are my own.

29. Robyn Horner, *Jean-Luc Marion: A Theological Introduction* (Farnham: Ashgate, 2005), 63.

30. Ibid., 17.

with futility. Ecclesiastes announces simply, "What exists is far-reaching; it is deep, very deep: Who can find it out?" (7:24). The utterance bespeaks humility more than resignation, because he acknowledges that there is a "deep, very deep" reality out there. Ecclesiastes' theology is concerned with the edges of human experience, to give expression to that "very deep." It is not futile to search for this something more.[31] It is, rather, the very basis of mysticism.

Even the wisdom of the sages cannot grasp the mystery that exists beyond its limits. It is left for sages, in Ecclesiastes' case, to sketch out those limits that hint at a mystery beyond them. This is a more modest and subtle theological agenda than that in Job or other portions of the Bible. As we noted earlier, St. Augustine captured this sense of yearning beyond the mundane in his opening of the *Confessions*: "Our hearts are restless until they rest in thee."[32] Defeat is not an option for Ecclesiastes or the mystic, and so the phrase "chase the wind" persists.

Elsewhere in Wisdom, breath is used as a cipher to locate the divine. In Job 32:8 and 33:4 breath and the spirit of God are equated, and in the Wisdom of Solomon 7:25, wisdom is viewed as the breath of God's power. Since Wisdom literature is imbued with creation imagery and theology, the use of breath in these instances recalls its importance for animating the cosmos and the human being in Genesis 1–2.

Biblically, breath signifies both the breath in a living being and the larger element of wind.[33] It was God's breath that first breathed over the watery deep at creation (Gen 1). And, in a gesture of profound intimacy, God breathes into Adam's nostrils to animate the creature with life (Gen 2:7). One of Jesus' final acts with his disciples involves breath as divine presence: "he breathed on them and said to them, 'Receive the holy Spirit'" (John 20:22). Breath is instrumental in the psalmist's definition of mortal life (Pss 39:6; 62:10; 144:4). When the breaths run out, life expires. These images of the cessation of breath serve as bookends to the enchanted story of human beginnings from dust and divine breath. In the psalms, without God, humans are but breathless corpses. But this is no nihilism; it is an anthropology born of creation theology. Breath has a presence after all.

---

31. See Michael V. Fox, *A Time to Tear Down and a Time to Build Up: A Rereading of Ecclesiastes* (Grand Rapids, MI: Eerdmans, 1999), 38.

32. Augustine, *The Confessions*, trans. Maria Boulding (Hyde Park, NY: New City, 2001), 1.1.

33. *Hebel* itself is onomatopoetic. With the aspirating *he* and the soft *bet*, it sounds like breath, *hevel*.

It is vital to life, yet this connotation has too often been glossed over in discussions of Ecclesiastes.[34]

Ecclesiastes' theophany of breath and wind at the liminal edges of human endeavor may well be an inner biblical commentary or midrash on the theophany that the prophet Elijah witnessed (1 Kgs 19:11-12). Not the theophany atop Mount Carmel where YHWH bests the Canaanite god Ba'al by licking up all the water and sending fire to scorch the entire mound. There, YHWH's power is on full spectacular display. Ecclesiastes' perspective may be a midrash on the theophany Elijah experiences in the aftermath. When Elijah returns to Mount Horeb, also known as Sinai, depressed and emotionally at his limit, he feels a sublime divine presence. Here, God was not in "a strong and violent wind rending the mountains and crushing rocks," the earthquake, or the fire (1 Kgs 19:11-12). But after that, YHWH was in "a light, silent sound" of wind. Divine presence is clear, as something fleeting, ephemeral, and much harder to detect than the noisy atmospherics of old theophanies. These are subtle theophanies that require human discernment.

Ecclesiastes scratches in search of that "light, silent sound" of the wind too. He is unsure whether or not YHWH is in it, but he allows a space for the possibility, a divine trace beyond human toil and its dissatisfactions. God, the numinous, may be present in this vapor of vapors, evanescence detectable at the edges of human activity. Ecclesiastes' vision of a "vapor of vapors" is an icon allowing mystery to manifest. This is animated presence, to which we continually yearn.[35] Vapor is a metaphor for a fleeting, moving presence. It is not a vacuum. The wind here, the vapor of vapors, is a metaphor in Ricoeur's sense, what he called "calculated error."[36] It is, then, sloppy, precise speech. The numinous is like a vapor, the vapor of

34. Biblical scholars continue to offer mostly pejorative translations of *hebel*: "futility" in James Crenshaw, *Ecclesiastes: A Commentary*, Old Testament Literature (Philadelphia, PA: Westminster, 1987), 57; "absurd" in Michael V. Fox, "The Meaning of *Hebel* for Qohelet," *Journal of Biblical Literature* 105 (1986): 409–27, at 409; "transience" in Daniel C. Fredericks, *Coping with Transience: Ecclesiastes on Brevity in Life* (Sheffield: Sheffield Academic Press, 1993), 11–32; "meaningless" in Tremper Longman III, *The Book of Ecclesiastes* (Grand Rapids, MI: Eerdmans, 1998), 59; and Klaus Seybold, "Hebhel," *Theological Dictionary of the Old Testament* (Grand Rapids, MI: Eerdmans, 1978), 3:313–20, at 320, who views the term's ubiquity in the book as nihilistic.

35. When Levinas laments that much twentieth-century religion has been reduced to the ethical, he importantly points out that Catholicism and Judaism offer exceptions in their attempts to restore the sacred, the sacramental, the numinous in theology.

36. Paul Ricoeur, *The Rule of Metaphor: Multi-disciplinary Studies of the Creation of Meaning in Language* (London: Routledge and Kegan Paul, 1978), 178.

vapors even. It retains its freedom while sliding through metaphor's depiction of it. The vaporous vapor is presence, not absence. It is a dwindled trace compared with God's thick glory but real nonetheless.

The book of Ecclesiastes seems to imply that divine mystery is manifest not only or even primarily in a cultic context but precisely at the edges of human activities. It uses many cognate accusatives—the "doing of doings," "toiling the toil," etc.—to underscore tedium *and* point to a horizon beyond it. For it is at the liminal spaces that theology begins to intuit mystery as presence. In Ecclesiastes, *hebel* marks the limit point of possible satisfaction from a variety of human endeavors, for example, wisdom, wealth, monarchic rule, dining, love, labor, etc. *Everything* on that plane is found wanting in some crucial respect; *everything* is now "in suspension" as noticeably fragile, temporary.[37]

The use of vapor throughout Ecclesiastes is, of course, a stark reminder that nothing is permanent, even the things humans consider vital. But impermanence is not judgment devoid of theology. It is assessment: "The eye is not satisfied by seeing / nor has the ear enough of hearing" (Eccl 1:8). Theologically, I should hope not! Empirical ways of knowing are limiting and can awaken desire for transcendence, for God, ungraspable as the wind. Ecclesiastes suggests a horizon *beyond* human endeavors, of a perspective that can see them all as a "vapor of vapors." Whoever God can be in this situation, God must be other than yet another object for investigation and inevitable disappointment. In the daring wisdom of Ecclesiastes, "spirituality is offered up not through a tangible substance, but through absence."[38] God must especially be more than a conceptual idol, for example, of omnipotence, or presence, or ground of being. In seeking to get past the metaphysical constructions of onto-theology, Marion probes this eerie site of Hiddenness in Ecclesiastes.[39] The Psalmist also gains access to this horizon when he cries out that "our lives are but a breath" (Ps 39:6). Such truth can only be seen from a perspective that transcends life's breathy shortness. The world is saturated or at least saturating at its edges with the ever new possibility of breath.[40]

---

37. Marion explores the philosophical function of *hebel* in delimiting human satisfactions (*God without Being*, 123–26).

38. Levinas, *Difficult Freedom*, 145.

39. For a substantial discussion of the theological issues involved with omnipotence in the modern and postmodern contexts, see Francis Schüssler Fiorenza, "Being, Subjectivity, Otherness: The Idols of God," in *Questioning God*, ed. John D. Caputo, Mark Dooley, and Michael Scanlon (Indianapolis: Indiana University Press, 2001), 320–50.

40. Marion, *God without Being*, 125.

Ecclesiastes offers a circumspect theology, one accepting the ineffable quality of the divine and wholly given over to the experience of yearning for it nonetheless. Systematic theologians would call this outlook "theological anthropology" with strong apophatic tendencies. In Paul Ricoeur's understanding, the everyday of Ecclesiastes is "the everyday as rediscovered by someone who has looked death in the face and renounced knowing. . . . [M]ade modest, divested of its pomp, wisdom is then tempted to an excess of humility."[41] Having come to such acknowledgment of the deep, Ecclesiastes' perspective on human activity changes, as it did for Paul later: "I tell you, brothers, the time is running out. From now on, let those having wives act as not having them, those weeping as not weeping, those rejoicing as not rejoicing, those buying as not owning, those using the world as not using it fully. For the world in its present form is passing away" (1 Cor 7:29-31).[42] Before the silence of the "deep, the very deep," human activity, including theological speech, becomes provisional. We live with Ecclesiastes and Paul *as if*, but not in escapism.

By discerning the fragile impermanence of human life, Ecclesiastes moves past it to something impossible and "not-yet."[43] Spliced within the perspective of impermanence is a vantage point with the divine: God has "put the timeless in their hearts" (Eccl 3:11). The spiritual quest is not always, or even often, reassuringly placid. There is no achieved goal of ecstasy or certitude. It involves tension and discomfort for the individual caught, in Emmanuel Levinas's phrase, between "jealously guarding its independence but thirsting after God."[44] Ecclesiastes exists in those tensions: chasing something *other than* what all his investigations have wrought. Chasing the wind, in Ecclesiastes, is an apt active description for discerning the holy. We encounter vapor, the Other, not to name it but to respond. Ecclesiastes' theology, then, embraces both the arduous experience of the spiritual heart and the destabilizing fluidity of the numinous.

Elijah had discerned a "light, silent sound" of wind as divine presence. Ecclesiastes discerns the vapor of vapors as its possibility. The vapor of vapors reflects the fleeting, intangible quality of finding life's purpose as well as any role divinity plays within it. It also reflects wisdom's practical and universal orientation as the elements of vapor and wind are natural, everyday realities experienced by all. Indeed, the postexilic community might

---

41. Paul Ricoeur, *Figuring the Sacred: Religion, Narrative, and Imagination*, trans. David Pellauer, ed. Mark I. Wallace (Minneapolis, MN: Fortress Press, 1995), 178.

42. Marion, *God without Being*, 127.

43. Caputo, *The Prayers and Tears of Jacques Derrida*, 117–60.

44. Levinas, *Difficult Freedom*, 16.

well have found solace in these images and their leveling effects. No situation—political, economic, or spiritual—was considered to be permanent. Though temporary, vapor and wind were paradoxically more reliable for a people now in flux than sovereignty, monarchy, and the temple had been. A vapor is even a little sweeter, moister than the wind. This is the potential of the numinous; it animates human life, revives a spent Elijah, and keeps Ecclesiastes yearning, "chasing" after it. The holy in Ecclesiastes is not as overwhelming as it is in Job, to be sure, but is sublime incandescence, of the ordinary being not quite only that but also extraordinary. The numinous is quiet, not absent. In Elijah's case, the holy had been a faint breeze—and God himself— hitting the prophet's cheek. For the postmodern, "God also comes as an ever-deeper Hiddenness—the awesome power, the terror, the hope beyond hope."[45] A gentle, ephemeral Hiddenness is present to Elijah and Ecclesiastes. Ecclesiastes has summoned the courage for a "theological speech" that "feeds on the silence in which, at last, it speaks correctly."[46]

Wind is *more* than atmospheric. Not less. It is life, breath, the beckoning of an elusive God. And isn't this what the sacramental principle tells us about our world: that things are more than what they seem, not sometimes, but often—even characteristically? The theological nuance in Ecclesiastes, while subtle, is a boon to understanding God in our world. What it lacks in obvious categories it more than makes up for in aptness. For this gentle, evanescent presence is the theophany most of us will or do experience, often unknowingly. Ecclesiastes instructs us on how to better read these subtle occasions and so encounter the divine.

45. David Tracy, "Approaching the Christian Understanding of God," in *Systematic Theology: Roman Catholic Perspectives*, ed. Francis Schüssler Fiorenza and John P. Galvin, 2nd ed. (Minneapolis, MN: Fortress Press, 2011), 110–27, at 125.
46. Marion, *God without Being*, 1.

The Dilemma of Suffering

Job in Crisis

Perhaps nowhere is God's absence felt more acutely than during periods of prolonged suffering. The experience of suffering would seem to give lie to the idea of providence, that is, God's active presence in history. When Abraham went on a three-day journey to sacrifice his only son, the God who had commanded this test remained silent (Gen 22:11). When Jesus endured a three-hour crucifixion with bystanders mocking him, his last words conveyed his loneliness: "My God, my God, why have you forsaken me?" (Mark 15:34). There is no question that God can be painfully silent sometimes.

"Often enough," as Michael Novak writes, "faith leads one to feel abandoned to darkness, isolated in inner dryness, undermined by a fear of having been seduced by an illusion."[1] There are myriad pastoral strategies for enduring these periods we all have. One is to keep talking and praying through life regardless of its conditions. The stability of faith comes to the fore here. We pray even while we don't feel like it does a thing to alleviate our pain. If nothing else, prayer shatters the isolation tank that prolonged suffering throws us into. In grief, after trauma, we are all convinced of our

---

1. Michael Novak, *No One Sees God: The Dark Night of Atheists and Believers* (New York: Doubleday, 2008), 17.

solitary confinement, that we will never laugh again, and that creation itself
had been cruelly oversold:

> The stars are not wanted now: put out every one;
> Pack up the moon and dismantle the sun.
> Pour away the ocean and sweep up the wood;
> For nothing now can ever come to any good.[2]

Job, of course, is the singular biblical example of a man who endured an
extended absence of God in suffering. He is credited with a legendary patience, though he never had much of a choice. Suffering is a theological issue
at its core. It goes well past the expertise of friends like Job's or our own and
forces us into the liminal, uncertain place of solitude. Hence, Job—or anyone
suffering—must deal with God. Jesus, though he felt abandoned, nevertheless
shouted to God. Someone more convinced of divine abandonment would
not have bothered with the exertion it must have taken him. I suppose that
is suffering's one consequential gift. Our theological questions cease being
academic. They grow real very fast or they wither and die. Job is a bit like
Peter who could not fathom leaving Jesus: "Master, to whom shall we go?
You have the words of eternal life" (John 6:68). Job too can find no answers
or pastoral strategies apart from his God. Amid all the thick hiddenness of
God, Job still can sing out, "I know that my vindicator lives!" (Job 19:25).

Assuming that he is not just putting on a brave face, Job demonstrates
an impressive confidence in God. Grief makes one crazed and preoccupied
with the self; praise is put on hold for the near future. Yet Job manages
the selfless effort of praise. And, just to recap the extent of this man's
suffering, he lost his farm, his servants, his flocks of animals, and all ten
of his children, *in a matter of hours*. Then, barely into the first stage of
grief—denial—blistering boils cover him so extensively that this wealthy
power player of Nob is reduced to sitting atop a dunghill, scraping those
boils with a shard, a broken piece of pottery. His wife's one acerbic line
in the entire book is surely no comfort to him: "Curse God and die" (Job
2:9). Her rage, though, is understandable, given that she is bereft of those
ten children as well, and so she advises Job to just get it over with.

Cursing God is the theist's version of "suicide by cop," where the besieged
refuses to disarm and surrender. Here, cursing God is antilife. So startling
is the advice of Job's wife that the Masoretic scribes charged with copying
scriptural texts skidded to a stop and could not copy her words. Instead, they

---

2. W. H. Auden, "Twelve Songs," in *Collected Poems*, ed. Edward Mendelson (New
York: Random House, 2007), 142. An alternative title for this poem is "Funeral Blues."

did what they rarely were so bold to do elsewhere with Holy Scripture: they substituted the verb in her mouth to "bless" (Job 1:5, 11; 1 Kgs 21:10, 13). They wished on her some pious goodwill, extending best wishes across the centuries, muting her despair. Perhaps they made the change too as prophylactic against *their* having to curse by proxy. This seems to be the case in the other instances, even when the satan speaks of cursing God (Job 1:5, 11). With that, Mrs. Job vanishes. The people who drop so quickly out of the Bible, never to be heard from again, could fill a book: Mrs. Job, Seth, Hagar, Ishmael, Lot's daughters, Zedekiah, Jeremiah, Vashti, the man who runs off naked at Jesus' arrest. As it is, her legacy is her contrast to Job's praise.

Job knows his vindicator lives. This is more than the practicing agnostics of modernity have. He has nothing left and he knows it. The sheer ardor of his faith is astonishing. He spends the majority of the book defending himself against his well-meaning friends in search of why such bad things happen to good people.[3] The suffering piles on. First, there is the loss, then the loneliness, his physical harm, and, to top it off, lectures from his bystanding friends. All of the aggravated conditions of human suffering are carefully detailed in the book of Job. Somebody has definitely been there; if not an actual person (Job), then certainly the nation of Israel victimized by the Babylonian destruction of Jerusalem and Judah in 586 BCE. The grief is palpable in Job, as is the loneliness and the loud silence of his God. And, to add insult to injury, the chatty friends who are there for the express purpose of comforting Job need, it turns out, *his* reassurances that their worldview is intact. Job's suffering has unnerved them, and they slyly work to attain comfort from him. All of this is endured beautifully by Job. Through that bleak, arid time when Job does not know his ordeal will end or *where* God is, he nevertheless knows his vindicator lives, the one who will come and set him free—from the suffering. And he is white-knuckle hanging on to this promise.

Grief is a kind of slavery for Job; he becomes a slave to emotional pain, to a spiritual ordeal of genuinely disturbing doubts, to despair about the pointlessness of life, to the indifference of God, and, of course, to the just discovered chasm inside his marriage. Most marriages do not survive the loss of a child. The Jobs endure the loss of ten. Their progeny is wiped out in one day. And for the "Be fruitful and multiply" crowd that this is, the loss is catastrophic. There is a restriction of outlook during grief. Our world narrows, along with our sense of competency, and our energy constricts. We aim to get through the day. Smaller goals. Babyier steps. In some ways we have been knocked back to the needy wobbling of a toddler, but with

---

3. Rabbi Harold S. Kushner's book, *When Bad Things Happen to Good People* (New York: Anchor, 2004), is quite instructive and highly readable.

the eyes of the weary, that is, toddlerhood as torture. The psalmist knew all about this plight:

> My heart pounds within me;
>> death's terrors fall upon me.
> Fear and trembling overwhelm me;
>> shuddering sweeps over me.
> I say, "If only I had wings like a dove
>> that I might fly away and find rest.
> Far away I would flee;
>> I would stay in the desert. I would soon find a shelter
>> from the raging wind and storm. (Ps 55:5-9)

Job is so engulfed by his pain that he cannot muster even the psalmist's "if only" of relief. He reminisces about his own babyhood, but only so that he could undo it:

> Perish the day on which I was born,
>> the night when they said, "The child is a boy!"
> May that day be darkness:
>> may God above not care for it,
>> may light not shine upon it! (Job 3:3-4)

He can envision no future and no dove's flight plan to safety as the psalmist could. Instead, life is all darkness and he would sooner be stillborn than endure this level of unremitting suffering.

When the friends first see Job they do not even recognize him. That is how much damage suffering can do. It can change a person utterly, ir-revocably: "They met and journeyed together to give him sympathy and comfort. But when, at a distance, they lifted up their eyes and did not recognize him, they began to weep aloud" (Job 2:11-12).

The bravest comfort they offer occurs when they first arrive. They sit with him in silence for seven whole days, the original shiva. They sit in profound, pregnant, communal silence. No sequence of verses could possibly describe the compassion this takes. Their companionable support is God-with-flesh. Although Job is considered the biblical go-to book for suffering, it is given no answer, even as its entire forty-two chapters try to marshal one. It is truly a heroic try that gives witness to the power of suffering. I am sure that the younger, blunt friend, Elihu, speaks for many readers too when he "was angry also with the three friends because they had not found a good answer and had not condemned Job" (Job 32:3). Such are the horns of the dilemma suffering exacts that the victim becomes a prime suspect in the cause of his own circumstances.

Most of the book of Job consists of talk about God, with the exception of the prologue (chaps. 1–2) and the epilogue (chap. 42). The reader of the book of Job knows something terrible that Job does not: that God *is* implicated in what befalls him. Since Job defends God throughout the entire book, this knowledge undoubtedly would have killed him and proven his wife correct with her advice to curse God. The narrator of the prologue (1:1–2:6) presents God in conversation with "the satan," who is not yet the personification of evil but is an adversary in a rather legal sense.[4] Satan is essentially doing his job by "[r]oaming the earth and patrolling it" and reporting back to God (Job 1:7). It is God, *not* the satan, who mentions Job as exemplary in faith and avoiding evil (1:8). The scene is uncharacteristic of Wisdom for a variety of reasons, not the least of which is that God is shown betting with satan.

The scene between God and satan is similar to theophanies found elsewhere in the Bible in that God appears to someone and engages in dialogue with them, but this time with sinister overtones. Since this divine appearance is confined to the heavenly realm, however, where satan has access but humans do not, it is technically not a theophany, for no revelation occurs. Satan is already fully aware that God exists (and vice versa!) and shows no deference toward—or even recognition of—the awe-filled divine presence. Instead, he is quite content "roaming and patrolling" in heaven too. There is no waiting, no bowing, and no imperial greeting for God who is Lord of all, including satan himself. Instead, we get traipsing familiarity, challenge, and insouciance. While historically it is too early for satan to be the personification of evil, his attitude before God here nevertheless shows him to be well on his way.

Scholarly consensus views the prologue and the epilogue of Job, both prose accounts, as originally independent traditions that were attached to the poetic dialogues comprising the rest of the book. In this instance, however, literary analysis of two traditions does nothing to diffuse the theological bomb their juxtaposition triggers: God is an accessory to satan in the torturous suffering Job undergoes. The two celestial beings wager over whether catastrophic suffering would alter Job's faith. Since exemplary faith has actually attracted catastrophe in this instance, the story would seem to counsel readers to aim safely lower for a spiritual mediocrity, beneath God's radar for praise. What began as an idle hypothetical between God and satan quickly turns deadly. Idle hands, it turns out, really are the devil's workshop.

The good news, I suppose, is that God bet *on* Job's perseverance rather than *against* it, as satan does. The bad news, of course, is the stake of the

---

4. It is not until later, with 2 Enoch and the New Testament, that the figure of Satan represents the embodiment of evil. See Elaine Pagels, *The Origin of Satan: How Christians Demonized Jews, Pagans, and Heretics* (New York: Vintage, 1996).

bet: overwhelming loss for Job. The worst news is to discover God in a compromising exchange with satan, wagering on his faithful servant. Indeed, it is difficult to imagine a more damning portrayal of a capricious God. From the standpoint of fidelity, how is this any different from Eve's tête-à-tête with the serpent? Both conversations have ghastly consequences. Eve, after all, at least had a defense, what with being brand new alive and seeing only "good" and "wisdom" in the fruit. God knows better, and yet he hands Job over to satan to do *whatever* he wants to him, short of killing him (Job 2:6). Except for his death, everything else is permitted.

God's image problem is not resolved by the attribution of independent literary traditions. The theological problem persists over who such a God is and why faith would even want to serve him. God remains silent as Job struggles to understand his suffering. Would that God had exhibited some of this legendary divine silence during his conversation with satan! The portrait of God in the prologue is an affront to our hearts and minds. It elicits ambivalence about God. Indeed, it forces the issue. This stark notion of God's complicity with evil remains in the text as is. It reveals not so much a doctrine of God-as-he-is-in-himself but, more tellingly, the hidden human fear that this is how it all really works behind the scene. The prologue exposes a truth all right, namely, that humans are often caught up short by uncomprehending pain, with their assumptions about God vacillating wildly.

The prologue and epilogue of the book reveal a dastardly God of retribution as the fear we harbor in our hearts. The rest of the book works to deconstruct that image. By laying it bare at the outset, the fearful image no longer festers in our souls. Israel had a pronounced Deuteronomistic tradition regarding divine retribution, namely, that God rewards the righteous and punishes the wicked (e.g., Deut 28) with all the neat predictability, as Rabbi Kushner noted, of a "cosmic vending machine."[5] After its devastating exile from the land, Israel worked hard to interpret the national tragedy as divine punishment—until it just would not wash. No amount of bad behavior, however calculated and persistent, could justify Israel's horrendous suffering.

The book of Job deconstructs the doctrine of retribution by demonstrating how bizarre its theology is in relation to innocent suffering. The prologue and epilogue function as a satire that reduces God to puppeteer, experimenting on his people and then grandly rewarding them punitive damages at the end. Job's ten children are still dead, even as he receives a second set in the epilogue (Job 42:13). Mrs. Job's silence in response to God's "reward" speaks volumes. The doctrine of retribution must be retired

<hr />

5. Kushner, *When Bad Things Happen to Good People*, 46.

if Israel—or any of us—is to move forward in faith. God is no sniper, picking off the innocent for no other reason than that he can, thinking all the while that they make for such easy targets they almost deserve what they get. One revelation offered in the book of Job is the severe ambivalence we have toward God and how that finds an outlet in our theological imaging of him.

Our minds can be way off about God. One of the symptoms of the Fall, that is, preferring our own will to God's, is that our versions of God suffer distortion. They are idiosyncratic, laced with psychological baggage, and multiple. On the inside, many of us are riotously conflicted about God. Images of a menacing, vindictive, wrathful deity vie for attention alongside images of love, mercy, and comfort. The theology inside our heads is a squally jumble. The Bible, because it is written with human hands, has some of these human distortions in it. It seems, as it were, to know this about humankind and so throws all of these images out onto pages for the entire world to see, and hopefully for us to recognize too. It would lance the distortions by first exposing them to the light of day.

Theology is, in part, human projection, as Feuerbach has charged.[6] We want the kind of God who meets our needs, so we project our images of God onto the sky. The biblical writers would have had these impulses too and filtered their understandings of the divine through the circumstances they knew. Divine inspiration would not have overpowered that human process or else the Bible would look like otherworldly gibberish. The God of the exodus, for instance, is power on full display, outstripping the Pharaoh of mighty Egypt. This image would comfort the Israelites whose nation was much smaller and poorer than that of Egypt. The God of creation in Genesis is, well, creative and loving toward the environment. That would encourage the Israelites toward skillful, sustainable methods of farming.

The Bible is not God's self-portrait. It is a mixture of human imagination, situation, inspiration, and sources. Theological humility is gained by encountering the Bible's rich and varied theophanies. For these have, in effect, prepared us not to cave in to a flat literalism when we reach the prologue to Job. Indeed, it is the premise of my book that the Bible teaches us dexterity, in the name of reverence, about imaging God that would spare us further distortions.

In the parable of the talents (Matt 25:14-30), the parsimonious servant buries his one talent rather than risk the *imagined* wrath of his master (God). He has assumed that the master is punitive and is too afraid to get on with the business of living fully. Frozen by fear, he cannot therefore choose life. He has buried much more than his talent. He buries his life, for without

---

6. Ludwig Feuerbach, *The Essence of Christianity*, trans. George Eliot (Lawrence, KS: Digireads, [1841] 2012), 20.

giving God a chance, he can never flourish. Our projections of God get in our way and block out God. The theology of this servant and that of Job's prologue is hamstrung by fear, with the result that God is pinned down to a predictability cycle of test, punish, reward, repeat. Such a constrained view is as wearisome for humans as I imagine it must be for God.

Scripture offers a complex, multitude of voices and is unflinching in portraying evil. But it nowhere approves of it. Instead, it throws characters right on in, and they are, as often as not, the primary instigators; they have jumped right in, swan dove. And, it often implicates God in the chaos: "I form the light, and create the darkness, / I make weal and create woe; I, the LORD, do all these things" (Isa 45:7). Evil and suffering are not resolved in Scripture, and that is as maddening to readers as it was to Elihu. They are, however, grappled with and respected as the enormities that they are, respected for the ways they can confound and cripple the believer. They are taken seriously throughout and not subsumed under breezy, unctuous platitudes.

A mere six chapters into Genesis, God sends a devastating flood, undoing much of the creation of the opening chapters. It is a harsh, unsettling reversal and, at the very least, a dubious start to the divine-human relationship. The flood story is an auspicious, haunting text without the least concern for any kind of divine public relations. In chapter 1, humans are made in the very image of God (Gen 1:27), and by chapter 6, their inclination is "nothing but evil" (Gen 6:5). This is a swift downgrade indeed! The cultural legacy of this story typically centers on Noah, the ark, and the rescued animals. It is a wonderful image of God's loving care as he is present—even personally shutting the door for Noah!—to ensure the ark's survival (Gen 7:16). It makes for a tender subject for mobiles hanging above infant cribs. But this is only because there are pandas, giraffes, and lions, smiling as they dangle. Outside of the ark, there were no survivors. *All* were washed away: panda corpses, giraffe corpses, human corpses.

When tragedy and loss happen, the experience is overwhelming for the victim. We only make any sense of it in hindsight, never right on the scene. So, when the Yahwist notes that human inclinations are "nothing but evil" (Gen 6:5), he reflects the wearied resignation of an Iron Age people (1200–586 BCE) who had already seen quite enough of this psychological truth to write about it. There are acts of cruelty then and now that beggar understanding of the human heart.

Since writing is partly about making sense of things, the human authors explain a flood by depicting God upset with humans.[7] They do

---

7. This is what they do as well in the older Mesopotamian flood stories, from which the Genesis flood story clearly borrows. In *Atrahasis*, the gods are upset by human

not anachronistically embrace the idea of chaos theory, that is, random events just sometimes happen. Nor are they privy to the science of meteorological forces at work in flooding. We cannot fault biblical writers for not availing themselves of ideas as yet undiscovered—chaos, meteorology, heliocentricity. What is striking is that they (humanity) assume the blame rather than offload it on God. The flood story is a remarkable testimony of human humility, as humanity all but covers for God. They finger God to explain tragedy, but then assume the blame for it; that is, God only acted so destructively because human mendacity left him with no other choice.

A close reading of the passage right before the flood account (Gen 6:1-6) reveals, however, that humankind did nothing wrong. In fact, the perpetrators were the "sons of God." They came down from heaven and slept with human women, and giants (the *nephilim*) were the result. *Human* inclinations, then, were not in play at all. If human desire "was always nothing but evil" (Gen 6:5), then this is not the story to make that case. The sons of God are clearly at fault. It is doubtful, anyway, that human women in such circumstances could reasonably give consent to divine wills. While patriarchal customary power *may* have vouchsafed a daughter's right to decline sexual advances, it also means the women's response is lacking in the patriarchal story. At any rate, given their celestial stature, we cannot assume that consent was even solicited by the divine beings, making this a possible rape scene with the resulting, unwanted offspring, namely, huge people. What is out of control and wholly unexplained in the story is the rapacious gang of God's sons. I am sure that feminist scholars have caught this misplaced rage of a father over his sons' sexual exploits, that is, that God would punish the victim—the daughters and their race—rather than control those randy bad boys.

Two contrasting images of God, as loving caretaker and wrathful avenger, collide in the flood story. They are smashed together in the text.[8] The image of a punishing God is to some extent undercut by the deity's lack of full control over events. God is wrathful, no question; drowning the world establishes that. But he is also misdirected in his wrath at humans, and the sons of God are not explained. Traditional interpretations, unfortunately, consider the sons of God mentioned here and elsewhere as the angels, but that only massively compounds the problem. Historical-critical scholars,

---

noisiness, and they hatch a secret plot of flooding. Stephanie Dalley, *Myths From Mesopotamia: Creation, the Flood, Gilgamesh, and Others* (New York: Oxford University Press, 2009), 20.

8. Source criticism is able to untangle two sources, with their different names for God, *elohim* and YHWH, but these do not explain the contrasts in God's behavior.

by contrast, see in the divine sons the polytheistic traces of a divine court as evidenced in Israel's surrounding cultures. The Israelite Priestly writers, having lived in Babylon after the exile, borrowed the Mesopotamian flood story in order to assert the supremacy of their God, over against the regnant polytheism. The power of God is thereby lauded in the tale, without concern for his motive.

Still, the theological conundrum of God's presence and evil persists. Blame, when it comes right down to it, is blurred in the flood story. Disturbing possibilities linger about God and how much control he does or does not have over his own house, let alone the creation. Uncertainty, confusion, and puzzlement are stitched within this tale. It is as if the writers themselves have not quite figured out who this God is. And that in itself is an important testimony to theological humility. God has not quite figured out who he will be to his creation—creator or destroyer—and yet the Bible proceeds, nevertheless, in medias res for theological depiction. The emphasis on relationship with the divine propels the story forward, overriding any conceptual concerns about God's essential nature.

This rough, complex story is revelatory of a host of theological issues. The first is the glaring limitation of theological efforts to describe God along with its attendant humility as the Christian apophatic tradition insists. Second, it offers nothing systematic or comprehensive in knowledge of God or of anthropology. It thrusts the assertion that humans are "nothing but evil" in their hearts, and therefore deserving of divine punishment, but then deconstructs it with the misdirected, even confused, blame by God. Divine discernment, both here and after the flood, is obliquely critiqued. For Noah, we recall, had been the only righteous man worth saving in God's eyes. Yet it is this same Noah who, after the flood, gets drunk, passes out, and exposes himself to his sons. Such a paternal loss of control may qualify more as grossly uncomfortable than as evil, but still it caused lasting damage, as Noah condemns one son to slavery for generations after (Gen 9:25).

Third, the story reveals the elusive, jostling, unstable enterprise that relating to the divine is—that uncertainty, projection, invisibility, and suspicion are written into the mixture of divine-human relationship. We are never sure of divine presence. In our lived faith, we always wonder if a decision is a God moment, something God wills for our lives to flourish, or merely prosaic as part of the bustling routine of life. We might wonder, for instance, "Does God want me out of this situation, because I am miserable? Or, does God want me to 'bloom where I am (supposedly) planted'?" In such circumstances, we are trying to second-guess providence, and God can feel exasperatingly like a quiet, nondirective therapist. The Ignatian discipline of the discernment of spirits, incidentally, does much to hone our attention to God's will in our lives, but uncertainty always remains characteristic of relating to the divine.[9]

Paul was clear on this point: "At present we see indistinctly, as in a mirror, but then face to face. At present I know partially; then I shall know fully, as I am fully known" (1 Cor 13:12). We necessarily relate to God before we have face-to-face clarity. Hence, part of what the Bible reveals, part of what makes it a "strange, new world," is its exposure of our theological distortions. To be clear, the Bible confounds us. It reveals human ambivalence about God. And since most people who go to the trouble of reading Scripture desire to know God better, the experience is often stupefying. As the flood story exemplifies, to our fear-based hearts God is both wrathful avenger and hands-on caretaker. We are split at the root by ambivalence but were so long before we started to read the Bible.

Scripture begins to correct our ambivalence by first laying it bare. Perhaps it has to happen so early in the Bible, in only its sixth chapter, because we have such a long way to go in healing our distortions. I am not claiming that this is a conscious, authorial intent or simply the happy coincidence of sloppily edited sources. I am saying that the effect of reading the text *as is*, that is, canonically, reveals plenty of truths—some on the page, some in our hearts. Revelation in this story and others like it is partly to excise the theological assumptions that harm us.

Theodicy in Christian Tradition

The dilemma of suffering remains an anguishing mystery, something beyond comprehension but demanding it all the same. And evil is closely linked with suffering as it is so often its cause. Theodicy is the branch of inquiry, be it philosophical or theological, devoted to the matter of God's presence or absence in the face of evil. Theodical questions arise out of an acute conflict, namely, that Scripture insists on the goodness of creation while human history would seem so handily to belie that perspective. Why *is* there so much evil, suffering, and wreckage in a world fashioned by God as good? The term "theodicy" (justice of God) was coined by Leibniz in the eighteenth century to address the issue of evil and God's presence during it. In 1755, a massive earthquake struck the city of Lisbon, killing an estimated fifty to seventy thousand people. And, because it struck on

9. Timothy M. Gallagher, *The Discernment of Spirits: An Ignatian Guide for Everyday Living* (New York: Crossroad, 2005). For a practical, motivating overview of Ignatian spirituality in general, see Tim Muldoon, *The Ignatian Workout: Daily Spiritual Exercises for a Healthy Faith* (Chicago: Loyola, 2004).

a Sunday morning, an extraordinary number of churchgoing folk perished while those who remained further out from the epicenter were spared. How could God let this happen? Theodicy tries to answer that question and is typically concerned with the justification of God in the face of evil and suffering. And that, as we all know, has only gotten harder since 1755.

Augustine's view of evil has had the most influence in Christian tradition. In essence, he argues that evil is the result of human sin. God certainly could not be the cause of it, since he is all good, omnibenevolent. Hence, evil must come from the human arena. Augustine reasons that humans were made good by God with free will (Gen 1:31). Our choices away from God distort us until evil becomes like second nature to us.[10] Everything in creation for Augustine is good. Evil exists as the privation of the good, *privatio boni.* In common parlance, the Augustinian view is often expressed as a necessary contrast, for example, we would not know the good, unless there were evil.

David Hume (d. 1776) later diagnosed the problem of theodicy and outlined it clearly: (1) if God cannot prevent evil, he is not omnipotent; (2) if God is not willing to prevent evil, then he is not omnibenevolent; and (3) there would be no evil if God were willing and able to prevent it.[11] In terms of God's presence, theodicies beget a host of responses, including Hume's schema. These run the gamut, including the following characteristic viewpoints: God is not involved at all, since evil is the privation of good, like a vacuum (Augustine); God is not involved because evil is the inevitable by-product, the toxic waste, of having created *ex nihilo,* from nothing; God is present but beyond emotional responses, that is, impassable, to what we do to one another;[12] God is evil or has an evil counterpart (Manichaeism); evil is in God, since he has his shadow side (Jung); God is otiose or semi-otiose, that is, essentially retired these days and away from the scenes of our destructiveness. Deism resolved theodicy in this way. Like a divine watchmaker, God's efforts principally went into winding the watch, the world he made. Once wound, though, people are on their own in that world, left to make good choices, or not.

10. Terrence W. Tilley, *The Evils of Theodicy* (Washington, DC: Georgetown University Press, 1991), 113–40.

11. David Hume, *Dialogues Concerning Natural Religion* (New York: Hafner, 1948), 66.

12. For a thorough and historical analysis of the notion of divine impassability, see Thomas G. Weinandy, *Does God Suffer?* (Notre Dame, IN: University of Notre Dame Press, 2000).

The limitation of theodicy should be fairly apparent. First, it is predicated on a central conundrum about omnipotence. The concern is chiefly metaphysical; it raises questions such as the following: How could God be good and all-powerful? How, if at all, is the holy present during times of catastrophic loss? But evil is much more than intellectual quandary. Would that it were. Theodicy tends to be a systematic concern to hammer out the conceptual issues that evil presents to notions of God's providence and omnipotence. But the suffering in the victims of evil is not intellectual; rather, it is an affective, soul-drenching assault. Anguish is not solved by more concepts. Reason cannot puzzle its way through here, and even if it could, it was woefully ill-equipped for twentieth-century evil. After the Holocaust, after the actual "invention" of genocide, theodical discourse proved futile. Natural disasters such as earthquakes, floods, and fires are one thing, and they certainly exact horrific human tolls. Still, as forces of nature, they lack the sickening, disheartening chill that human evil manages. Natural disasters are still listed on insurance policies as "acts of God," but no one is spooked by this upon signing. It is merely a euphemism for what the policy is not going to cover.[13]

Theodicy has served a corrective function all the same. It has enabled us to rule out at least what evil is not. It is first and foremost not Punishment-from-God, and for two reasons. First, God wills human flourishing while evil hobbles it. A God who did need to punish would do so in a manner not so self-sabotaging to his own life-affirming agenda. And second, the collateral damage alone suggests that God is wildly inefficient as a punitive enforcer, as inefficient as a "smart" bomb taking out the innocent along with the wicked. Further, evil is not a social pressure gauge needed to be unleashed occasionally to level off the energy build up. It is also not personal or related in any way to the victim. We might be desperate enough in our pain to trade incomprehension for some focused self-blame, but it is a false certainty. Victims do not deserve what they get. If the book of Job proclaims nothing else, it is this truth—he did not deserve what happened to him. Jesus did not either. Nor did the six million Jews. Evil is not the result of God's insufficient management of victims because we would have protested the loss of freedom in being so classified.

With modern atrocities, theodicy proved bankrupt, even obscene. Human evil flourished before the twentieth century, of course, but the grandness of scale and grisly creativity put to its use was novel. Human evil did what it always had done, namely, wreak havoc on innocent lives. But this time, it went further, wreaking epic havoc and baffling damage,

13. It is bad theology, nonetheless, with God again relegated to the role of sniper.

with no rational explanation at hand. But before turning to this mystery, we must first examine the variety of atheisms that haunt the landscape of late modernity, especially since one of them is a response to modern atrocities.

Varieties of Atheism

Twentieth-century atrocities, I believe, put an end to theodicy as an intellectual discipline, and a new breed of atheism—"protest atheism"—came into its apex.[14] It is captured by Dostoevsky in *The Brothers Karamazov*, namely, that a God who would allow the suffering of even one child cannot be believed in: "Listen: if everyone must suffer, in order to buy eternal harmony with their suffering, pray tell me what have children got to do with it? It's quite incomprehensible why they should have to suffer, and why they should buy harmony with their suffering."[15]

This form of atheism protests that a God who allows such suffering is not worth knowing. God's existence is not in dispute here, as it is for atheism broadly construed. Instead, protest atheism is the boycott of faith in such a negligent God, whose depraved indifference has finally gone too far. Protest atheism bears witness to the human spirit. It has within it a kind of strong faith—against degradation, for life, for meaning, and for a God who would protect his creatures. There is, I think, even a nobility to protest atheism because it insists on the inherent goodness of the world, one closer to that described in Genesis, even as humanity wrecks it. If mysticism is the felt experience of God, as discussed in chapter 1, then protest atheism is the felt experience of God's absence. All the same, it is not nihilism—the absence of meaning—because it witnesses to meaning. It is much more serious than nihilism because it witnesses to a felt absence of where God *should* go if this were a world worthy of his creation. It is a mysticism of absence.

Nihilism, for its part, Marxism, and varieties of hedonism are atheisms as well, but these were not born of a felt sense of God's absence. Instead, they advertise as improved, replacement systems for God in the name of progress. God is not so much missed or lamented as he is simply passé. He may even be murdered, as Nietzsche had prophesied long ago: "Do we not hear anything yet of the noise of the gravediggers who are burying God? Do

---

14. Jürgen Moltmann, *The Crucified God: The Cross of Christ as the Foundation and Criticism of Christian Theology* (Minneapolis: Augsburg Fortress, 1993), 221.

15. Fyodor Dostoyevsky, *The Brothers Karamazov*, trans. Constance Garnett (New York: W. W. Norton Inc., 1976), 244.

we not smell anything yet of God's decomposition? Gods too decompose. God is dead. God remains dead. And we have killed him."[16]

Protest atheism, by contrast, decries the murder. There is a searing illustration of protest atheism in Elie Wiesel's *Night*:

> Then the march past began. The two adults were no longer alive. Their tongues hung swollen, blue-tinged. But the third rope was still moving; being so light, the child was still alive. . . . For more than half an hour he stayed there, struggling between life and death, dying in slow agony under our eyes. And we had to look him full in the face. He was still alive when I passed in front of him. His tongue was still red, his eyes were not yet glazed. Behind me, I heard the same man asking: "Where is God now?" And I heard a voice within me answer him: "Where is He? Here He is—He is hanging here on this gallows. . . ." That night the soup tasted of corpses.[17]

This account is crushing, and *filled* with faith, a faith in something much greater than the debasing bowels of the Holocaust. It resists the atrocity it cannot stop. It stands as testimony against it and for something elided, absent, a love for life. It indicts God only secondarily. God becomes an accessory after the fact of human brutality. Protest atheism is not merely a philosophical stance. It grips the heart and stands as memorial to those who perished.

"New Atheism" emerged within the last decade and enjoys considerable notoriety today, in part because it offers the satisfying "relief of revolt."[18] Its primary spokespeople—Christopher Hitchens, Sam Harris, Daniel Dennett, Richard Dawkins—are provocateurs, happy to relegate biblical faith to a best-forgotten past.[19] With sarcastic relish, they call themselves the "four horsemen of the apocalypse" after Revelation 6. But this is atheism lite. It lacks any theological and philosophical engagement, preferring instead a

16. Friedrich Nietzsche, *The Gay Science*, in *The Portable Nietzsche*, ed. Walter Kaufmann (New York: Penguin Books, 1968), 95. His words are painful even to type.

17. Elie Wiesel, *Night* (New York: Hill & Wang, 2006), 78. But his words are excruciating to type. Here, a modern miracle is clearly evident, namely, that Elie Wiesel did not go mad.

18. Charles Taylor, *A Secular Age* (Cambridge, MA: Belknap Press of Harvard University Press, 2007), 306.

19. For a critical analysis of the New Atheist thought, see David Berlinski, *The Devil's Delusion: Atheism and Its Scientific Pretensions* (New York: Basic Books, 2009); Terry Eagleton, *Reason, Faith, and Revolution: Reflections on the God Debate* (New Haven, CT: Yale University Press, 2010); and Alister McGrath and Joanna Collicut McGrath, *The Dawkins Delusion? Atheist Fundamentalism and the Denial of the Divine* (Downers Grove, IL: Intervarsity, 2007).

sequence of straw-man arguments, which all revolve around an overbearing, petulant, tyrant God whom few believers would recognize. And so, instead of loving presence, a power greater than ourselves, a sense of profound peace passing understanding, a transcendent awe, a God greater than that which can be thought, New Atheists construct a cartoonish Supreme Being, a pastiche of the best scoundrels who ever chased Bugs Bunny, who is one big, pompous incompetent.

These New Atheists are popular but not persuasive because of this fatal misrepresentation. Dawkins is representative of their general viewpoint.[20] He believes that religion is infantile and science has superseded the need for it. God, for Dawkins, was just the question mark about life that ancient peoples resorted to because they had nothing else. With the age of science, that is all thankfully behind us now. All that is left is a so-called God of the gaps, the placeholder for the unknowns science has yet to solve. Even here, Dawkins is angry that it is taking us too long to say our goodbyes to this diminishing God.[21] Religion under science is really nothing more than planned obsolescence and so the smart play is to drop God now. Dawkins' argument, however, is yet another triumphalism, with science as the new, better idol we can serve.

Dawkins is especially piqued that people would believe in anything without evidence. He sports a simplistic dualism with science as the polar opposite of religion. In tone, he is angry, mocking, narrowly empiricist—in short, anything but scientific. Faith, he says at various points, is a delusion, a throwback, a virus infecting our minds. It is all of the above and it does not seem to matter which as long as we get the larger polemical point that religion is just so wrong. Dawkins and the other three horsemen all have an ax to grind—his is just the biggest—and it fully mangles their argumentation. So too does a preference for truculence, profiteering, and glibness.

It is difficult to imagine if the New Atheists would stipulate to any theological views since they remain delightedly insular in their debates. The petulant make really poor students. One theological question for the New Atheists would be: Why assume that belief in a God known since biblical times is somehow more primitive than secularism, which has a vast, bulging, storehouse of its own crudeness? Dawkins calls God "jealous and proud of it," "a vindictive, bloodthirsty ethnic cleanser," "genocidal,"

---

20. Overall, Dennett and Harris are more subdued in tone, and their primary target is institutional religion rather than God, even though he bears some responsibility for institutional religion as well.

21. Richard Dawkins, *The God Delusion* (New York: Mariner, 2008), 17.

"sadomasochistic," and a "malevolent bully."[22] If his tone weren't so churlish and adolescent, these words might qualify as hate speech.

The traditional, "old" atheists of the nineteenth and early twentieth centuries were the genuine lions of doubt—Nietzsche, Feuerbach, Marx, and Freud. They launched much graver assaults on God and threw into question the very motives of religion. Whereas Dawkins views faith as willful infantilism, these traditional atheists respected religion's existential heft, that is, that it had persisted because it addressed the fundamental questions about the meaning of life. They offered rigorous philosophically based disquisitions on the impossibility of God or the rather hidden motives for religious belief. For Feuerbach, religion is projection. There is no God but only a blank screen upon which we project our best qualities magnified, that is, goodness, truth, beauty, fatherhood. For Freud, it was an illusion born out of humankind's fears about the precariousness of existence. Nietzsche primarily castigated Christianity for twisting human natural power. It offered a slave morality, born of resentment, that made a virtue out of weakness, and this only stymied human actualization. Marx famously noted that religion was the "opiate of the masses," meaning that God was something we tell ourselves to numb the dissatisfying pain of life. He agreed with Nietzsche that belief in a Supreme Being only robbed humanity of its autonomous power and created a false consciousness to accept the material status quo.

All of these critiques have truth in them or else they would not have had the staying power they have. When my car skids on ice, my image of God quickly becomes a strong Midas-sized father protector, as Freud claimed. And the truth of Feuerbach is evident in art. Michelangelo projected a masculine, bearded, buffed, and frowning God on the Sistine Chapel, and even lifelong feminists have that image flash through their minds at the word "God." It is much harder to envision God as the large, happy black woman of Wm. Paul Young's popular book *The Shack*, even if we are large, happy black women ourselves.[23] The damages of a false consciousness are well attested in priggish, passive surrender to one's circumstances, in rationalizing tragedy as God's will, and in religion as yet another form of escapism. These traditional atheists are far more compelling than the new ones.

22. Ibid., 51.

23. And that is leaving aside the whole other problem of the rank stereotyping in the book. The author has conjured God as an Aunt Jemima, complete with her actually cooking pancakes for the grieving protagonist! Projections will always exist in our theological descriptions. Stereotypes, on the other hand, are optional and wholly to be discouraged.

In the wake of Auschwitz, Emil Fackenheim noted, theodicy is ship-wrecked.[24] Modernity's wishful scenario had been that the march of human progress would certainly render evil controllable and probably extinct. With tragic consequences, though, human reason had both underestimated evil and overestimated humanity.[25] We are in unchartered territory about evil and God's presence. This level of human cruelty makes questions about God's providence look like distractions from the spectral truth before us, namely, how far humanity had sunk from being in God's image. The Holocaust was revelatory, horrifically so, and not of a welcomed truth. Evil was real and theodicies only deflected from this truth; they did nothing to pierce it.

The hard biblical testimony is that evil exists as part of the landscape of human life. Good *and* evil already exist in the Garden of Eden where knowledge of them is momentarily contained. Evil is not mentioned in the six days of creation, but an enigmatic "knowledge of good and evil" lay dormant in a tree. Christian theology has long viewed evil as a byproduct of human free will. The cost of having *free* will is that some choose against God. Evil is human-caused. There are sociopaths living next door and hatreds boiling elsewhere.[26] By eating the forbidden fruit, humankind discovered a knowledge of good and evil that it was not at all ready for. Beyond the garden, this becomes instantly clear, as so much is done on impulse. Cain is jealous of Abel, so he kills him (Gen 4). Murder is one way to deal with an emotion, but not a finessed one. Noah gets drunk and creates slavery (Gen 9). Abraham, frightened that Egyptians *might* hurt him, pushes his wife into forced adultery with Pharaoh (Gen 12). We could blame God here for not cleaning up all these messes for them, but the messes themselves make a strong case for *human* recklessness.

God warned Job long ago that the chaotic, destructive force in the world, in the figure of Leviathan, was something God could control, but not easily: "Can you lead Leviathan about with a hook, / or tie down his tongue with a rope?" (Job 40:25). This is a precarious image of divine power. Yes, God has Leviathan on a leash and the beast is otherwise too "fierce" for any man to rouse (Job 41:2). At the same time, this destructive force

---

24. Fackenheim cited in Zachary Braiterman, *(God) After Auschwitz: Tradition and Change in Post-Holocaust Jewish Thought* (Princeton, NJ: Princeton University Press, 1998), 164.

25. Terrence Tilley makes a strong case that the intellectual moves, like the either/or choice of the diagram, betrays it as an enlightenment concern where reason was supposed to reign and not be utterly confounded by issues; see Tilley, *The Evils of Theodicy*.

26. Martha Stout, *The Sociopath Next Door* (New York: Three Rivers, 2005).

is *only* controlled by a leash. It is contained, barely. What goes unsaid until Auschwitz is how all hell breaks loose when humankind grabs the leash.

Auschwitz revealed several deep truths about the nature of evil. First, it is most definitely real, a malicious, potent force that goes well beyond any conceivable socioeconomic hardship of its perpetrators. Second, it is a mystery in the sense that it is more and more dangerous than all the talk we sling at it. Third, evil is more than the privation of good. Rather, it is parasitic, an intruder on the good. It is in play, in movement, and would devour the good. It has a threatening, palpable presence that overtakes life and innocence *without concern*. Even though we are schooled not to think in such dramatic terms as devils and demons, the magisterium has officially affirmed the existence of the devil and evil spirits to give expression to evil's potency. These are not spooky poltergeists but the presence of something unexplainably malevolent. A presence as real as Yeats's "rough beast":

> A gaze blank and pitiless as the sun,
> Is moving its slow thighs, while all about it
> Reel shadows of the indignant desert birds.
> The darkness drops again; but now I know
> That twenty centuries of stony sleep
> Were vexed to nightmare by a rocking cradle,
> And what rough beast, its hour come round at last,
> Slouches towards Bethlehem to be born?[27]

It would be a kind of depraved indifference to ignore evil's reality, so perhaps the Catholic Church is out in front on this one. As Baudelaire had once remarked, the best trick Satan ever played was in convincing us all that he wasn't real.

Fourth, evil is more than sin. The notion of original sin is that humans prefer their self-will over that of God's. It is essentially a preference for the self over God and, therefore, a rejection of relationship.[28] A self-focus generates sins but need not lead to evil. Evil lunges after others, extinguishing life and hampering the flourishing of life wherever it can. Such outward aggression may be born from narcissism. Erich Fromm suggests that psychologically a "malignant narcissism" can form that harbors a love

27. W. B. Yeats, "The Second Coming," in *The Collected Poems of W. B. Yeats*, ed. Richard J. Finneran (New York: Scribner, 1996), 187.

28. Pope Benedict, *Introduction to Christianity*, trans. J. R. Foster (San Francisco: Ignatius Press, 2004), 66.

of death and seeks to extend its range.[29] Malignant narcissism, he argues, is always predatory. It does not stay on its own turf. An evil person, though he loves death and decay, causes death only for others, not for himself.[30] Instead, he goes after others. He is a hypocrite of course, but that is the least of our problems.

Fromm's notion of malignant narcissism differs from Freud's death drive, namely, a human instinct to return to inorganic matter. In Freud's view, life is a series of decisions skillfully steered between the competing instincts of pleasure and death, with the necrophiliac apparently streamlining his urges.[31] Evil results when the death instinct holds greater sway over the pleasure instinct. In Freud's view, these instincts for death and for pleasure are hardwired in our psyches and so there is an element of determinism over whether we can avoid evil. By contrast, Fromm argues that a love for death, Thanatos, is not instinct. Instead, it develops when a love of life, Eros, is thwarted in a failure to adapt successfully. For Fromm, evil is a malignant, real phenomenon but not one that is original to the human makeup. Fromm's perspective is, in the end, more hopeful than Freud's, without being naïve,[32] and it is consonant with the biblical perspective.

Evil, then, is baffling, unnerving, and powerful. It desires the death of life, of others, of the life force, of spirit, of faith, and lots more. We could ask where malignant narcissism comes from, why God allows it to emerge, but that again picks at free will—that we want it until we want to be rescued from it. Free will has a frightening responsibility to it. We are to act in the image of God and tend to the creation bestowed to us, knowing full well that perpetrators reject this worldview and play by their own sadistic rules. Tending to creation means fending off evil, marshaling forces of life against it, and witnessing wherever it snuffs out the breath of life, as Elie Wiesel has done.

Faith after Desolation

Auschwitz revealed a horrific truth: that human mendacity exists on such a scale as, in Martin Buber's terms, to eclipse God. Buber argued that

---

29. Erich Fromm uses the term "necrophilous" to describe this kind of personality; see *The Heart of Man: Its Genius for Good and Evil* (New York: Harper & Row, 1964), 38.

30. Fromm also notes an obsession about feces and all forms of nonliving matter. Hitler apparently was fastidiously attracted to this entire, inorganic bonanza. And, he committed suicide for other reasons.

31. Fromm, *The Heart of Man*, 49.

32. Ibid., 50.

God is neither dead nor complicit in evil but that humanity is destructive enough to block God out.[33] There are times when life goes all dark: the crucifixion, the Holocaust, the rape of a child, the slaughter in Rwanda, etc. During an eclipse we witness, perhaps for the first time, not the absence of God, but rather what the world would look like without God. From this juncture, faith has to be decided again. Martin Buber again: "How is a life with God still possible in a time in which there is an Auschwitz? The estrangement has become too cruel, the hiddenness too deep. One can still 'believe' in the God who allowed those things to happen, but can one speak to him?"[34]

Faith is trust; it is voluntary, genuine, and about relationship. If the decision should be negative, then we cast our hopes in humankind with its various utopias and distractions. A decision for faith after such desolation of hope begins again, a somber, fledgling experiment. As Abraham Heschel correctly noted, "We are in greater need of a proof for the authenticity of faith than of a proof for the existence of God."[35] Authentic faith is willing to interrogate any conceptual assumptions that wound it and, where necessary, dismantle them. Such assumptions include: humanity is basically good; progress is some shared and mutually agreed-upon goal; omnipotence; impassability. But perhaps the most destructive assumption is that providence must be interventionist to be real. Such a view supports God's omnipotence, as Hume noted, namely, if God is all-powerful, then he will intervene to prevent evil. This sounds reasonable on the face of it, but it subtly puts God on-call for us, thereby robbing God of freedom. Interventionist providence becomes a human insurance policy, that is, if we really mess things up, God will intervene and stop us. Further, if we do something truly horrific, this will bring God out of the sky and provoke a reaction. After the wreckage of the twentieth century, this idol has to be melted down. When theological concepts are defended over and above faith's relationship with God, they become mere scaffolding around God, just as galling as a tower of Babel. It was never about what we could build with our hands, still less our intellects; it was always about relationship.

In the Bible, faith, as we have said, means trust, but we should not be misled that trust is in any sense easy. Trust in a numinous presence is very

---

33. Zachary Braiterman provides an excellent detailed discussion of the varieties of Jewish response to the holocaust in *(God) After Auschwitz*.

34. Martin Buber, *On Judaism*, ed. Nahum N. Glatzer (New York: Schocken, 1967), 224–25.

35. Abraham Joshua Heschel, *God in Search of Man: A Philosophy of Judaism* (New York: Farrar, Straus and Giroux, 1955), 36.

difficult indeed. It is never a *blind* faith but rather faith in an invisible, real presence. Abraham is deservedly the father of faith because he trusted God throughout the journey to Mount Moriah, where he would have sacrificed his son, Isaac. His was a faith that was never simplistic or robotic. With his beloved son on the line, it could not afford to be. Abraham and Jesus take their long, gritty journey in a faith that is arduous. Such ardor is clear too in Job's feisty commitment: "Slay me though he might, I will wait for him" (Job 13:15). The faith we have biblically has always been to love God completely, without conditions: "Therefore, you shall love the LORD, your God, with your whole heart, and with your whole being, and with your whole strength. Take to heart these words which I command you today" (Deut 6:5-6). In other words, to give it all we've got, hold nothing back, and spend all our trust on this God. Invest it all, even and *especially* the mess of suffering.

Jesus

God Made Visible

"The proximity of God," Samuel Terrien argues, "created a memory and an anticipation of certitude, but it always defies human appropriation."[1] This happened throughout the Old Testament in encounters with divine presence and it happens as well in the New. There is a definite presence lurking, even when Jesus is not on the scene. It yields the "anticipation of certitude" which is the very definition of faith: "Faith is the realization of what is hoped for and evidence of things not seen" (Heb 11:1).

As Paul states in Colossians, Jesus is "the image of the invisible God, / the firstborn of all creation" (Col 1:15). And the author of 1 John adds sharper, tangible testimony to this effect:

> we have seen with our eyes,
> what we looked upon
> and touched with our hands
> concerns the Word of life—
> for the life was made visible;
> we have seen it and testify to it
> and proclaim to you the eternal life
> that was with the Father and was made visible to us. (1 John 1:1-2)

---

1. Samuel L. Terrien, *The Elusive Presence* (San Francisco: Harper & Row, 1978), 43.

Both New Testament writers suggest that the spiritual period of invisibility is now in the past. That being the case, it would seem that the ongoing interplay of divine absence and presence that we have been tracing in the Old Testament could now come to a satisfying Christocentric close. Yet, it cannot. We do not find closure in the New Testament, despite this easy assumption of many Christians.

The figure of Jesus remains tantalizingly enigmatic throughout a New Testament that is nevertheless devoted to him. This concrete manifestation of God—Jesus, who is visible in the flesh, incarnate—is still quite elusive, just like his father. Mystery is constitutive of his person, because it is of God. Even the incarnation, as Karl Barth insists, retains its mystery: "In his revelation in Jesus Christ, the hidden God has indeed made himself apprehensible. Not directly, but indirectly. Not to sight, but to faith. Not in his being, but in sign."[2] The temple curtain is torn at the end of the gospel, but it still remains protecting the mystery of divine presence.

If Jesus were fully seen, grasped, and understood, the disciples would have replaced God with him and turned Jesus into an idol, reifying his name as a new Apollo. But that is not what happens. Instead, Jesus confounds them, foiling their expectations at every turn. He cannot be domesticated either, though this remains a persistent Christian temptation. In certain respects, Jesus must be incomprehensible to the disciples if he is truly God. To make this theological point, the gospels insist on depicting the disciples' limited understanding. They bear their incomprehension out with multiple stories of distrust, parables that have to be explained, Peter's denial, Judas' betrayal, Jesus' entire hometown turning on him, groups of followers leaving before his arrest, etc. Despite Paul's belief that Jesus is "the revelation of the mystery kept secret for long ages but now manifested through the prophetic writings" (Rom 16:25-26), Jesus retains a divine presence unknowable even by those closest to him. Jesus, then, is not God made clear; he is God made *clearer*.

"Jesus" is no placeholder for God; nor does he, in effect, replace the God of the Old Testament for Christianity. There is always a danger for Christian readers to reduce Old Testament materials to a preview for the New Testament. Such a narrowing, however, misses the richness of revelation and unwittingly supports a heresy known as Marcionism. In the second century,

---

2. Karl Barth, *Church Dogmatics*, vol. 2, bk. 1, trans. Harold Knight, G. W. Bromiley, J. K. S. Reid, and R. H. Fuller (Edinburgh: T & T Clark, 1960), 199. Barth's notion is similar to that of Edward Schillebeeckx, who called Jesus the "sacrament of God"; Francis Schüssler Fiorenza and John P. Galvin, eds., *Systematic Theology* (Minneapolis: Fortress Press, 2011), 56.

Marcion argued that the Gospel superseded all previous revelation and so the Old Testament could be discarded in favor of a one testament canon comprised only of writings of the New Testament. The church argued against this view for several reasons: (1) the God of the New Testament is the same God of the Old—God does not change over time; (2) The Old Testament reveals the father of Jesus and was the Bible of Jesus and the disciples; (3) God's communication in revelation may look sequential to us since we live in historical time, but for God there is no time line. Divine truths are evident in the Bible, regardless of Testament. God's truth is not bound by time. And Christians, as "spiritual Semites," needlessly impoverish ourselves when we use Jesus as a spiritual shortcut. He may be a clearer sign of God's presence to Christians, but he is still invisible as well. Christians stumble around in the absences of Jesus all the time, even as art has put a facial image in our minds. The Old Testament and the New aid believers in relating to invisible presence. In this way, both Judaism and Christianity are partners in a sophisticated, nimble project and can always benefit from dialogue.

Prayers addressed to Jesus are speech within a triune relationship that includes God the Father and is aided by the Holy Spirit. Therefore, the elusiveness of divine presence is evident as well, even in the testimonies about Jesus. If we turn our attention to the mystery in the New Testament as we have in the Old, we gain an appreciation of the gospels' own testimony, namely, that something truly new happens. Something truly new happens in the Old Testament as well, a God who wants relationship with his creatures and communicates his love. Now, in the New Testament, that same living God becomes flesh. Surely God's daring outreach through both Testaments is a mystery of tremendous plenitude and not a cause for Christian triumphalism. Several key facets of the New Testament demonstrate its preservation of divine mystery.

In the first place, it is worth noting that the duration of Jesus' earthly ministry was quite short: one year according to the Gospel of John, three years according to the Synoptic Gospels. The rest of his thirty some years, though average for the standard life expectancy of the day, is lost to obscurity.[3] There are the nativity accounts in Matthew and Luke, but these shed more light on the role of the Christ than they do on Jesus' own humble beginnings. A poor child born in a manger and from a no-good town like Nazareth (John 1:46) would have been unremarkable except to his parents. The only other episode, found only in Luke's gospel, from Jesus' early years occurs when he is twelve years old and his distraught parents find him in

3. John Dominic Crossan, *Jesus: A Revolutionary Biography* (New York: Harper-One, 2009), 22–23.

the temple (Luke 2:46-50). But this too reflects Christological construal as Jesus pronounces the temple "my Father's house" (v. 49). Much of the rest of the gospels is given over to Jesus dying and rising, ascending and leaving and promising to be with us always. Indeed, the notable New Testament scholar Martin Kähler once remarked that the gospels were essentially "Passion narratives with extended introductions."

The entire project of the incarnation, then, was relatively short in terms of historical time and detail. The very notion that God somehow zeroed in on one specific time and culture is referred to as the scandal of particularity: first for the Jewish people, one group of Semitic tribes amid all the peoples of the world, and then for Jesus, a poor, rural carpenter in the backwater of the Roman Empire. What are the odds that divine presence would touch down so particularly? In terms of human logic, this is incredible or, as Paul said, foolish: "Has not God made the wisdom of the world foolish?" (1 Cor 1:20). The particularity gives way quickly to Jesus' vanishing. *All* of Paul's letters are written in Jesus' physical absence, as Paul knew only the resurrected Jesus through a blinding vision that was more real to him than the entirety of his life. Paul's moment of encounter with the risen Jesus, then, is an even smaller window of opportunity on the stage of human history to witness divine presence in the flesh.

Second, no gospel account goes indisputably back to Jesus himself, and so the enigma of Jesus remains even while there are four gospels devoted to him. One facet of the gospels that is often overlooked is that Jesus did not write a word of them. With the exception of one passage in the Gospel of John, there are no depictions of Jesus writing or asking others to record anything for posterity's sake. In John 8:6, Jesus writes in the sand, but even here the gospel does not mention what he wrote, and he uses the unstable medium of sand, which will not survive the day. The only detail is that he writes in the sand while poised between an adulterous woman and the angry mob that would stone her. Again and again, it is not writing but Jesus' speech that makes the life-saving difference: "Let the one among you who is without sin be the first to throw a stone at her" (v. 7). That no one in that gathering hurls a stone anyway is testimony to even a mob's honesty. Rage sputters off into silent dispersal, as the mob walks away one by one, from the oldest to the youngest (v. 9). Divine presence in this scene is evident by its effect, in just what it is able to diffuse. We can assume that the forgiven woman is not the only dumbstruck witness to this effect. Something new has entered the scene, something vastly superior to any rhetorical cleverness or crowd control.

A third issue is that the New Testament is written in Greek, while Jesus and his disciples spoke Aramaic. There are only two quotations by Jesus stated in Aramaic: *Talitha koum* ("Little girl, . . . arise!"; Mark 5:41); and *Eli, Eli, lema sabachthani?* ("My God, my God, why have you forsaken me?"; Matt 27:46). These two verses retain either a memory of Jesus having uttered them or instill an air of verisimilitude to the gospel accounts. The language of the New Testament, then, represents a level at least once removed from that spoken by Jesus and his followers. It is a Greek rendering of the events of God's presence in Jesus.

Fourth, along with the language difference, the passage of time creates a further degree of separation. The gospels are written forty to fifty years after Jesus' earthly life, roughly between 70 CE (the Gospel of Mark) and 90 to 95 CE (the Gospel of John). They emerge decades after the events depicted, the result of memory, storytelling, and oral transmission of traditions about Jesus.

The early followers of Jesus were convinced that he was returning to them shortly, and so there was really no need for written accounts, no thought given to posterity. But as the original witnesses began to die off and Jesus still had not returned, some followers undoubtedly thought it best to construct gospel accounts from the oral materials they knew. Another factor was the destruction of the temple in 70 CE, which shook Jewish faith—including followers of Jesus, of "the way"—to the core. Written materials could offer a substitute stability that the temple no longer could. The period in between Jesus' crucifixion and the writing of the first gospel, that of Mark, consisted of shared eucharistic meals in house churches where followers would recount stories of Jesus and hand them down to the younger generations as they awaited Jesus' imminent return. The gospels themselves, then—the fact that they get written—are a kind of backup plan to the original anticipated return of Jesus. Somewhat ironically, the gospels present Jesus because they mark the divine absence of Jesus' delayed return.

None of the gospels were written by the original twelve disciples; the current titles are all second-century ascriptions added to distinguish between them. For Matthew, the ascription comes from the mention of Matthew the tax collector in 9:9; for Mark, it comes from an associate mentioned with Peter (1 Pet 5:13) and Paul (Acts 12:12); for Luke, from a greeting sent by Paul (Col 4:14; Phil 1:24); and for John, from the "beloved disciple" mentioned in 19:26. The literary conventions about authorship in antiquity were different from our own. Authenticity was established by the message, not the author. The anonymity of the gospels, then, is not a mark against their credibility. In fact, it reflects a modest deference to the message. At any rate, the secured identity of an author would be no more solid proof of divine presence than deferential anonymity. If Jesus is God, we do not need the authorial chain of evidence going back to a disciple.

A fifth and final facet of the gospels is simply their number. There are four gospels, not one, and so their differences necessarily preserve a lively tension of wonder. The presence of four different gospels does not lessen divine mystery; it preserves it through multiple, shifting lenses. We are blocked by the gospels themselves from reduction to any supposed more reliable gospel, to a biography of Jesus culled from them, or to Jesus' own words, as the red letter versions of the New Testament try to do. The presence of four gospels in the Bible protects and portrays an enigmatic, divine presence that is not reducible to one account or to language itself.

The New Testament has a built-in safety against fundamentalism. Its creation in a different language and at a later time than that of Jesus and its multiple gospels act as gift containing a surplus of meaning and not a lack. Its very complexity offers testimony, perhaps backhanded, that divine mystery dwelt among us, someone for whom biography at any rate was wholly unsuited. No quest for the historical Jesus gets us any closer to his holiness, his divine, life-changing impact.[4] Instead, the holy floods the New Testament writers. It overwhelms them, heart, soul, and might, spilling into their gospels as if to say, "How can we describe a man who *is* the burning bush?" Whatever happened on the scene during the historical life of Jesus, it is not contained even by the gospels themselves. Jesus left an indelible mark not in writing but in the consciousness of witnesses and the swift gathering of followers after him. Rodney Stark has estimated the growth of Christianity to be at an astonishing 40 percent per decade, and this all happens *after* Jesus' life, in his absence, as it were.[5]

Reading the New Testament gives us multiple angles on Jesus. It ushers us into a rich enigmatic presence to ponder his own question, "Who do *you* say that I am?" When we read about Jesus, we allow wonder about the holy and about how it is present in Jesus and in our world to emerge. For example, in Matthew, Jesus says, "Come to me all you who labor and are burdened and I will give you rest. Take my yoke upon you and learn from me, for I am meek and humble of heart; and you will find rest for yourselves. For my yoke is easy, and my burden light" (Matt 11:28-30). In other words, "Come in, sit down, and rest with me." The holy is welcoming;

---

4. We are currently in the third quest, which began in 1985 when Robert Funk established the Jesus Seminar. The first quest occurred in the eighteenth and nineteenth centuries with Albert Schweitzer, the second in the mid-twentieth century, and the current, third quest continues with the ongoing work of the Jesus Seminar.

5. Rodney Stark, *The Rise of Christianity: How the Obscure, Marginal Jesus Movement Became the Dominant Religious Force in the Western World in a Few Centuries* (New York: HarperOne, 1996), 7.

it is restful. There is nothing in Jesus' words about how we are undeserving, or better try harder, or should be prepared to *earn* time with God. There is just invitation, hospitality, and gentleness. I recognize this *as* holy because I have seen it before: it is the third commandment, to keep holy the Sabbath, to rest. God commanded his people to rest, just as he had rested on the seventh day of creation, and now Jesus calls for it too. Rest is an elemental part of creation: "In green pastures he makes me lie down; / to still waters he leads me; / he restores my soul" (Ps 23:2-3). And now, Jesus invites all to rest from their burdens.

God's Torah and Jesus' yoke are both easy; they offer guidance rather than burden. Like the Torah, Jesus' yoke is "instruction," a gift offered to meet the holy in the ordinary. I recognize this *as* God because it is entirely characteristic of him. It turns out that the God who is steadfast and consistent in the Old Testament is here as well. God is not going anywhere. Both God and Jesus are in unison in their instruction: "Be still and know that I am God!" (Ps 46:11).There is a reassuring stability of character in this man Jesus and in God.

The saying in Matthew is yet another invitation to come and encounter divine presence and to be caught up in it. Another example occurs in the parable of the Good Shepherd who "walks ahead of them, and the sheep follow him, because they recognize his voice. But they will not follow a stranger. . . . I came so that they might have life and have it more abundantly" (John 10:4-5, 10). The passage contains a comforting message about the gentle protectiveness of Jesus, and it evokes a faint feeling for sheep, and, oddly, it is awe. Awe, as Abraham Heschel said, is "an intuition for the creaturely dignity of all things."[6] There is a slight stirring of awe for the sheep who follow only a voice they know. It bespeaks a tender dignity, a divine attention to details about all creatures, including farm animals. I first recognize the holy from this stirring of awe, and then with the stirring of memory, I recognize God as described in Psalm 23: "The LORD is my shepherd; / there is nothing I lack." Further associations follow when God "walks ahead" of his people in the exodus and leads them out of slavery, and in Deuteronomy when he called them to choose life *with* him, to have life *"more abundantly."* Divine presence is not intrusive or invasive, but it starts to take on familiar resonances in these biblical accounts. It is uncanny how similar the Jesus of the New Testament is to the God of the Old. The similarities quickly begin to mount until it becomes clear that God and Jesus are the same character, the life force flowing through existence itself. The

---

6. Abraham Joshua Heschel, *God in Search of Man: A Philosophy of Judaism* (New York: Farrar, Straus and Giroux, 1955), 75.

movement toward this God in faith is not coerced but, in the end, comes from our own accord, freely.

The aim of the gospels is much higher than that of biography; it is somehow to depict the enigmatic, compelling character of Jesus and elicit a response to him from readers. Within the accounts of his ministry career, the gospels take care to emphasize Jesus' need for frequent retreat and solitary prayer (e.g., Luke 5:16; 6:12; 9:28). Jesus, though divine himself, needs prayer. His own need for divine presence in solitude is the counterpoint in the gospels to the divine presence so evident in his sermons, miracles, and patience. Had the disciples been able to remain awake at Gethsemane on Jesus' last night, they might have learned how to endure God's absence through prayer as rehearsal for the loss they would soon suffer.

Of Jesus' short ministry career, Pope Benedict notes that "paradoxically, public activity always entails isolation."[7] For Jesus, prayer is of a piece with healing, preaching, and loving all. All of the gospels reflect Jesus' need to go off alone to pray; for example, "After doing so, he went up on the mountain by himself to pray. When it was evening he was there alone" (Matt 14:23). The isolation of Jesus must have been painful for him at times. He was human, yet so often misunderstood, even hated. At times, the gospels report that he must withdraw because the crowd is pressing on him: "Since Jesus knew that they were going to come and carry him off to make him king, he withdrew again to the mountain alone" (John 6:15). At other points, we catch a glimpse of how lonely it must have been for him: "When it was evening, the boat was far out on the sea and he was alone on shore" (Mark 6:47). We can only imagine the lonely isolation behind these cryptic verses.

At Gethsemane, before his impending arrest, he asks the three disciples to remain with him as he goes off to pray alone: "He took along Peter and the two sons of Zebedee, and began to feel sorrow and distress. Then he said to them, 'My soul is sorrowful even to death. Remain here and keep watch with me' " (Matt 26:37-38). They famously cannot manage it, falling asleep three different times during their very last chance to be with Jesus. Jesus is "sorrowful," asking for support in the form of companionship from his disciples; in prayer he asks God three separate times to "let this cup pass from me; yet, not as I will, but as you will" (Matt 26:39, 42, 44). Nicholas Lash argues that the darkness Jesus endures here is even more severe than that of Job, because Jesus receives no answer from God, just silence.[8]

---

7. Pope Benedict XVI, *The God of Jesus Christ: Meditations on the Triune God*, trans. Brian McNeil (San Francisco: Ignatius Press, 2006), 79.

8. Nicholas Lash, *Holiness, Speech, and Silence: Reflections on the Question of God* (Aldershot, England: Ashgate, 2004), 76.

The divine absence he faces is compounded by the human abandonment in his hour of real need. Before this moment, he has asked nothing of the disciples the entire time he has been with them. Jesus endures the loneliness of being misunderstood even by those closest to him. Though divine, he is also human, and the deafening solitude of Gethsemane causes him pain, for he was "sorrowful even to death." Jesus knows what is coming and that his disciples will continue to "sleep through" it, abandoning him during his arrest, trial, and execution: "Behold, the hour is coming and has arrived when each of you will be scattered to his own home and you will leave me alone" (John 16:32).

Much later, as Christians read the gospels, the disciples' behavior comes to represent our own failures of faith: that we remain oblivious to important moments when Jesus is really present. This biblical scene becomes symbolic of a deeper truth about our own presence before the numinous, how *we* fail *it*. And this has been my point throughout the book, that biblical symbols do not represent only something far back there in time; rather, they encode something perennially, spiritually true for us today. As Elizabeth Johnson notes, "Symbols open up levels of reality that would otherwise be closed to us, and simultaneously open up depths of our own being that would remain otherwise untouched."[9] Upon reading this particular scene at Gethsemane, a new "depth of our own being" is sounded, a desire for ourselves to be more present. We have been sleeping through faith in complacency and missing these hard, true moments. We fill pews and our eyes are opened, but we too have been sleeping disciples.

Nicholas Lash sees this particular passage as uniquely suited to the modern situation in its struggle with God's silence. He writes, "Our task, as Christians, is to help each other to acquire the courage to be still, to keep our eyes open in the dark. Gethsemane would be the paradigm of the attentiveness we need. In the garden, Christ remained attentive to the father's silence—while the disciples, unfortunately, slept."[10]

The Father's Silence

Jesus withstands divine absence in his temptation in the desert, even though the Holy Spirit led him out there (Matt 4:1). Those forty days are dead, hot, ringing silence. Jesus' exchange with the devil breaks the silence only at the end of the forty days. Jesus' contribution in breaking

9. Elizabeth Johnson, *Quest for the Living God: Mapping Frontiers in the Theology of God* (New York: Continuum, 2007), 20.

10. Lash, *Holiness, Speech, and Silence*, 93.

the silence is all scriptural. He undergoes three tests, after which the devil leaves and angels come to care for Jesus (Matt 4:11). The rest of the ordeal, the majority of it, is given over to silence, hunger, thirst, and whatever are the unstated emotional and spiritual torments that Jesus endures. As fully human, Jesus would have had to have felt those days of divine absence as forcefully as we do or else the scene is a faux temptation only, a docetic mime that insists Jesus cannot feel divine absence because he is divine. If this were true, then clearly during his temptation and crucifixion Jesus would be just biding his time, silently mocking the devil for his futile efforts. Jesus is not playacting through his own suffering. He is present to the devil, answering him with Scripture. He engages the devil and does not mock or deride him. Jesus is present, open, and invincible all at the same time. He endures genuine suffering and the suffering of God's absence in the desert, again at Gethsemane, and finally at the cross.

The most blistering scene of divine absence for Jesus is his cry of dereliction from the cross in the Gospel of Mark: "And at three o'clock Jesus cried out in a loud voice, '*Eloi, Eloi, lema sabachthani?*' which is translated, 'My God, my God, why have you forsaken me?'" (Mark 15:34). Jesus feels utterly abandoned at this point, wracked with pain by an ordeal that has brought him fully to his limits. This riveting, awful scream is jarring, conclusive witness to the truth of God's periodic absence from humankind. That his absence does turn out to be temporary is no comfort during the moment Jesus endures. Christians made uncomfortable by Jesus' cry of dereliction have long sought to soften this scene of forsakenness by noting that it is the first line of a psalm (Ps 22) that ends on a more uplifting note of praise: "And I will live for the LORD; / my descendants will serve you. / The generation to come will be told of the Lord, / that they may proclaim to a people yet unborn / the deliverance you have brought" (Ps 22:31-32). Hence, they suggest that Jesus is really just speaking in a kind of shorthand to the crowd with the first line of a psalm everyone would know.

But this kind of sentiment is misdirected piety, offered in an effort to protect the savior from harm, as Peter tried to do whenever Jesus mentioned that he would have to suffer and die (Matt 16:23). It is dishonest caretaking because it seeks to minimize Jesus' suffering for our own comfort. We would erase Jesus and replace him instead with the gnostic Jesus of the Apocalypse of Peter, where Jesus taunts his executioners from the cross: "He whom you saw on the tree, glad and laughing, this is the living Jesus."[11] We might

11. James Brashler and Roger A. Bullard, trans., "Apocalypse of Peter," in *The Nag Hammadi Library*, ed. James M. Robinson, rev. ed. (San Francisco: HarperCollins, 1990); available at ttp://www.gnosis.org/naghamm/apopet.html.

mean well, but we rob the scene of its core revelation, namely, that God is not absent even in this harrowing, deathly moment, *in extremis* of all sorts. Pope Benedict reminds us that "not only God's speech but also his silence is part of Christian revelation. God is not only the comprehensible word that comes to us; he is also the silent, inaccessible, uncomprehended, and incomprehensible ground that eludes us."[12]

Jesus' response to divine absence is instructive but terribly difficult: he accepts it. We too could surrender all the concepts and the grasping after God and just yield to being embraced or abandoned, flooded, overcome, enveloped, speechless, led to a place that is a full silence past fright. Jesus has to be frightened, even a little unnerved perhaps by the deafening silence, but he rests in it nonetheless.

The Vanishing Jesus

In the gospels, Jesus spends a considerable portion of his ministry preparing for his departure. After his resurrection, the remainder of the New Testament is about Jesus' physical absence. Paul never even knew Jesus during Jesus' earthly ministry. His conversion is the result of experiencing the risen Christ in a vision that left him temporarily blind for three days. This Christ is surplus, a presence beyond the empirical, who nevertheless overloads the senses, showing Paul more than his eyes could handle. The letters by Paul and others in the New Testament contain frequent messages about living *in* Christ Jesus, waiting for Christ Jesus' return, and what the Gospel of Christ Jesus can do for all the new churches Paul and others are establishing throughout the Mediterranean basin. There is, however, surprisingly little about Jesus himself, his actions, his teachings, the events of his life. Revelation, the last book of the Bible, is a vision of how Jesus will return, but the entire vision is predicated on his visual absence. What is striking in these Scriptures is how quickly Jesus himself vanishes, even as the entire New Testament is about him. Those seeking to learn about this man are in for a complex path of hearsay, testimony, letters, the Holy Spirit, and the slow, steady recognition scenes after the resurrection, where a presence is revealed beyond vision.

It is an odd feature of the New Testament, that its central character should prove to be elusive, largely missing in the writings even as he is the driving force behind them. Jesus is the Christ, the firstfruits of the resurrection; the head of the church; the reason for unity, hope, and love; the lamb

---

12. Pope Benedict XVI, *Introduction to Christianity*, trans. J. R. Foster (San Francisco: Ignatius Press, 2004), 296.

of God; the subject of all the acts in Acts. But he himself is nowhere to be found, because he is everywhere. In other words, Jesus is not physically present as subjective agent in the texts but rather is "there" in the hearts and minds of all the people whose lives have been so dramatically altered by this man. Peter had been so frightened the night of the crucifixion that he denied having known Jesus at all. The disciples as a group are frightened after the crucifixion, holing up in an upper room with the door locked. Yet within only a few chapters into Acts, those frightened men all emerge fearless, articulate preachers to anyone and everywhere. They are changed people. Peter, who had feared imprisonment at the crucifixion, now takes it in stride, seeing it as an opportunity to convert the prison guards. The threats of arrest, imprisonment, and martyrdom make no impression on him now. Jesus vanishes physically from the scene of Peter's life, only to overwhelm him with another kind of fully real presence. Jesus is invisible to Peter now, but he powerfully saturates Peter's every action and speech. The disciples who live without their master, whom they had known in the flesh, now live truly in him *in* Christ. They have become indomitable, utterly focused, and certain. But the disciples have not occasioned this change themselves; the living Christ has, and he dwells within them and all over in the peripheral visions of the New Testament.

Throughout the period of Jesus' ministry, Peter has been there. He is sincere, impulsive, cowardly, and brave all in one mercurial mixture. This is a man you want to know, even as he would be exhausting. In his imperfect genuine responses, you feel the Christ effect, that is, that something tremendous has happened by the impact it is having. Peter wants to cling; he denies; he walks on water until he doubts. He is all over the place, excited. Jesus takes Peter, James, and John up a mountain for his transfiguration:

> Then Peter said to Jesus in reply, "Lord, it is good that we are here. If you wish, I will make three tents here, one for you, one for Moses, and one for Elijah." While he was still speaking, behold, a bright cloud cast a shadow over them, then from the cloud came a voice that said, "This is my beloved Son, with whom I am well pleased; listen to him." When the disciples heard this, they fell prostrate and were very much afraid. But Jesus came and touched them, saying, "Rise, and do not be afraid." And when the disciples raised their eyes, they saw no one else but Jesus alone. (Matt 17:4-8)

The moment of transfiguration is a conclusive, affirming, and temporary display of divine presence made clear and blinding. Peter would like to make the holy presence last by pitching tents. But the kind of encounter holy presence requires is an aptitude for presence and absence, a spiritual abiding, shorn of any need to make camp.

Jesus' physical absence in much of the content of the New Testament is certainly no lack of presence; it is, instead, witness to a saturating real presence, suffusing every person and every page. It is making a profound theological point often overlooked because Western thought has privileged presence over absence, as Derrida and other postmodern thinkers have noted.[13] One need not wade far into postmodern readings to be able to see the limitations of this perspective, namely, that presence can occlude the truth by rendering the Word as static. "Deconstruction is organized around the idea that things contain a kind of uncontainable truth, that they contain what they cannot contain."[14] This, it seems to me, is precisely what the New Testament reveals with all its marked occasions of Jesus' putative absence. The gospels are a different kind of literature because this is a different, new story. You do not have to be a deconstructionist to see that in important ways, the New Testament itself cannot contain its central character, cannot contain its joy. Jesus is too big, too enveloping, too true. Nor, for that matter, could the Old Testament contain its elusive character.

Jesus is the profound encompassing life force of the gospel, but he is not contained by it. Fundamentalism would make an idol of the Bible, a bibliolatry, and thereby miss the surpassing, uncontainable truth that Jesus is elusively real, just as God is. This aspect of his character is consistent with the claim that he is God. The very elusiveness lends credibility to Jesus' divine nature.

His absence is necessary as faith continues to be and always has been based on things unseen: "Faith is the realization of what is hoped for and evidence of things not seen" (Heb 11:1). Faith in Jesus, in God, is not empirically based; it is not reducible to data or even tangible presence ever. If it were, then only Jesus' contemporaries would have benefited. Even when Jesus walks and breathes among his people, even then, with empirical presence standing right before them, the people keep asking who he is, and he does not tell them. They are left to answer for themselves in the climax of the gospels, which reveal themselves now to be interactive; the clueless disciples had been us all along: "Who do you say that I am?"

Jesus never plays by the empirical rules: healings, walking on water, saying something mystically incomprehensible about his body and blood being bread and wine his last night on earth. And, according to the logic of the thing, that is, the numinous, Jesus cannot stay, teaching into his sixties, retiring peaceably in Galilee. His continued presence would thwart faith.

---

13. John D. Caputo, *What Would Jesus Deconstruct? The Good News of Postmodernism for the Church* (Grand Rapids, MI: Baker Academic, 2007), 62.

14. Ibid., 28.

The writer of John's gospel grasps this point beautifully. He contrasts the reaction of Mary Magdalene and Thomas to the mysterious vanishing of Jesus' corpse inside the garden tomb.

When Mary discovers the risen Jesus only after he calls her by name, she excitedly touches Jesus. Her joy is instantly redirected by him. "She thought it was the gardener and said to him, 'Sir, if you carried him away, tell me where you laid him, and I will take him.' Jesus said to her, 'Mary!' She turned and said to him in Hebrew, 'Rabbouni,' which means Teacher. Jesus said to her, 'Stop holding on to me, for I have not yet ascended to the Father'" (John 20:15-17). Mary must let go. Her moment of reunion is to be short-lived. Grasping, clinging, holding on will not change all that. The followers of Jesus must be taught still—to let go, to let seeming absence overtake presence in trust, in the rhythm that is faith. Jesus is not the same as before. He is no longer Mary's rabbi, and she cannot return this transformed Jesus back to the past they had enjoyed together. Instead, he summons her toward something new and astonishing. If she can let go of what she had, Mary will discover a plentitude beyond comprehension, namely, that there is something even better, fuller for her soul, than Jesus' earthly presence had been and that is his absent-aliveness, his suffusing, radiating love.

With Thomas, the tangible need is there as well, but it is an obstacle to his faith. Thomas is called Didymus in the gospel but is better known since then as the "doubting" one. He was absent when the risen Christ visited the disciples and so exclaims "Unless I see the mark of the nails in his hands and put my finger into the nail marks and put my hand into his side, I will not believe" (John 20:25). Thomas is quite bold to put conditions on his faith in Jesus and honest about it. Jesus returns to give Thomas just this opportunity. He will permit empirical verification of the wound sites in his body: "Jesus came, although the doors were locked, and stood in their midst and said, 'Peace be with you.' Then he said to Thomas, 'Put your finger here and see my hands, and bring your hand and put it into my side, and do not be unbelieving, but believe.' Thomas answered and said to him, 'My Lord and my God!'" (John 20:26-28). Curiously though, when Jesus presents the opportunity to investigate his wounds outright, Thomas no longer seems to need the verification. He simply exclaims, "My Lord and my God." The text is silent on whether Thomas then put his fingers and hands into Jesus. It is only clear that he has seen him: "Jesus said to him, 'Have you come to believe because you have seen me? Blessed are those who have not seen and have believed'" (John 20:29).

Encounter with Christ overrides empiricism. It always did with Jesus. He writes only once and in sand, yet his words are indelible. The disciples had followed Jesus during his ministry, often without understanding him. They were in the dark by his light and were compelled to it nonetheless. Their pilgrimage of understanding and not understanding who Jesus is represents the faith journey for us all. Their journey of faith and ours all share in a growing tolerance and then acceptance of divine silence. Gregory of Nyssa describes this shift in attitude, from intellectual grasp to contemplation that accepts "incomprehensibility as by a kind of darkness." He continues, "For leaving behind everything that is observed, not only what sense comprehends but also what the intelligence thinks it sees, it keeps on penetrating deeper until by the intelligence's yearning for understanding it gains access to the invisible and the incomprehensible, and there it sees God."[15] From the darkness of mystery, the light of presence shines, ever uncontainable. Jesus' fleeting, changed presence is not a hindrance at all. It is helping to cement the faith of the first witnesses.

We notice a vital contrast between what Mary Magdalene and Thomas Didymus call the resurrected Jesus. Mary exclaims, "Rabbouni!" ("Teacher!"; John 20:16). Indeed, it is obvious that he is the best teacher she has ever had. Yet rabbi is still the role Jesus played during his earthly ministry. But Thomas, who with his skeptical temperament had further ground to cover in his avowal of faith, says "My Lord and my God" (John 20:28). His terms of divine presence fit this Jesus. The new, unthinkably new, really has happened. Thomas is not holding on to the past, as Mary tries to do, or to Jesus' presence in the past. He has let go into the larger reality, a presence that is divine and all-encompassing. Thomas had been the last holdout of the disciples to believe in the resurrection. When he sees the wounds and is invited by Jesus to place his hands upon them, he proclaims that Jesus is God. It is more than enough to see the wounds, the gaps in flesh that had died for him.

Jesus again instructs on a faith beyond the empirical, saying to Thomas, "Have you come to believe because you have seen me? Blessed are those who have not seen and have believed" (John 20:29). The response of Thomas reflects a man moved by Jesus beyond the seeing. It could well be that the encounter with Christ, the conversation with him, changes Thomas. Standing before Jesus, his only action is speech, namely, a proclamation of Jesus' divinity. Thomas recognizes Jesus as God; the bodily investigation simply stops. While Mary needs to let go, Thomas needs to stop testing. Both are being reminded that the God of Scripture is beyond grasping.

15. Gregory of Nyssa, *The Life of Moses* (New York: HarperCollins, 2006), 80.

The new element to their understanding of holiness is that this risen man has been God all along. And God cannot stay tangibly present to them.

Jesus could not remain on the scene in biblical texts any more than God could. We recall from chapter 4 that the biblical tradition of not seeing God is protective rather than punitive. Humankind cannot withstand continued divine presence, for it would arrest its faith and life. At the transfiguration, Peter would have been happy to stop his life and live in a tent before the holy presence. This greatest story ever told has written into it a bittersweet, ongoing loss that on our brighter days we term yearning, on the darker ones, the silence of God. They, we, are being taught that faith and love and hope consist in abiding.

It may be Paul who understood best the ineffable quality of Jesus. He was, after all, the only apostle who did not know Jesus when he was physically alive. He is shaped by that lack, perhaps even compensates for it through preaching zealously. In any other organization, the original eleven followers would have an advantage in authority and insight over a latecomer convert who would be considered to have entry-level status. But it is Paul who grasps clearly, famously, how murky the truths of this faith are empirically: "At present we see indistinctly, as in a mirror, but then face to face. At present I know partially; then I shall know fully, as I am fully known. So faith, hope, love remain, these three; but the greatest of these is love (1 Cor 13:12-13).

His own vision of the risen Christ causes his conversion as it blinds him temporarily (Acts 9:3-9). Paul's own experience of a truth transcends the empirical as Jesus always had. Indeed, the effect of blindness is even more revealing of Jesus than the conspicuous display of light knocking Paul to the ground (Acts 9:4). Jesus imbues a teaching beyond sight. Paul is blind for the next three days and does not eat or drink. His other senses, it seems, are minimized, perhaps so that he can learn to listen and take in this larger truth.[16]

The Road to Emmaus

The presence of the resurrected Jesus is the foundation stone of Christianity: "And if Christ has not been raised, then empty [too] is our preaching; empty, too, your faith" (1 Cor 15:14). Depicting this presence as

---

16. Northrop Frye notes that Paul's conversion is the loss of his (considerable) ego; see *The Great Code: The Bible and Literature* (New York: Harcourt Brace & Company, 1982), 231.

visible yet different from that during Jesus' earthly life is paramount for the gospel writers. It is a challenging literary task since they must also respect the aniconic tradition of preserving divine mystery. The resurrected Jesus is visible in some manner because he is human but also not grasped fully because he is God. In the episode with Thomas and the disciples above, Jesus' presence is tangible, yet he manages to come through a closed door. In the scene with Mary Magdalene, Jesus again is visible, and someone she can physically touch but not at first recognize. Jesus is at once there but not there, and then he is recognized as really there in these postresurrection scenes. In miniature, these postresurrection scenes replicate the moments of divine presence and absence that have been occurring throughout the entire Bible. A dynamic God is both present and transcendent, and our trust must be correspondingly agile.

The elusive yet sure presence of the resurrected Jesus is given masterful expression in the road to Emmaus pericope in Luke 24. Two disciples are walking the road in sadness over their loss of Jesus at the crucifixion three days ago. "Jesus himself drew near and walked with them, but their eyes were prevented from recognizing him" (Luke 24:15-16). The disciples then start telling this "stranger" all about Jesus (vv. 19-21), putting them in the unique position of having preached the Gospel to Christ himself! Jesus is absent to the two men as their grief indicates but present to them incognito.

The disciples had heard from the women who had gone to the tomb that Jesus was alive. There, Jesus was absent to the women yet also present, in that he was alive. When they did not find his body, they came back and reported that they had indeed seen a vision of angels who had announced that Jesus was alive (Luke 24:23). Hearsay, then, first from angels and then from the women, occurs as the enticing substitute for Jesus' physical presence. Both the women and the disciples thus far are experiencing simultaneously the presence and absence of Jesus, but they are only conscious of the absence. Nothing is clear yet on the road to Emmaus, but something is definitely breaking new.

"As they approached the village to which they were going, he gave the impression that he was going on farther. But they urged him, 'Stay with us, for it is nearly evening and the day is almost over.' So he went in to stay with them" (Luke 24:28-29). Jesus "gave the impression that he was going on farther," but something in the disciples makes them stop and invite him to stay. Their response to this enigmatic stranger is a parallel to Moses having given the burning bush a second look. They demonstrate initiative and a desire for more from this encounter. On Jesus' part, he waits for that response, as God had with Moses earlier. The divine, here on the road, is as compelling, nonintrusive, and invitational as it has been all along throughout Scripture.

These disciples are quietly snagged by some enigmatic quality about this stranger even as they are demonstrating customary biblical hospitality. They act, in other words, without the certainty or even expectation of divine presence. Yet divine absence, in the stranger, has created the opportunity for its presence to be manifest. They will later describe this snag quite well: "Were not our hearts burning [within us] while he spoke to us?" (Luke 24:32). When they invite this stranger in, their world utterly transforms and symbolically we are asked to do the same. The road to Emmaus is a symbol for us that "opens up levels of reality that would otherwise be closed to us."[17] So far in the story, this has all been invisible, divine presence, but the stranger is about to become known: "So he went in to stay with them. And it happened that, while he was with them at table, he took bread, said the blessing, broke it, and gave it to them. With that their eyes were opened and they recognized him, but he vanished from their sight" (Luke 24:29-31).

Here, at the climax to the story, Jesus is revealed and fully known, recognized for who he is. It happens through what he does, namely, give himself in Eucharist. This is how Jesus is recognized in the bread and wine that are so much more; they are his real presence. Divine presence, hidden in the stranger, now manifest, is again shifting, this time toward the Liturgy of Eucharist, where Jesus will always be known and at the same time invisible. The empirical limitations are expressly addressed in this passage as their eyes are opened with divine presence, and then he vanishes "from their sight" (v. 31). Jesus did not vanish. He only vanished *from their sight*: "behold, I am with you always, until the end of the age" (Matt 28:20). This is the essence of sacramental faith, where exegesis and Eucharist combine for full translucent sight.

---

17. Johnson, *Quest for the Living God*, 20.

Real Presence

Remaining Present with God

We have been arguing that biblical descriptions of God's presence and absence are, in part, simply ways to negotiate divine mystery. Theophanies convey the real presence of God without in any way delimiting the divine. The presence and absence of the divine, God's fluidity, is experienced or construed not by statues, pantheons, or conceptual abstractions but by effects, impact, and memory. Fire, speech, and breath are particularly apt metaphors throughout Scripture because they are vital, powerful, and, by their nature, ungraspable. If, as Martin Buber claimed, "God is above all the name for the pressure to be alive to the world," then God is inherently of interest to us all.[1] Once we become attuned to and accepting of this pulsating, living realness of God, he then begins to stir our own yearning for aliveness. God prompts us to more life, more than we could envision on our own. Divine presence and absence is crucial for preserving God's mystery and for drawing out our interest. This combination gives the numinous its tantalizing quality. The bush deserved a second look from Moses. The stranger on the road to Emmaus deserved an invitation. A biblical passage deserves a second look from us.

---

1. Martin Buber, *Eclipse of God: Studies in the Relation between Religion and Philosophy* (New York: Harper, 1952), 9.

There are moments—in life and in Scripture—when divine presence is so palpable that faith is given foundation, evidence of things not seen (Heb 11:1). The moments of absence do not erase that knowledge of sure, real presence, nor do they "balance" them out so as to cancel the effort of faith. The effort of faith is the effort of love. It can wait and even wants to as Jesus advised simply, "Remain in me, as I remain in you" (John 15:4). For then the absences begin to soften into something closer to companionable silence, a trust in communion. This is what the Bible has been teaching all along, first with God in the Old Testament and then with God in Jesus in the New: that love and communion include periods of silence and that these do not constitute proofs of divine nonexistence. Remaining even in what feels like total dereliction yields to a silent presence, often as subtle and as real as Elijah's light, silent sound.

God's presence was patently manifest in the scene of the burning bush and atop Mount Sinai, and it also did not remain there for Moses and the people. The Sinai revelation of God, then, included both momentous divine presence in the theophany and divine absence in the invisibility that is memory. God is not limited either by place or time. This is why tourist spots based on the life of Jesus can be inherently disappointing, as we saw in chapter 5 with Jesus' tombs. Jesus is not there. God cannot be found on empiricism's terms. That same insight, which at first comes with a sense of disappointment, then yields to a new threshold of possibility where we are liberated from assumptions about place and presence. As Jürgen Moltmann asserts, "To know God means to endure God." He further explains, "To know God in the cross of Christ is a crucifying form of knowledge because it shatters everything to which a man can hold and on which he can build, both his works and his knowledge of reality, and precisely in so doing sets him free."[2]

We need not travel far away to find God or practice hard at meditation if our goal is divine presence. We must be willing instead to remain, to enter into solitude, and to do so without a mental stopwatch, without in any way assessing the experience. This God is not *in* the bush or the fire, still less is he in a tomb. The firmness or situatedness of faith is internal, regardless of where we happen to be standing.

There is another moment when Moses encounters God in community, without spectacle, but where the ordinary blends easily with the extraordinary: "Moses then went up with Aaron, Nadab, Abihu, and seventy elders of Israel, and they beheld the God of Israel. Under his feet there appeared

2. Jürgen Moltmann, *The Crucified God: The Cross of Christ as the Foundation and Criticism of Christian Theology* (Minneapolis: Augsburg Fortress, 1993), 212.

to be sapphire tilework, as clear as the sky itself. Yet he did not lay a hand on these chosen Israelites. They saw God, and they ate and drank" (Exod 24:9-11).This theophany is an intimate celebration of sight of the divine and, *as if they go together*, sharing a meal. The closeness of divine presence here sanctions worship, since at least three of those men are priests, namely, Aaron, Nadab, and Abihu. Worship bridges the gap between God and the people as it subsequently mediates divine-human encounter. The people "saw God, and they ate and drank" (v. 11), and this is no haphazard sequence of verbal actions. These actions are vitally linked, first by God in this passage, then again by Jesus at Emmaus. Both encounters are temporary but substantial and real nonetheless. In the revelation at Mount Sinai in chapter 20, the people had been too frightened to be present to God and so they sent Moses. But here, in chapter 24, they are not.[3] Their own human tendency to be "present and absent" to their God, that is, their ambivalence, is accepted as fright gives way to communion. Humankind never has to stop being human to meet God. The Bible gives testimony to the human desire to want to be close to God and, at the same time, the reality of being too scared of it.

Empirical Bias

The empirical slant of modernity, while incalculably helpful in advancing knowledge, has at the same time impoverished our awareness of the numinous. It views the world and the Bible as objects for study and sees study as largely acquisitive. The "I" of the thinker is the primary locus of meaning. It acquires information; it understands; it decides whether or not God is real. Under this perspective, divine invisibility feels like absence, which then fuels an understandable futility about faith. A "why bother?" attitude pervades in a host of endeavors, faith included. Free-floating dissatisfaction signals a human limit, that we are not getting what we want and need. It hints that maybe there is a myopia involved in the isolation of the thinker to determine meaning, because something like yearning persists even after all our acquisition and mastery. The biblical alternative is to view the self as fundamentally in relationship with an Other, God. The self still matters but is submerged in a dynamic relationship as its defining posture: "Man's walled mind has no access to a ladder upon which he can, on his own strength, rise to knowledge of God. Yet his soul is endowed with translucent

---

3. The seventy elders accompanying the three priests, in my reading, represent the people as a whole. The number seven, in the Bible, indicates completeness, so that seventy would function as a representative sampling.

windows that open to the beyond. And if he rises to reach out to Him, it is a reflection of the divine light in him that gives him the power for such yearning. We are at times ablaze against and beyond our own power."[4]

Faith is a decision to trust in maybe nothing more specific than this sensation of being "ablaze against and beyond our own power." It surfaces over and over again in life and is neither delusion nor easy, as the atheists contend. It is, in fact, quite hard to be a believer today. As Pope Benedict asserts, "What Israel had to do in the early days of its history, and the church had to do at the beginning of her career, must be done afresh in every human life."[5] From joining the journey within Scripture, he said, we come to realize that "Both the poverty of human existence and its fullness point to God."[6]

Paradox of Faith

The entire Bible is built on a paradox, one slipped in at the beginning of Genesis (chap. 3) before readers have had a chance to acclimatize fully to its strange world. The paradox is that faith *requires* distance in order to exist and flourish. Adam and Eve, humankind, would never know faith unless they left the garden. They alone had certainty about God and a familiarity that precluded doubt and prayer. Any questions they had could simply be checked out with God the next time they saw him. And God further allays any potential anxiety by letting the couple know when he takes his daily stroll. But this certainty of divine presence is not faith; it is a kind of infancy. A baby does not *trust* that her mother will not drop her. Instead, there is a merciful cluelessness to being an infant, similar to the worldly naiveté that Adam and Eve enjoyed. It is, however, fully unworkable to go through life naked, talking to animals, eating whatever is on hand. There is a necessary distancing between God and humankind in the garden in order for the journey of faith to begin.

The trust that is faith cannot emerge without divine distance. Without that distance, Scripture would be replete with scenes of the same harmonious stasis of garden life over and over and over again rather than the choppy, furtive dance of divine presence and absence where faith really dwells. We learn to accept from these biblical cadences a divine presence as fluid and

---

4. Abraham Joshua Heschel, *God in Search of Man: A Philosophy of Judaism* (New York: Farrar, Straus and Giroux, 1955), 138.

5. Pope Benedict XVI, *Introduction to Christianity*, trans. J. R. Foster (San Francisco: Ignatius Press, 2004), 151.

6. Ibid., 105.

not subject to human terms. Surely, Mother Teresa is a saint just for abiding as she did in this stark truth.

The awareness of human limits provides an opportunity for discovery. Anthropologists term this psychic threshold "liminality," a kind of suspended state between the past and a present not yet secured. Liminality is particularly evident in cultural rites of passage, where marking social transitions occasions reflection on both the transition and the mystery outside the regularity of daily life.[7] It occasions awareness of mystery previously undetected, which includes religious mystery.[8] Part of the reason for reflection is due to the increased vulnerability felt during important transitions. A vulnerability to doubts, Pope Benedict notes, occurs with the persistent question if one is "only dealing with the reflections of his own consciousness or whether it is given to him to reach out beyond himself and to encounter God himself."[9]

The soul in its encounter with the Otherness of God is one such liminal situation. It is unsettling in large part because the limit or threshold being crossed is that of the ego. Divine encounter exceeds our cognitive grasp but also our very desire *to* grasp. Elizabeth Johnson is clear on this point: "Far from being a pessimistic experience, however, encounter with Holy as mystery is laced with the promise of plenitude: more fullness exists than we can grasp."[10]

There is an advantage to experiencing a liminal state in that it allows us to glimpse a place beyond ourselves. We discover *in extremis* not the abyss we so feared but rather a state beyond the ego's controlling grip, a peace or sense of well-being greater than that furnished by our control. Culturally, we prefer our forays into the unknown in small, managed doses, such as bungee jumping, rollercoasters, video games, indoor rock climbing. We want the rush of the unknown, but only in controlled environments. Yet simulated adventures into the unknown deny us liminality, which is often where God meets us. Uncontrolled Scripture reading begets us this liminality. "If we

7. Victor Turner, *Dramas, Fields, and Metaphors: Symbolic Action in Human Society* (Ithaca, NY: Cornell University Press, 1975), 231–42. Turner identifies three phases of a change in social status: (1) separation, (2) existing at the margins or threshold for a period of time, and (3) reaggregation into the social unit (231–32).

8. "In liminality resides the germ . . . religious askesis, discipline, and mysticism" (Ibid., 242).

9. Pope Benedict, *Introduction to Christianity*, 164.

10. Elizabeth Johnson, *Quest for the Living God: Mapping Frontiers in the Theology of God* (New York: Continuum, 2007), 9.

wish to come to grips with the contents of the Bible," Barth asserted, "we must dare to read far beyond ourselves."[11]

The freedom revealed in liminal experience is described by Jesus perhaps too baldly: "Whoever finds his life will lose it, and whoever loses his life for my sake will find it" (Matt 10:39). His message sounds extreme and reckless and like a summons to eager martyrdom. But the image encourages us to life's limit for the sake of a greater freedom.

A psyche defined primarily by self-interest, that is, original sin, cannot help thinking it a shame that Jesus was so reckless in not even resisting his captors. With a bare modicum of political savvy, he could have lasted longer, healed more, preached to more people. To the ego, martyrdom is admirable to a point but is mainly wasteful. The point of Jesus' message was to bring us past the ego, past the fear of nonexistence. The Cistercian monks of Tibhirine, the subjects of the film *Of Gods and Men* (2010), got there, past the ego and its fears, and gave bodily witness to Jesus with their lives.[12]

The single most repeated commandment in Scripture is "be not afraid." It is used forty-eight times within the Old and New Testaments. Fear holds us back. It cripples trust and so is faith's opposite. Pope John Paul II knew this truth well and used the phrase frequently to challenge the young and old alike to notice the level of corrosive fear in their lives. True trust gains "the courage to face the abyss of being . . . to affirm, at the risk of assuming all risks, the will to gamble away . . . one's ego."[13] Fear evaporates and the numinous surrounds the ego-less consciousness; it is to this joy that Jesus and the martyrs witness.

Real Presence

The real presence of God cannot be staid, fixed into certainty, but has instead pockets of perceived absence, of opaqueness, and of uncertainty that enable divine liveliness to blow through. God becomes another idol if we insist that he be a firm, permanent fixture. Faith's challenge is to remain supple to the divine élan and resistant to idols. John Caputo here lends philosophical support for faith's effort, which nicely honors the divine name, YHWH: "The name of a God is not the name of an abstract logical

---

11. Karl Barth, *The Word of God and the Word of Man* (New York: Harper & Row, 1957), 33.

12. Their dilemma was one all martyrs face, namely, to choose with Jesus for life, even though it means their own death.

13. Samuel L. Terrien, *The Elusive Presence* (San Francisco: Harper & Row, 1978), 83–84.

possibility but of a dynamis that pulses through things (*rei*), urging them, soliciting them, to be what they can be, and it is in that sense what is most real about them. The name of God is not the name of the most real thing but of what is most real *in* things."[14] Facets of God remain mysterious and hidden within revelation.[15] However much this can feel like a divine power outage to humankind, it is not. Since revelation is inseparable from God's self-communication, it is intrinsically salvific, simply because it is God. That is, if I have sensed both God and God absent, I have still sensed him as real. "I know my vindicator lives," even if I cannot track his whereabouts. The believer learns to relate to an elusive God with a nimble trust, one that accommodates absences, not in pious concession, but in love. God, as Rahner claimed, is always "past all graspness" but not aloof.

God is really present in the bread and wine of Eucharist. These visible signs do not mean more simply because believers say they do. Their assent is, of course, part of it. A community agrees to the meaning of Eucharist, a community established by Christ whose body and blood nourish it forever. But Eucharist is a sacrament, because it holds divine mystery within it. There is literally more than meets the eye and it is that more of mystery that feeds the soul. Somehow, out of view, far from forensic analysis, taking bread and drinking from this cup alter our vision of what is possible, of what truly is. In the simple creaturely act of chewing and sipping "is a syntax of the silence in which our souls mingle with the divine."[16] That silent, untraceable mingling is more real than everything else surrounding it.

This always-new habit of Eucharist guides us deeper into Christ's real presence animating the world. Real presence spreads out from communion to the world incandescent with grace. Jacob dreamed one night of "a stairway rested on the ground, with its top reaching to the heavens; and God's angels were going up and down on it" (Gen 28:12). Notice that God's angels are not coming down first; they are ascending. They are opened pathways to God from the human level. Sacraments allow our lithe ascent into the plenitude of God's presence. Sacrament and mystery are the blessings of Catholicism. They bestow not medieval intransigence, but a resting place, a homing station, a docking station where I go back to the real.

When a slight breeze blows through our day, it can simply be a pleasant sensation, one with a meteorological stimulus and a physiological response.

---

14. John D. Caputo and Gianni Vattimo, *After the Death of God* (New York: Columbia University, 2009), 65.

15. Avery Dulles, *Models of Revelation* (Maryknoll, NY: Orbis, 1983), 87.

16. Abraham Joshua Heschel, *I Asked for Wonder: A Spiritual Anthology* (New York: Crossroad, 1983), 9.

A gentle breeze is all that, certainly. And sometimes it is much more. When Elijah felt it on his cheek, it fully revived him. It did more than cool him; it rescued him from full despair. He had wanted to die, to be left alone to expire in a cave, and that is rock-bottom despair. What he experienced was more than physiological stimulus to an environmental variable. It touched his soul. Breeze in that instance was a both/and phenomenon rather than an either/or. It packed meteorology, physiology, and divine presence all into one gentle life-giving experience. I cannot chart the progression of providence or map out precisely how this packing occurs. I know it the way we know love, that is, beyond the empirical or love does not get off the ground. A relationship dies by daily proofs of its sincerity. Elijah felt something extraordinary in the ordinary and it brought him back to life. If a breeze can do that, so can a piece of bread and a sip of wine. For the Holy is lurking in creation with the sole intent of loving us. Part of its gift is anticipation, as Heschel so clearly saw: "The presence of God is a majestic expectation, to be sensed and retained and, when lost, to be regained and resumed. . . . Every moment is His subtle arrival, and man's task is *to be present*. His presence is retained in moments in which God is not alone."[17] God becomes present in our waiting, in our efforts to be present. God is present always but often undetected in prayer because we have the enormous rock face of our own self-consciousness to climb over first.

Catholicism is flamboyant about the possibility of divine presence. The whole creation is chock-full of grace, the potential of delighted encounter with the holy lurking everywhere. Catholics have the boldness to expect that everyday details are full of sacramental moments. An elementary school Mass, for instance, is full of sacramental presence: on the altar, to be sure, but also in the fidgeting of little hands, struggling not to be adults about religion, there is the sacrament of what it is to be God's child, and "unless you turn and become like children, you will not enter the kingdom of heaven" (Matt 18:3).

We are entranced at times just by the possibilities, the delicious mystery of not knowing what is about to happen, who this person is, when the rain or sun will break open the sky. I would bet that Catholics pay less attention to meteorologists than other demographic groups. We relish or at least acquire a taste for the unexpected, even if caught by a downpour. It was still worth it for the shiver of mystery.

Once the bread and wine become Christ himself, you expect to see more of this profound, divine simplicity all around you. If that could happen, then kindness could, or giggling, or a sense of being truly known. Your

17. Ibid., 31.

expectations quietly expand rather than diminish in the regular ritual of Eucharist. Even as we adult-wriggle in inattention, we acquire a taste for grace in the everyday. We expect to be caught by surprise and hope for it as we delve into God's mysterious presence and absence. We glimpse or catch a little, release, and then praise. Eucharist habituates us to this reality in the bread and wine and nourishes us to see it elsewhere in the world, the body of Christ, the face of Christ, the image of God, the teeming creation, the extraordinary amid the ordinary. Real presence has always been real, palpably experienced, revealed, loved, and invisible rather than forensic. It means more in the receptivity of our souls, also not forensically available.

Both Catholicism and Scripture insist on the details because they contain more than they seem. There is much more to the ordinary if we are attuned to it. It is a Catholic impulse and witness to let the world be animated, full of mystery, to see it biblically as creation. Then you see the holy lurking. You begin to care; you begin to handle with care. This is not the vision of willful naiveté, as Dawkins believes, or arrested emotional development à la Freud. Nor is it the blind hope of life-delayed gratification in heaven. It is a steely eyed vision that can see both the good and the evil in the world and fight off the latter. As Rahner was convinced, "man's ground lies in the abyss of mystery. The only question is whether he lives with mystery willingly, obediently and trustingly."[18] I swim in this mystery, within a vast expanse of some delectable barely detectable presence, the invisibility of God, with the bravery of faith.

The broader biblical revelation has always been that the details matter, the concrete fabric of life matters to this God who is not abstraction. Our lives matter down to the smallest detail to this God. The incarnation made divine care clear, but it had been there all along, as God-with-us, Immanuel. God had always been really present: to Abraham and Sarah, a couple in their nineties giving birth at once to Isaac and to monotheistic faith; to puny, armor-less David against Goliath; to a poor, tiny country in the Fertile Crescent; to Jacob, the younger, less important son; to Joseph, the favored younger brother of the twelve; to some battered slaves in mighty Pharaonic Egypt; to the little sparrow who is more fabulous in splendor than King Solomon; to Solomon, a baby conceived in the grief of a first, stillborn child; to a Palestinian baby being born in a stall with animals; to the widows, orphans, aliens, unknown, and wounded on roadsides whom Jesus heals.

---

18. Karl Rahner, "Mystery," in *Sacramentum Mundi: An Encyclopedia of Theology*, ed. Karl Rahner, vol. 4 (New York: Herder & Herder, 1968), 135.

Each of us walks past burning bushes, little heroes, and dirty mangers mostly clueless to their life-altering dazzle but less clueless for having read of these tiny, divine real encounters in Scripture.

> *Earth's crammed with heaven,*
> *And every common bush afire with God:*
> *But only he who sees, takes off his shoes.*[19]

19. Elizabeth Barrett Browning, *Aurora Leigh*, ed. Kerry McSweeney (New York: Oxford University Press, 2008), 246.

Bibliography

Allen, John L., Jr. "Benedict Battles the 'Dictatorship of Relativism.'" *National Catholic Reporter*, September 16, 2010. http://ncronline.org/blogs/ncr-today /benedict-battles-dictatorship-relativism. Accessed June 29, 2012.

Altizer, Thomas J. J. *Radical Theology and the Death of God*. Indianapolis, IN: Bobbs-Merrill, 1966.

Auden, W. H. "Twelve Songs." In *Collected Poems*, edited by Edward Mendelson. New York: Random House, 2007.

Augustine. *The Confessions*. Translated by Maria Boulding. Hyde Park, NY: New City Press, 2001.

Balentine, Samuel E. *The Hidden God: The Hiding of the Face of God in the Old Testament*. Oxford: Oxford University Press, 1983.

Barth, Karl. *Church Dogmatics*. Vol. 2, bk. 2. Translated by G. T. Thomson. Edinburgh: T & T Clark, 1936.

———.*Church Dogmatics*. Vol. 2, bk. 1. Edited by G. W. Bromiley and T. F. Torrance. Edinburgh: T & T Clark, 1957.

———. *Church Dogmatics*. Vol 3, bk. 2. Translated by Harold Knight, G. W. Bromiley, J. K. S. Reid, and R. H. Fuller. Edinburgh: T & T Clark, 1960.

———. *Dogmatics in Outline*. New York: Harper Perennial, 1959.

———. *The Word of God and Theology*. Translated by Amy Marga. Edinburgh: T & T Clark International, 2011.

———. *The Word of God and the Word of Man*. New York: Harper & Row, 1957.

Benedict XVI. *The God of Jesus Christ: Meditations on the Triune God*. Translated by Brian McNeil. San Francisco: Ignatius Press, 2006.

———. *Handing on the Faith in an Age of Disbelief*. San Francisco: Ignatius Press, 2006.

———. *In the Beginning . . . : A Catholic Understanding of the Story of Creation and the Fall*. Grand Rapids, MI: Eerdmans, 1995.

———. *Introduction to Christianity*. Translated by J. R. Foster. San Francisco: Ignatius Press, 2004.

Beyerlin, Walter. *Origins and History of the Oldest Sinaitic Traditions*. New York: Oxford University Press, 1965.

Blenkinsopp, Joseph. *Treasures Old and New: Essays in the Theology of the Pentateuch*. Grand Rapids, MI: Eerdmans, 2004.

Blumenthal, David. *Facing the Abusing God: A Theology of Protest*. Louisville, KY: Westminster/John Knox Press, 1993.

Braiterman, Zachary. *(God) After Auschwitz: Tradition and Change in Post-Holocaust Jewish Thought*. Princeton, NJ: Princeton University Press, 1998.

Brashler, James, and Roger A. Bullard, trans. "Apocalypse of Peter." In *The Nag Hammadi Library*, ed. James M. Robinson. Rev. ed. San Francisco: HarperCollins, 1990. Available at http://www.gnosis.org/naghamm/apopet.html.

Brenner, Athalya, and Carole Fontaine, eds. *A Feminist Companion to Reading the Bible: Approaches, Methods and Strategies*. London: Routledge, 2001.

Brisman, Leslie. "On the Divine Presence in Exodus." In *Exodus*, edited by Harold Bloom, 105–22. New York: Chelsea House, 1987.

Brueggemann, Walter. *Theology of the Old Testament: Testimony, Dispute, Advocacy*. Minneapolis: Fortress Press, 1997.

Buber, Martin. *Eclipse of God: Studies in the Relation between Religion and Philosophy*. New York: Harper, 1952.

———. *On Judaism*. Edited by Nahum N. Glatzer. New York: Schocken, 1967.

Bultmann, Rudolf. *Theology of the New Testament*. Waco, TX: Baylor University Press, 2007 [1951].

Burnett, Joel. *Where Is God? Divine Absence in the Hebrew Bible*. Minneapolis: Fortress Press, 2010.

Burrell, David. *Knowing the Unknowable God: Ibn-Sina, Maimonides, Aquinas*. Minneapolis: Fortress Press, 2007.

Caldwell, Christopher. *Reflections on the Revolution in Europe*. New York: Doubleday, 2009.

Caputo, John D. *The Prayers and Tears of Jacques Derrida: Religion without Religion*. Bloomington: Indiana University Press, 1997.

———. *What Would Jesus Deconstruct? The Good News of Postmodernism for the Church*. Grand Rapids, MI: Baker Academic, 2007.

Caputo, John D., and Gianni Vattimo. *After the Death of God*. New York: Columbia University Press, 2009.

Chauvet, Louis-Marie. *The Sacraments: The Word of God at the Mercy of the Body*. Translated by Madeleine Beaumont. Collegeville, MN: Liturgical Press, 2001.

Childs, Brevard S. *Biblical Theology of the Old and New Testaments*. Minneapolis: Fortress Press, 1992.

———. *The Book of Exodus: A Critical, Theological Commentary*. Philadelphia: Westminster, 1974.

———. *Old Testament Theology in a Canonical Context*. Philadelphia: Fortress Press, 1985.

Cooper, Terry D. *Dimensions of Evil: Contemporary Perspectives*. Minneapolis: Fortress Press, 2007.

Crenshaw, James. *Defending God.* New York: Oxford University Press, 2005.

———. *Ecclesiastes: A Commentary.* OTL. Philadelphia: Westminster, 1987.

———. "In Search of Divine Presence." *Review and Expositor* 74, no. 3 (1977): 353–69.

Cross, Frank Moore. *Canaanite Myth and Hebrew Epic: Essays in the History of the Religion of Israel.* Cambridge, MA: Harvard University Press, 1973.

Crossan, John Dominic. *Jesus: A Revolutionary Biography.* New York: HarperOne, 2009.

Dalley, Stephanie. *Myths from Mesopotamia: Creation, the Flood, Gilgamesh, and Others.* New York: Oxford University Press, 2009.

Dawkins, Richard. *The God Delusion.* New York: Mariner, 2008.

Dillenberger, John. *God Hidden and Revealed: The Interpretation of Luther's Deus Absconditus and Its Significance for Religious Thought.* Philadelphia: Muhlenberg Press, 1953.

Dostoyevsky, Fyodor. *The Brothers Karamazov.* Translated by Constance Garnett. New York: W. W. Norton, Inc., 1976.

Douglas, Mary. *Leviticus as Literature.* Oxford: Oxford University Press, 1999.

Downey, Michael. *Understanding Christian Spirituality.* New York: Paulist Press, 1997.

Dulles, Avery. *The Craft of Theology: From Symbol to System.* New York: Crossroad, 1995.

———. "Faith and Revelation." In *Systematic Theology*, edited by Francis Schüssler Fiorenza and John P. Galvin, 2nd ed., 79–108. Minneapolis: Fortress, 2011.

———. *Models of Revelation.* Maryknoll, NY: Orbis, 1983.

Dupré, Louis, and James A. Wiseman, eds. *Light from Light: An Anthology of Christian Mysticism.* New York/Mahwah, NJ: Paulist, 2001.

Eagleton, Terry. *Reason, Faith, and Revolution: Reflections on the God Debate.* New Haven, CT: Yale University Press, 2010.

Eichrodt, Walther. *The Theology of the Old Testament.* Philadelphia: Westminster, 1967.

Ellul, Jacques. *Reason for Being: A Meditation on Ecclesiastes.* Translated by Joyce Main Hanks. Grand Rapids, MI: Eerdmans, 1990.

Ellwood, Robert S. *Mysticism and Religion.* New York and London: Seven Bridges Press, 1999.

Feuerbach, Ludwig. *The Essence of Christianity.* Translated by George Eliot. Lawrence, KS: Digireads, 2012 [1841].

Flannery, Austin, trans. *Vatican Council II: The Basic Sixteen Documents.* Northport, NY: Costello Publishing Co., 1996.

Fox, Michael V. *A Time to Tear Down and a Time to Build Up: A Rereading of Ecclesiastes.* Grand Rapids, MI: Eerdmans, 1999.

———. "The Meaning of *Hebel* for Qohelet." *Journal of Biblical Literature* 105 (1986): 409–27.

Fredericks, Daniel C. *Coping with Transience: Ecclesiastes on Brevity in Life.* Sheffield: Sheffield Academic Press, 1993.

Fretheim, Terence E. *The Pentateuch*. Interpreting Biblical Texts 1. Nashville: Abingdon, 1996.

Friedman, Richard Elliott. *The Disappearance of God: A Divine Mystery*. New York: Little, Brown and Company, 1995.

Fromm, Erich. *The Heart of Man: Its Genius for Good and Evil*. New York: Harper & Row, 1964.

Frye, Northrop. *The Great Code: The Bible and Literature*. New York: Harcourt Brace & Company, 1982.

Gallagher, Timothy M. *The Discernment of Spirits: An Ignatian Guide for Everyday Living*. New York: Crossroad, 2005.

Gerrish, Brian. *The Old Protestantism and the New: Essays on the Reformation Heritage*. Chicago: University of Chicago Press, 1982.

Gilson, Etienne. *The Spirit of Mediaeval Philosophy*. South Bend, IN: University of Notre Dame, 1991.

Glueck, Nelson. "Incense Altars." In *Translating and Understanding the Old Testament: Essays in Honor of Hubert Gordon May*, edited by Harry Thomas Reed and William L. Reed, 325–41. Nashville, TN: Abingdon, 1970.

Greeley, Andrew. *The Catholic Imagination*. Berkeley: University of California Press, 2001.

Green, Barbara. *Makhail Bakhtin and Biblical Scholarship: An Introduction*. Atlanta, GA: Society of Biblical Literature, 2000.

Gregory of Nyssa. *The Life of Moses*. New York: HarperCollins, 2006.

Gschwandtner, Christina M. *Reading Jean-Luc Marion: Exceeding Metaphysics*. Indiana Series in the Philosophy of Religion. Bloomington: Indiana University Press, 2007.

Gunkel, Hermann. *Genesis*. Macon, GA: Mercer University Press, 1997.

Harmless, William, ed. *Augustine in His Own Words*. Washington, DC: Catholic University of America Press, 2010.

Hart, David Bentley. *Atheist Delusions: The Christian Revolution and Its Fashionable Enemies*. New Haven, CT: Yale University Press, 2009.

Heschel, Abraham Joshua. *God in Search of Man: A Philosophy of Judaism*. New York: Farrar, Straus and Giroux, 1955.

———. *I Asked for Wonder: A Spiritual Anthology*. New York: Crossroad, 1983.

Higgins, Gregory C. *Christianity 101: A Textbook of Catholic Theology*. New York/Mahwah, NJ: Paulist, 2007.

Hillesum, Etty. *An Interrupted Life: The Diaries, 1941–1943, and Letters from Westerbork*. New York: Henry Holt, 1996.

Horner, Robyn. *Jean-Luc Marion: A Theological Introduction*. Farnham: Ashgate, 2005.

Hume, David. *Dialogues Concerning Natural Religion*. New York: Hafner, 1948.

International Committee on English in the Liturgy. *The Roman Missal*. 3rd ed. Collegeville, MN: Liturgical Press, 2011.

James, William. *The Varieties of Religious Experience: A Study in Human Nature*. New York: Macmillan, 1961.

Jeremias, Jörg. *Theophanie: Die Geschichte einer alttestamentlichen Gattung.* Neukirchen-Vluyn: Neukirchener Verlag, 1965.

John of the Cross. *The Dark Night of the Soul.* In *The Collected Works of St. John of the Cross*, translated by Kieran Kavanaugh and Otilio Rodriguez. Washington, DC: Institute of Carmelite Studies, 1991.

Johnson, Elizabeth. *Quest for the Living God: Mapping Frontiers in the Theology of God.* New York: Continuum, 2007.

Kasper, Walter. *The God of Jesus Christ.* Translated by Matthew J. O'Connell. New York: Crossroad, 1986.

Kinnell, Galway. "St. Francis and the Sow." In *A New Selected Poems.* New York: Houghton Mifflin, 2001.

Krüger, Thomas. *Qoheleth: A Commentary on the Book of Qoheleth.* Hermeneia. Minneapolis: Fortress Press, 2004.

Kugel, James L. *The God of Old: Inside the Lost World of the Bible.* New York: Free Press, 2004.

Kushner, Harold S. *When Bad Things Happen to Good People.* New York: Anchor, 2004.

Lakeland, Paul. *Postmodernity: Christian Identity in a Fragmented Age.* Minneapolis: Fortress Press, 1997.

Lash, Nicholas. *Holiness, Speech, and Silence: Reflections on the Question of God.* Aldershot, England: Ashgate, 2004.

Levinas, Emmanuel. *Difficult Freedom: Essays on Judaism.* Translated by Seán Hand. Baltimore: Johns Hopkins University Press, 1997.

Longman, Tremper, III. *The Book of Ecclesiastes.* Grand Rapids, MI: Eerdmans, 1998.

Louth, Andrew. *Discerning the Mystery: An Essay on the Nature of Theology.* New York: Oxford University Press, 1990.

de Lubac, Henri. *The Mystery of the Supernatural.* Translated by Rosemary Sheed. New York: Herder and Herder, 1998.

———. "Spiritual Understanding." In *Theological Interpretation of Scripture: Classic and Contemporary Readings*, edited by Stephen E. Fowl. Hoboken, NJ: Wiley-Blackwell, 1997.

Mann, Thomas. *Divine Presence and Guidance in Israelite Traditions: The Typology of Exaltation.* Baltimore and London: Johns Hopkins University Press, 1977.

———. "The Pillar of Cloud in the Reed Sea Narrative." *Journal of Biblical Literature* 90 (1971): 15–30.

Marion, Jean-Luc. *God without Being.* Translated by Thomas A. Carlson. Chicago: University of Chicago Press, 1991.

Martinez, German. *Signs of Freedom: Theology of the Christian Sacraments.* New York/Mahwah, NJ: Paulist Press, 2003.

Mazar, Amahai. "Cult Stands and Cult Bowls." In *Excavations at Tell Qasile*, 87–100. Qedem 12. Jerusalem: Hebrew University Press, 1980.

McBrien, Richard P. *Catholicism.* San Francisco: HarperSanFrancisco, 1994.

McFague, Sallie. *Speaking in Parables: A Study in Metaphor and Theology.* Minneapolis: Fortress Press, 2000.

McGinn, Bernard. *Foundations of Mysticism*. New York: Crossroads, 2004.

Midrash Tanhuma Genesis. Edited by Samuel Berman. Hoboken, NJ: KTAV Publishing, 1996.

Miles, Jack. *God: A Biography*. New York: Vintage, 1996.

Milgrom, Jacob. *Leviticus: A Continental Commentary*. Minneapolis: Fortress Press, 2004.

Moltmann, Jürgen. *The Crucified God: The Cross of Christ as the Foundation and Criticism of Christian Theology*. Minneapolis: Augsburg Fortress, 1993.

Moule, C. F. D. "Mystery." In *The Interpreters' Dictionary of the Bible*, edited by George A. Buttrick, vol. 3, 479–81. Nashville, TN: Abingdon, 1962.

Newsom, Carol A. *The Book of Job: A Contest of Moral Imaginations*. New York: Oxford University Press, 2003.

Nietzsche, Friedrich. *The Gay Science*. In *The Portable Nietzsche*, edited by Walter Kaufmann. New York: Penguin Books, 1968.

———. *Will to Power*. Translated by Walter Kaufmann. New York: Vintage Books, 1968.

Noth, Martin. *Exodus*. Translated by J. S. Bowden. Philadelphia: Westminster, 1962.

Novak, Michael. *No One Sees God: The Dark Night of Atheists and Believers*. New York: Doubleday, 2008.

Otto, Rudolph. *The Idea of the Holy*. New York and Oxford: University of Oxford Press, 1950 [1923].

Pagels, Elaine. *The Origin of Satan: How Christians Demonized Jews, Pagans, and Heretics*. New York: Vintage, 1996.

Pascal, Blaise. *Pensées and Other Writings*. Edited by Anthony Levi. Translated by Honor Levi. New York: Oxford University Press, 2008.

Perdue, Leo G., Robert Morgan, and Benjamin D. Sommer. *Biblical Theology: Introducing the Conversation*. Nashville, TN: Abingdon, 2009.

Perl, Jeffrey M. *A "Dictatorship of Relativism"? Symposium in Response to Cardinal Ratzinger's Last Homily*. Durham, NC: Duke University Press, 2007.

Pieper, Josef. *Leisure: The Basis of Culture*. San Francisco: Ignatius, 2009 [1963].

von Rad, Gerhard. *The Problem of the Hexateuch and Other Essays*. New York: McGraw-Hill, 1966 [1938].

———. *Theology of the Old Testament*. San Francisco: HarperSanFrancisco, 1962.

———. *Wisdom in Israel*. Nashville, TN: Abingdon, 1972.

Rahner, Karl. "Mystery." In *Sacramentum Mundi: An Encyclopedia of Theology*, edited by Karl Rahner, vol. 4, 133–36. New York: Herder & Herder, 1968.

———. "Mystery." In *Theological Investigations*, translated by Cornelius Ernst, vol. 4, 34–73. Baltimore: Helicon Press, 1961.

———. "The Spirituality of the Future." In *The Practice of Faith: A Handbook of Contemporary Spirituality*, edited by K. Lehmann and A. Raffelt. New York: Crossroad, 1986.

Ricoeur, Paul. *Figuring the Sacred: Religion, Narrative, and Imagination*. Translated by David Pellauer. Edited by Mark I. Wallace. Minneapolis: Fortress Press, 1995.

————. *The Rule of Metaphor: Multi-disciplinary Studies of the Creation of Meaning in Language*. London: Routledge and Kegan Paul, 1978.

————. "What Is a Text? Explanation and Understanding." In *Hermeneutics and the Human Sciences: Essays on Language, Action and Interpretation*, translated by John B. Thompson, 145–64. Cambridge: Cambridge University Press, 1981.

Rogerson, John W. *A Theology of the Old Testament: Cultural Memory, Communication, and Being Human*. Minneapolis: Fortress, 2010.

Rubenstein, Richard L. *After Auschwitz: History, Theology and Contemporary Judaism*. 2nd ed. Baltimore, MD: Johns Hopkins University Press, 1992.

Savran, George W. *Encountering the Divine: Theophany in Biblical Narratives*. JSOTSS. London: T & T Clark International, 2005.

Schneiders, Sandra M. *The Revelatory Text: Interpreting the New Testament as Sacred Scripture*. Collegeville, MN: Liturgical Press, 1999.

Schüssler Fiorenza, Elisabeth. *Bread Not Stone: The Challenge of Feminist Biblical Interpretation*. Boston: Beacon Press, 1995.

Schüssler Fiorenza, Francis. "Being, Subjectivity, and Otherness: The Idols of God." In *Questioning God*, edited by John D. Caputo, Mark Dooley, and Michael Scanlon, 320–50. Indianapolis: Indiana University Press, 2001.

Scott, James C. *Domination and the Arts of Resistance: Hidden Transcripts*. New Haven, CT: Yale University Press, 1992.

Seitz, Christopher R. *Figured Out: Typology and Providence in Christian Scripture*. Louisville, KY: Westminster/John Knox, 2001.

Seow, Choon-Leong. *Ecclesiastes*. Anchor Bible. New York: Doubleday, 1997.

van Seters, John. *The Life of Moses: The Yahwist as Historian in Exodus-Numbers*. Louisville, KY: Westminster/John Knox, 1994.

Seybold, Klaus. "Hebhel." In *Theological Dictionary of the Old Testament*. Vol. 3: 313–20. Grand Rapids, MI: Eerdmans, 1978.

Smith, Huston. *Why Religion Matters: The Fate of the Human Spirit in an Age of Disbelief*. San Francisco: Harper Collins, 2001.

Smith, Mark S. *The Early History of God: Yahweh and the Other Deities in Ancient Israel*. 2nd ed. Grand Rapids, MI: Eerdmans, 2002.

Stark, Rodney. *The Rise of Christianity: How the Obscure, Marginal Jesus Movement Became the Dominant Religious Force in the Western World in a Few Centuries*. New York: HarperOne, 1996.

Steyn, Mark. *America Alone: The End of the World as We Know It*. Washington, DC: Regnery, 2008.

Stout, Martha. *The Sociopath Next Door*. New York: Three Rivers, 2005.

Stroup, George W. *Before God*. Grand Rapids, MI: Eerdmans, 2004.

Taylor, Charles. *A Secular Age*. Cambridge, MA: Belknap Press of Harvard University Press, 2007.

Mother Teresa. *Come Be My Light: The Private Writings of the "Saint of Calcutta."* Edited by Brian Kolodiejchuk. New York: Doubleday, 2007.

Terrien, Samuel L. *The Elusive Presence*. San Francisco: Harper & Row, 1978.

Tilley, Terrence W. *The Evils of Theodicy*. Washington, DC: Georgetown University Press, 1991.

Tracy, David. *The Analogical Imagination: Christian Theology and the Culture of Pluralism*. New York: Crossroad, 1998.

———. "Approaching the Christian Understanding of God." In *Systematic Theology: Roman Catholic Perspectives*, edited by Francis Schüssler Fiorenza and John P. Galvin, 2nd ed., 110–27. Minneapolis: Fortress Press, 2011.

———. "Fragments of the Spiritual Situation of Our Times." In *God, the Gift, and Postmodernism*, edited by John D. Caputo and Michael J. Scanlon, 170–84. Bloomington: Indiana University Press, 1999.

Turner, Denys. *The Darkness of God: Negativity in Christian Mysticism*. Cambridge: Cambridge University Press, 1995.

Turner, Victor. *Dramas, Fields, and Metaphors: Symbolic Action in Human Society*. Ithaca, NY: Cornell University Press, 1975.

Voltaire. *Toleration and Other Essays*. Translated by Joseph McCabe. London: G. P. Putnam's Sons, 1912.

Wallace, Mark I. *The Second Naiveté: Barth, Ricoeur, and the New Yale Theology*. Macon, GA: Mercer University Press, 1990.

Walsh, Carey. "Theological Trace in Qoheleth." *Bulletin of Biblical Theology: Journal of Bible and Culture* 42 (2012): 12–17.

Weigel, George. *Witness to Hope: The Biography of Pope John Paul II*. New York: HarperPerennial, 2005.

Weinandy, Thomas G. *Does God Suffer?* Notre Dame, IN: University of Notre Dame Press, 2000.

Wellhausen, Julius. *Prolegomena to the History of Ancient Israel*. New York: Meridian Books, 1957.

Westermann, Claus. *Praise and Lament in the Psalms*. Louisville, KY: John Knox, 1981.

Wiesel, Elie. *Night*. New York: Hill & Wang, 2006.

Wright, G. Ernest. *God Who Acts: Biblical Theology as Recital*. Studies in Biblical Theology 8. London: SCM, 1952.

Subject Index

159

Scripture Index